STRATEGIES FOR BUSINESS AND TECHNICAL WRITING

Third Edition

KEVIN J. HARTY
La Salle University

Harcourt Brace Jovanovich, Publishers
San Diego   New York   Chicago   Austin   Washington, D.C.
London   Sydney   Tokyo   Toronto

ISBN: 0-15-583926-8

Library of Congress Catalog Card Number: 88-80614

Printed in the United States of America

FOR JAMIE

You may grow old and trembling in your anatomies, you may lie awake at night listening to the disorder of your veins, you may miss your only love, you may see the world about you devastated by evil lunatics, or know your honour trampled in the sewers of baser minds. There is only one thing for it then—to learn. Learn why the world wags and what wags it. That is the only thing which the mind can never exhaust, never alienate, never be tortured by, never fear or distrust, and never dream of regretting. Learning is the thing for you.

—T. H. White
The Once and Future King

Preface

T his third edition of *Strategies for Business and Technical Writing* is a thorough reworking of the previous edition. The number of selections has been increased from 28 to 30, with 10 appearing for the first time or in revised form.

These new and revised essays broaden the book's coverage of both business and technical writing and increase its usefulness as a textbook and as a reference. In particular, the new and revised essays:

- make even more explicit the previous editions' emphases on the *process* of writing,

- discuss the role computers and word processors can play in solving the problems of writing for the world of work,

- increase the coverage of graphics by adding materials on additional kinds of visual aids and on computer-generated graphics,

- offer fresh perspectives on such topics as audience analysis and adaptation, word choice, business and technical correspondence, resumes, and letters of application,

- extend coverage to such important new topics as business and technical writing style, the writing of procedures, and the kinds of writing samples appropriate for inclusion as part of an employment application.

Also, the extensive annotated bibliography has been expanded and updated to make it more helpful in locating further information on specific topics for reference or for library research. Finally, this third edition includes introductory essays for each of the first five parts, as well as a general introduction to the book itself.

Like its predecessors, this third edition of *Strategies for Business and Technical Writing* can be used in three ways: 1) as a supplement to a business or technical writing textbook, 2) as a supplement to a composition textbook or handbook, and 3) on its own as a textbook or as a reference source.

Strategies for Business and Technical Writing is designed to appeal to practical-minded instructors, students, and people already working in business and technical occupations. Its contributors write with the kind of purpose and understanding that come only from a career dedicated to improving the effectiveness of business and technical communications. As a result, the selections in this anthology not only teach professional writing; they are themselves fine examples of the genre.

In selecting essays, I have been guided by the belief that all courses in business and technical writing should firmly implant one ideal in students' minds: *All* successful writing consists of clear and effective prose. However, students should recognize that business and technical writing differs in important ways from the expository prose usually taught in freshman composition courses. Since business and technical writers communicate with multiple audiences and with a variety of intentions, learning to write well for the world of work requires some adjustments in technique. Therefore, in addition to touching on such broad problems as style, jargon, and diction, *Strategies* includes comprehensive discussions of specific forms of writing—for example, resumes, letters of application, letters that sell, memos, reports, and procedures. Students learn the specific techniques used by successful executives in business and industry who communicate information as part of their jobs. In Part 1, for instance, Herbert Popper sets forth six guidelines for professional writers that his extensive experience as a technical editor has enabled him to distill from many possibilities. In Part 3, Marvin H. Swift recreates the time-saving process by which an efficient manager composes a routine memo.

The essays in this third edition of *Strategies* have survived the most rigorous scrutiny—that of my students in seminars and courses in business and technical writing at La Salle University, Temple University, Rhode Island College, the Federal Reserve Bank of Philadelphia, Philadelphia Life Insurance Company, the Board of Pensions of the United Presbyterian Church (USA), First Pennsylvania Bank, Blue Cross of Greater Philadelphia, and Philadephia Newspapers, Inc. I am grateful to these former students for being such willing and helpful critics.

I wish to thank several others for their advice and assistance while this revision was in the making. Charles T. Brusaw of NCR Corporation, Dana L. Fox of the University of Missouri, and Roberta R. Gribbon of Chesapeake College wrote detailed reviews of the second edition from which I benefited greatly. At La Salle University, I am fortunate to have in Brother Emery Mollenhauer, FSC, Brother James Muldoon, FSC, and James A. Butler, a provost, a dean, and a chairman, respectively, who have always supported my efforts on this and other projects. I owe a similar debt of gratitude to my colleagues at La Salle: John Keenan, John Christopher Kleis, Richard Lautz, Margot Soven, and Howard Hannum.

Over the years I have had the good fortune to have the help of four Aquisitions Editors from Harcourt Brace Jovanovich—a numerical imbalance not indicative, I hope, of the difficulties editors encounter when working with me, but of the care with which Harcourt Brace Jovanovich treats its authors. I am grateful to Drake Bush and Bob Beitcher for their assistance on the first edition; Paul Nockleby for his assistance on the second edition; and Susan L. Mease for her continued support and tireless assistance on the third. My thanks, too, to Debbie Hardin, Manuscript Editor; Cindy Simpson, Production Editor; Kay Faust, Designer; Lesley Lenox, Production Manager; and Cindy Robinson, Art Editor.

Finally, I am indebted to Martin J. Piccoli, whose good humor, patience, and word processing skills made this revision possible, and to Jamie, to whom this edition is dedicated with love and repeated thanks.

Contents

2

PROBLEMS WITH LANGUAGE   **65**

3

BUSINESS AND TECHNICAL CORRESPONDENCE   113

4

REPORTS AND OTHER DOCUMENTS   153

5

RESUMES AND OTHER WRITTEN MATERIALS FOR A JOB SEARCH

Cover letters must be grammatically correct and typographically perfect; they must also be written in an appropriate style.

Candidates for certain jobs may have to submit a writing
sample along with their other application materials. Typical
samples include a policy-oriented paper, a program-oriented
paper, a paper using numbers, and a paper using theoretical or
complex ideas.

ANNOTATED BIBLIOGRAPHY   **289**

As a supplement to the readings in this anthology, here is an
annotated list of more than 330 sources of more information
on specific topics for reference or for library research.

INTRODUCTION

Writing consumes a substantial portion of the working day for almost all college-educated workers.[1]

Ability to express ideas cogently and goals persuasively—in plain English—is the most important skill to leadership. I know of no greater obstacle to the progress of good ideas and good people than the inability to compose a plain English sentence.[2]

Whether you are planning a career in business, in industry, or in some technical field, or whether you already have such a career, you may be ill-prepared for what is perhaps the most difficult part of your job. Although you may be an excellent accountant, salesperson, manager, engineer, or scientist, all of your training may not help you when you sit down to write. If this is the case, you are not alone in being frustrated by the writing demands of your job. Nevertheless, writing is essential to most technical and professional occupations; the ability to communicate effectively both in person and on paper can help you advance in your profession. Good writing can mean the difference between winning or losing a major sale, a pleased customer, or a challenging new position with a higher salary.

The selections in this book will help you make your letters, reports, memos, and other professional documents more effective. The selections represent some of the best advice veteran teachers and practitioners of business and technical writing have to offer. None of the selections, however, offers a quick cure for writing ills. There is no such cure. Like any worthwhile skill, good professional writing requires time, practice, and, most of all, discipline.

To begin with, we need to realize that there are only two kinds of professional writing:

1. clear, effective writing that meets the combined needs of the reader and the writer, and

2. bad writing.

Bad writing is unclear and ineffective; it wastes time and money. Even worse, it ignores its readers, usually raising more questions than answers.

To be effective writers, each of us needs to develop a variety of strategies for the different writing situations we face. We must also respect writing as something more than words typed or written on the page or fed into a dictaphone or word processor. Writing takes thought and planning.

[1] Paul V. Anderson, "What Survey Research Tells Us about Writing at Work," in *Writing in Nonacademic Settings*, ed. Lee Odell and Dixie Goswami (New York: Guilford, 1985), p. 30.

[2] The late John D. deButts, former Chairman, AT&T. Quoted as the epigraph to the third edition of the Bell Laboratories' *Editorial Style Guide* (Whippany, NJ: 1979).

THREE KEY QUESTIONS

Business and technical writing situations present us with a variety of challenges. One of the ways to meet these challenges is to begin by asking ourselves these three key questions:

1. Exactly who is my audience?

2. What is the most important thing I want to tell my audience?

3. What is the best way of making sure my audience understands what I have to say?

Exactly who is my audience?   Whatever we write on the job, somebody—across the hall, across the city, across the country, or even across the world—will eventually read what we have written. Most likely, our readers will receive our message in their own offices or homes. Since we won't be on hand to explain anything that is unclear or that doesn't make sense, our message will have to speak for itself.

Whenever we sit down to write, we become experts. That is in large part why we are the writers and not the readers. Our readers depend on us for clear, effective writing, so that they may share in our expertise. Although this seems obvious, business, industrial, and technical practice shows that the single most common cause of bad writing is ignoring the readers. There are any number of ways to ignore our audience: we can talk over their heads; we can talk down to them; we can beat around the bush; we can leave out important details—and, as a result, we can undermine our credibility.

When you next sit down to write, therefore, it is important to ask yourself what you know about your audience—you must determine your audience's situation and anticipate your audience's potential reaction to your message. To paraphrase the golden rule, make sure you are prepared to write unto others the way you would have them write unto you.

What is the most important thing I want to tell my audience?   Whether you write one page or one hundred pages, you should be able to condense your most important idea into about 25 words. If you can't, you aren't ready to write, since you haven't figured out what you are trying to say. You may not be able to explain every reason for a decision or a proposal in 25 words, but 25 words should be enough for a statement of the decision or proposal itself. For instance, you may have several reasons for recommending that your company replace its Brand X word processors with Brand Y word processors. You can make that recommendation in 22 words flat:

I recommend that we immediately replace all our Brand X word processors with new Brand Y units for the reasons presented below.

In short, you can cut through all the bull and come right out with your recommendation. Then, in the body of your memo or report, you can present the relevant facts. Busy people dislike having their time wasted, and they hate surprises. So, in professional writing, the bottom line should also be the top line.

What is the best way of making sure my audience understands what I have to say? Different writing situations require different strategies. After answering the first two questions, you may decide that you shouldn't write at all—that you should phone instead or make a personal visit. But once you do commit yourself to writing, you need to determine how to put the particular document together. You will need to use one strategy for good news and a different one for bad news, one for giving information and another for changing someone's mind, one for accepting a job offer and another for turning the offer down. But in each case you will need to get your main idea out as soon as possible in as few words as possible, and then later defend or elaborate on that idea as clearly and as effectively as possible.

To illustrate the importance of answering these three key questions properly, let's look at a brief excerpt from a booklet formerly used by the New York State Income Tax Bureau:

> The return for the period before the change of residence must include all items of income, gain, loss or deduction accrued to the taxpayer up to the time of his change of residence. This includes any amounts not otherwise includable in the return because of an election to report income on an installment basis.
>
> Stated another way, the return for the period prior to the change of residence must be made on the accrual basis whether or not that is the taxpayer's established method of reporting. However, in the case of a taxpayer changing from nonresident to resident status, these accruals need not be made with respect to items derived from or connected with New York sources.

How did you respond to this information? If you were a taxpayer in need of quick and concise information to solve a particular problem, you would surely be disappointed and probably even annoyed. Tax forms need not be complicated; since ordinary people normally fill out these forms, they should be written for the average taxpayer, not for a trained accountant. In fact, all professional writing should be reader-directed.

Furthermore, the result of such convoluted writing is that these two paragraphs do not fulfill their purpose: they do not tell taxpayers how to adjust their returns when changing residence. Although the grammar is correct, the message is certainly not effective. Among other faults, the writer forgot to ask, "Who is my audience?" Unfamiliar words or usages such as *includable, accrual basis,* and *election* appear without explanation. If taxpayers cannot understand such language, they will complete their returns incorrectly and cheat either themselves or the state out of money. In the end, these two paragraphs—and others like them in the tax booklet—will have missed their mark, and unnecessary complications for both taxpayers and the state will be the result.

GUIDELINES FOR EFFECTIVE WRITING

To make sure you answer the three key questions correctly, keep these guidelines in mind:

- *Put your main idea up front.* Then give whatever background or evidence your reader needs to understand your main idea.

- *Avoid using technical terms with nontechnical readers.* If you are an accountant writing to another accountant, use all the technical terminology you need. But if you are an accountant writing to a lay person, use ordinary language that the lay person will understand. If you must use technical terms, define them carefully.

- *Limit the length and complexity of your sentences.* Whenever possible, try to include only one main idea in each sentence. More mechanically, try also to limit your sentences to 25–35 words (or about 2½ typed lines). Generally speaking, the shorter the sentences, the fewer the difficulties you and your reader will get into. To ensure that your sentences are easily understood, move the main subject and verb to the front of the sentence and cut out any unnecessary words.

- *Limit the length and content of your paragraphs.* Nothing intimidates a reader more than a half-page-long block of dense prose. Rather than using one paragraph to discuss *every* aspect of a topic, use a separate paragraph for each aspect of your topic. In that way, you can limit your paragraphs to five or six sentences. If you really need a longer paragraph, use indentation or enumeration so that your subpoints stand out from the pack.

- *Give your reader all necessary information in a clear and unmistakable way.* If your reader needs to let you know something by June 12, tell the reader so plainly. If you want your reader to check back with you for additional information, make sure you provide your address or telephone number, and your travel or vacation schedule if you are going to be out of the office. If you are attaching or enclosing anything, specify exactly what. If your letter is a follow-up to some previous correspondence or to a recurring problem, make sure you give the reader this information too.

The selections that follow suggest many ways in which you can make your professional writing more effective. They also suggest ways you can make the process more enjoyable. If you view your professional writing as a chore, its effectiveness will be limited. But the more you get into the habit of asking the three key questions before you write your memos, letters, reports, and other documents, the easier, the more effective—and the more enjoyable—writing will become for you.

1

PROCESS AS WELL AS PRODUCT

The old adage tells us to think before we speak. We should also think before we write. Actually, we should think before we write, while we write, and after we write. Thinking is what the writing process is all about. A process approach to writing is simply a writing strategy that asks us to make sure that we carefully plan each written message, rather than simply letting the words fall where they may in the hope that they will somehow organize themselves effectively.

People in business and industry are, however, trained to think in terms of finished products and deadlines, so at first you may react with skepticism—if not total antagonism—to a process that requires you to slow down and think, especially when it's 4:30 and you need to get a memo to your boss by 5:00. Sometimes, sheer momentum and adrenaline will actually help, and a writer will produce an acceptable, even an effective, document. More times than not, though, the document will fail to achieve its purpose. Then the writer who balked at spending an extra ten minutes thinking a document through ends up spending an additional hour writing a follow-up document to clarify what should have been clear in the first document or, even worse, to mend fences because the original document created new problems.

In the introduction, I suggested an approach to the writing process that involved having writers ask themselves three key questions:

1. Exactly who is my audience?

2. What is the most important thing I want to tell my audience?

3. What is the best way of making sure my audience understands what I have to say?

My three key questions are simply one of any number of approaches to the writing process. The essays that follow offer several other approaches. Drawing on his long experience as a technical editor, Herbert Popper suggests a six-part approach to the writing process. Popper argues that it can actually take less time to produce an effective rather than an ineffective letter, memo, or report.

John Keenan and Michael E. Adelstein present two different five-part approaches to the writing process. The number of steps involved is, of course, unimportant. What is important is that there be a conscious effort to understand that, in business and technical writing, the process is as important as the goal. Keenan's approach is more open ended, allowing writers considerable freedom in the amount of time they spend on the different steps in the writing process. While allowing for some variation among writing situations, Adelstein suggests a more regimented approach that will appeal to other writers.

Peter Elbow takes a different tack by simply dividing writing time in half. Using what Elbow calls "the direct writing process," writers spend the first half of their available time "fast writing" in an attempt to get their ideas on the page before worrying about organization, correctness, or precision. Elbow suggests that these latter issues are best left to the second step in his approach to the writing process, revision.

Revision is the key to successful writing, but it is often the step busy writers claim they don't have the time to carry out. Andrew Fluegelman and Jeremy Joan Hewes maintain that advances in word processing can help even the busiest writers plan, write, edit, and revise their documents.

The first and last essays in Part 1 sound a common note that is repeated at least implicitly in all of the selections in this anthology: Consider your audience and the impact your message will have on that audience. John D. deButts, the late Chairman of AT&T, addresses the issue of audience by discussing the need to talk to not at customers. While this essay's comments are not specifically aimed at business and technical writing, they lie at the heart of all successful professional communication.

Echoing deButts is Linda Flower, one of the most respected teachers in the field of writing. Flower reminds us that writers, precisely because they are writers, are in a position of being experts, and being experts they need to consider their audience so they can ensure the effectiveness of their message. They know something their readers don't, and they must, therefore, translate what they have to say into terms that make sense to their readers.

When We Tell Customers, "We hear you," We'd Better Be Listening

JOHN D. DEBUTTS

When he wrote this article, the late John D. deButts was Chairman of the Board of the American Telephone and Telegraph Company (AT&T).

I f you were to sit at my desk and read and answer the mail I get about telephone service, you'd come to realize, if you don't already, how much "little things" mean; how sometimes lifelong impressions of the character of our business are formed on the basis of a single contact with just one employee. Rather significant, I'd say, when you consider that the Bell System employs more than a million men and women.

You know, it's only natural when a customer feels service is poor or when he thinks his bill is too high that he is going to register a complaint with someone. But in all my years in this business, I can't recall ever receiving a letter that complained solely about cost or service. No, the key element in all the letters of complaint I get is how the customer was treated by an employee of the company. As a matter of fact, I'm sometimes amazed at just how tolerant our customers are of situations that to me would seem intolerable, before poor treatment by an employee finally pushes them to write to me or to one of the other officers, or to a public utility commissioner.

So that I don't give the wrong impression, let me add that intermixed with those complaints are a goodly number of commendation letters. And commendation letters, of course, always talk about how an employee treated the customer in a manner so unusually satisfying that the customer felt compelled to write to me about it.

I'd like to share portions of some of those letters with you. Here's one from a man in New Jersey:

> Today, Saturday, at approximately 9:30 a.m., my next door neighbor rang my door bell to advise me that either my power or telephone line had pulled

WHEN WE TELL CUSTOMERS, "WE HEAR YOU," WE'D BETTER BE LISTENING   By John D. deButts. Reprinted from *Bell Telephone Magazine*, 52 (September–October, 1973), pp. 2–5. Reprinted by permission of AT&T.

loose from my home and was lying across the street where cars coming and going could have caused a serious problem.

I went out to investigate, when, at the same time, one of your New Jersey Telephone trucks was approaching. He immediately pulled his truck to the curb, hopped out and raised the line from the road. Without any words from me, he took his ladder down from the truck and proceeded to reinstall the line to the house and make necessary repairs.

I then spoke to him for the first time. He had been in the vicinity making a phone installation, and spotted the trouble . . . I thanked him . . . I feel that AT&T and New Jersey Bell should be mighty proud to have a man like that working for you.

The customer was right. We *are* proud to have such a man—the kind of employee who epitomizes the Spirit of Service we used to talk so much about in the old days, and who possesses that "sense of proprietorship" we've been talking about more recently. We wish all our employees showed the same sense of judgment and concern for a customer's problem. However, in an organization as large as ours, there are bound to be some weak links.

Here's a letter from a customer who also happens to be a share owner:

My telephone has been out of order for the past four days. On April 8, 1973 at 7:00 p.m., I made my fifth call to your service department and was told, as I had been told four times previously, "We'll take care of it." I asked for his name and he refused to give it. I asked for the identity of his supervisor and again was refused . . . I asked, "Do I have to go to New York to get my phone service restored?" He retorted, "You can call whoever the hell you want, but it won't get your service a damn minute sooner." Further discussion was pointless and I hung up.

The policy of permitting employees that have contact with customers to retain anonymity from behind Ma Bell's skirts is poorly conceived and poor customer relations. I cannot imagine any other company operating with this policy.

Now, consider this letter for a moment. The customer had been without service going on five days when he wrote. Subsequent investigation showed that one of our own cable crews working in the area was causing the problem, and that the customer was without service for still another day. Repair had been diligently searching for the cause of the problem from the time of the customer's first call, but no one thought to tell the customer what was being done. Obviously, the customer has *every* right to complain about being without service, but what is it that he is really complaining about here? Not lack of service, but an apparent lack of concern for his predicament, and the rude treatment he received from an employee.

When you get right down to it, there's really nothing very complicated about maintaining good customer relations. The guideline has been around a long time. Just follow the Golden Rule. If we treat the customer as we ourselves would like to be treated under the same set of circumstances, our actions are bound to meet with his approval. When I look through the letters I get from customers, I simply ask myself, "How would I like to be treated if I were in that customer's shoes?" The answers are usually fairly obvious.

Back when I was president of Illinois Bell, we had a saying there that "You not only have to give good service, but you've got to convince the customer that he's getting it." Here's a letter to illustrate what I mean.

> I am sorry to bother you but you should know about the poor service I had on the weekend.
>
> Saturday, April 28, about noontime, I found I could not use my phone . . . I reported on my neighbor's phone, immediately. I asked them to please fix it right away as I am an elderly lady—83 years old—and live alone. They said they would come before 5 p.m. I waited for them all Saturday and at 6 p.m. a man came and said he would come back later. He never came into my home. I waited for him until 11 p.m. and then went to bed. This was very upsetting and frightening for me and I didn't sleep. After I called again, they finally came . . . at 3 p.m., Sunday. I have large telephone bills and want better service than this.

In this case, Repair dispatched a man to investigate, and he found a short circuit in a cable on a pole outside the home. He worked on the trouble from Saturday afternoon into the early evening but couldn't finish the job and told the lady he'd return. He came back the next day, completed the splicing by early afternoon and left. The lady, not realizing that the repair had been completed, called again from the neighbor's phone. Another man was sent to check the problem, found everything in order, and reported to the lady that her phone was back in service. At which point, the lady took up her pen to write and tell us how we had let her down.

Now, I'm entirely sympathetic with this lady and can understand how such a thing can occur. A colleague of mine had a similar experience with an air-conditioning repairman. The man came into the home, looked briefly at the air conditioner, put the cover back on, picked up his tools and left. My friend's wife thought he had gone to get something from his truck, but when she looked out, the truck was gone. She waited all day for him to return, but he never came back. A second call to the repair shop the next day brought the information that a new part had to be ordered and, until it was received, the repair couldn't be completed. How easy it would have been, in both of these cases, for the repairman to give the customer a progress report.

Here's an excerpt from a letter I received from another share owner, one who had recently moved, relating an experience he had in merely inquiring about the types and cost of phone service:

> . . . I encountered a faceless voice that first demanded answers to a long list of questions, many of them personal, very few of them that could have any bearing at all on the answer to my inquiry. Rightly or wrongly, I became irritated

by the manner of my interrogator and when I recognized she was more interested in obtaining answers than she was in being helpful, and the questions had become so absurdly irrelevant to my request . . . I terminated the interview.

Now service representatives, obviously, must ask some questions if they are to do their jobs properly. But they should be flexible enough to know when to draw the line. When a customer begins to show irritation, as this one did, it's time to put aside the set routine. Fewer customers would have to be put through such prolonged fact-gathering if we spent just a little more time listening to what it is that the customer wants from us.

Finally, in the interest of balance, here's a note with a happy ending—from a customer who had a disappointing experience with one operator, only to have her faith restored later by the patient, resourceful service she received from another operator.

In contrast to her experience with the first operator, the customer had this to say about the second:

> . . . [She] listened to me, investigated the situation and had the courtesy to call me and explain that the number was out of order, that no report had been made to that effect earlier, but that she had done so.

Note the key word in this letter. The operator *listened* to her. The operator not only heard a problem described, but recognized how important it was for this customer to determine why she could not complete this particular call. The second operator, like the first, could have let the matter drop, but didn't. She followed through, determined the phone was out of order and reported it to the appropriate people.

Getting away from the letters for a minute, far more of our customer contacts come by phone. And of course, a certain number are in person. Our Operations-Commercial group ran a check on some 200 business offices around the country recently to see how "reachable" the business office manager was to the customer.

Well, I'm happy to say that the calls placed were handled properly more than 80 percent of the time. If the caller was not passed along, he was not only told why, but also informed when he could expect the manager to return the call. Although I'm happy that the majority of the calls did go through, I'm equally concerned about the 20 percent that didn't, and I worry about why they didn't.

We've got to stop building walls around our managers. These are the people who have the authority to correct the things the customers are complaining about. In all my years in this business, I've always had my home telephone number published in the directory. I know this isn't generally true of executives in other industries, but I've always felt it was the right thing to do. Over the years, I've received my share of crank calls, but I've also gotten calls from people just seeking help with their phone service. I've always been more than happy to help solve their problems whenever I can.

The Pacific Company, one time, made a study of some 150 written customer complaints. These complaints had been mailed either to company executives at Pacific, or directly to a public utility commissioner. In tracing the complaints back to see what kind of treatment the customer got along the way, the company discovered that more than half of the letter writers, 58 percent, as I recall, had contact with only one employee before taking up their pens.

Like the 20 percent of the calls that didn't get through to the managers in the Operations test, these letter writers didn't get the chance to have their problems reviewed by supervisors or managers at the local level. Well, you can bet that, following the written complaint, the customer got the attention from the people who should have given it to him the first time.

Again, don't misunderstand. I'm not suggesting that we capitulate to unreasonable demands, simply to curtail the number of complaints this company receives. We have rules and regulations to live by, and generally they must be observed. What does concern me, though, is that too often our employees hide behind the rule book and fail to honor some very sound requests simply because they are afraid to risk doing what they know is right, because it's not covered by the rules. In the final analysis, rules are there to guide us, not to govern us.

Take the case of the man in Brainerd, Minnesota, one of the very few places left in the country where equipment shortages still require 8-party service. As he was a year-round resident in an area primarily inhabited by summer vacationists, he asked if it wouldn't be possible to tie his line in with some of theirs. He reasoned that for most of the year, at least, when they were gone, his telephone wouldn't be ringing as often. You can't fault the logic. But do you know what our initial response was—absolutely not! You know why? If the other permanent residents found out, they'd want similar consideration. By the way, once he took the trouble to write me about his suggestion, we took another look at the rule book and found no reason why we shouldn't honor his request. He's a much happier man, today. And thinks a little better of us, too.

On the other hand, a Brooklyn customer, an elderly man, wrote telling how upset he was that his local bank had decided not to act as a collection agency for the company, and that he would now be forced to spend 70 cents in subway fares to come into the business office to pay his bill. While we couldn't force the bank to continue collecting his bill, as he suggested, we did ask the local business office manager to look into what could be done. Since the customer didn't believe in checking accounts, there was no safe way the manager could advise mailing in payments which would not incur costs almost as high as the subway fare to which the customer objected. In looking over the customer's payment record, the manager observed that over many years he always paid his bill promptly, and in full. In addition to providing this customer with the addresses of two other collection points nearer his home than the business office, the manager suggested, in light of the customer's fine credit record, that he remit payment every other month. Here's a manager willing to take a collection risk in an effort to do the right thing by this customer. And I find that very commendable indeed.

If we want to encourage employees to take such independent action in response to specific customer needs and requests, we, as managers, must set the climate. We'll never convince our customer contact-employees that we are sincerely interested in having them use their own good judgment in dealing with customers if we force a strict adherence to the rules and require double-checking of the most trivial matters up the line for higher level approval. While it is a manager's responsibility to see that his staff is adequately trained and can be relied upon to use common sense in dealing with customers, once that task is accomplished, managers should not keep intruding their presence. Following the careful selection, training and placement of the most competent employees in positions of trust and responsibility, nothing ruins initiative faster than to have managers who insist on second-guessing every decision and require that everything be run by the book. Again, we shouldn't throw the book away, but, I reiterate, the rules are there to guide us, not to govern us.

Over the past year, I've held more than 30 large, formal, employee meetings around the country and quite a number of smaller, informal, higher-level management meetings. At these meetings, I've stressed that I know of nothing more important to providing top-notch service than the *sense of proprietorship* each Bell System employee brings to his or her job.

Just recently, we embarked on a major national advertising campaign built around the simple phrase, "We Hear You." Through these three words we hope to convey to customers our determination to be responsive to their needs and concerns. Customer opinion, of course, will not be swayed one hair's breadth by any advertising campaign unless it is backed up by people who are ready and willing not only to listen, but to follow through with a satisfactory performance from the customer's point of view. When we say, "We Hear You," it carries the promise that we will listen. Employees who have that sense of proprietorship will see to it that the promise is kept.

I remind you that where that sense of proprietorship has been lost, you and I have no more important responsibility than to restore it; and where it has not, no more important responsibility than to see that it is maintained.

When that's done, the customer will know that we're listening.

Six Guidelines for Fast, Functional Writing

HERBERT POPPER

Herbert Popper was a senior editor of the
journal *Chemical Engineering.*

Some types of improvement in the quality of one's writing can only be achieved at the expense of quantity—for instance, by spending more time on the editing of drafts. However, regardless of whether you use longhand or some form of dictation, there are several areas where quantity and quality go hand in hand, and where it can actually take less time to produce an effective piece of communication than an ineffective one. The six guidelines that follow take aim at that area.

Because writing problems vary in kind and degree from person to person, you may find that some of these suggestions either don't apply to you or appear self-evident. However, "fast, functional" writing skills are so important to most engineers and technical managers that even if you only find one or two of the suggestions really useful, this should more than repay you for your reading time.

1. Know What Your Audience Expects

A vice-president of operations was making his annual tour of the company's outlying facilities. At one plant, he chatted with the assistant manager about the upcoming labor negotiations with the local union.

"I wish you'd send me a fairly detailed report of those negotiations," asked the vice-president. Flattered by this request, the assistant plant manager resolved to do an outstanding job of reporting. By the time negotiations were over, he had more than 50 pages of handwritten notes, which he decided to amplify with background information on some of the points the union or the management team had raised.

It took him two weeks after the close of negotiations to organize this material into a rough handwritten draft. Because of a secretarial bottleneck, it took him two more weeks to get this draft typed and edited, and then another two weeks to get the massive document typed up in final form. Nevertheless, as he signed the letter of transmittal in which he apologized for imperfections in the typing and commented on the shortage of good secretarial help, he felt rather proud of himself: The report read like a courtroom drama, and had a great degree of polish.

Unfortunately, before the report could even reach headquarters, the vice-president had made an acid phone call to the plant manager. Apparently, what the vice-president had really wanted was brief, day-by-day reports that he could review while negotiations were still in progress, and that he could pass on to another plant that started negotiations a week later. When he finally got the assistant plant manager's monumental opus, a lot of the information was old hat, the key points having been already passed along by the plant manager in a lengthy, long-distance phone call just before the close of negotiations.

Next year, the plant manager decided to handle the job of reporting himself; at the close of each day's session, he dictated his notes into a recorder—his secretary would type them up on the next day, so that he could ink in some comments and send them out as soon as he finished that day's negotiating. Since he didn't use a draft, his daily reports were not particularly polished; the inked-in comments and corrections looked rather informal—and yet these reports were acclaimed by the vice-president.

Moral of the story: Make sure you know what the audience wants. Don't be afraid to ask. There are times when speed, rather than quality or quantity, may be of the essence. In the example above, which is based on an actual situation, the assistant plant manager could have saved himself hours of toil by finding out what sort of details the vice-president did or did not want to know about, and whether quick dictation without a draft was acceptable.

Failure to find out or to really understand the audience's expectations is perhaps the single biggest time-waster in technical writing. An example of such inefficiency involves the engineer who uses exactly the same writing approach regardless of whether his report is primarily intended for the departmental archives, his immediate supervisor, or a financial executive on the appropriations committee.

If the report is just intended for a supervisor, for instance, there is nothing wrong with using technical jargon, and for keeping background information very brief. But if the report is to go to a financial executive—particularly one who lacks any sort of technical background—the engineer must avoid technical jargon, and explain some things that he would not need to explain to his boss, while leaving out technical details. In such a report, it is particularly important to make the first page or two tell the bulk of the story, in terms that are meaningful to the administrator.

If you are writing a dual-function report—say, one intended for both a financial executive and your boss—by all means get squared away with the latter on how the two approaches can be reconciled (e.g., by eventually giving your boss additional sections or informal notes that are omitted from the administrator's copy, by coming up with a preliminary version of the first two pages that you and your boss can review jointly before finalization, etc.).

When writing for publication, rather than for internal use, finding out the audience's expectations can be an equally great timesaver. Many magazines have booklets that discuss their "expectations" in regard to such things as writing style, quality of drawings, compatibility with readers' interests[1]—and are further prepared to conserve the author's time by reviewing outlines in some detail so as to minimize the need for revision of the final manuscript.

2. Mobilize Your Subconscious

Legend has it that on the day the opera "The Magic Flute" was scheduled to get its first performance, someone reminded Mozart that there still wasn't any overture, whereupon the composer calmly sat down and dashed off the magnificent overture just in time to give the score to the orchestra before the curtain went up. Actually, I think if this legend is true, the chances are that Mozart must have "precomposed" the overture in his mind days before he set it down on paper, so that leaving the actual writing until just before the deadline may not have been as risky as it seemed to others at the time.

Unfortunately, many of us tend to display a Mozart-like confidence in being able to meet a last-minute deadline regardless of whether we have done any precomposing or not.

If you have a writing project with a far-off deadline, and you don't feel like starting the actual writing right away, then don't. But I would still suggest that you draw up a rough outline as soon as you can, see how much information you already have available and how much more you will have to dig out, decide when you should start this digging out so that the information will be available at the proper time, and discuss the outline for the project with your boss or with a colleague. That way, you will not only get a feel for the emphasis needed (as discussed in the previous section), but you will be giving your subconscious mind a chance to come up with ideas while the project is incubating.

To come up with useful ideas, your subconscious should have some sort of framework—that way, perhaps some of the framework will be filled in for you while you shave in the morning. But if you wait till the last minute, even to prepare an outline or think about an approach, all your subconscious can do is to provide you with a feeling of anxiety.

Another constructive use for the prewriting period is to do some preselling. People hate shocks—which is what may happen when your recommendations based on a full year's work are coldly dropped on your department head's desk. It is fairer to him, and kinder to you and your writing time, to use the "let's let him in on part of the secret" technique. So, give your boss some inkling of what your report is going to recommend. Don't try to do a complete job of selling, but do give him a chance to get some exposure to your ideas. From his initial comments, you may also be able to obtain pointers on how to best link your ideas to his, and to the current objectives of the department. This can save a great deal of writing time in the long run, and will often let you get the constructive involvement of the reader much sooner than if you use the "This may come as a shock, but . . ." approach.

3. Build Up and Exploit Your Momentum

"I sit down with a fountain pen and paper and the story pours out. However lousy a section is, I let it go. I write on to the end. Then the subconscious mind has done what it can . . . The rest is simple effort . . . going over a chapter time and time again until, though you know it isn't right, it is the best you can do." That's how W. Somerset Maugham said he got his thoughts down on paper. If you have trouble getting started and building up momentum on a writing project, then the Maugham approach of putting down your thoughts in any old undisciplined way and eventually going back to polish them up, has a lot to recommend it. . . .

What do you do if you still don't succeed in unplugging your thoughts, regardless of whether you are using pen, pencil, stenographer or dictating machine? Here are a few additional pointers:

- Go over your outline . . . and pretend a good friend asked you to explain each point to him. If he were to ask questions such as "Why don't we just stick with the old process?" or "How does this gimmick work?," the chances are you wouldn't be at a loss for words—you would just say it like it is. So, pretend your friend is asking you questions that correspond to your outline, and write it like it is.

- Pretend that this is an examination, and that you have five minutes to get something down on paper for each thought on your outline—i.e., that if after five minutes you have nothing down on paper on the first point, you have nothing that you can be graded on, and you would thus get zero. (A couple of years ago, I took an aptitude test in which I was given a cast of two or three characters and had to shape them into a plot for a short story within ten minutes; then stop and shape another cast of characters into a new plot; then do this a few more times. Not considering myself a really fast writer, I was amazed at how much I could get down in ten minutes when the pressure was on, and when I knew I would be graded on content rather than style. It occurred to me that if I could pretend that I was in a similar situation when starting on a writing job, it would get me going—and it works!)

- Pick the best time to get started on a tough writing project. For most people, this may be the very beginning of the day, before things have come up to distract them. Others work best right after lunch. Still others find that the best time to unlock their thoughts is after dinner at home, and that once they get started that way, they can continue the project at work without much difficulty. If you haven't already done so, try to find a time pattern in the daily periods during which you feel sharpest and loosest; then exploit these periods to get started on tough projects.

Of course, getting started does not necessarily mean writing a brilliant beginning; it means getting started on the "meat" of the project. Very often a meaty fact-filled beginning is the most brilliant one anyway. But if you do feel the urge to think up something particularly striking or original, you may be better off doing this after most of the project is down on paper, rather than letting it be an initial stumbling block.

Once you have built up your momentum, how do you keep it?

First of all, try not to stop. Let someone take your phone messages. If you see a chance to finish the project by working late, do so. Resist the temptation to take a break until you start slowing down. (Personally, I find that sipping coffee or puffing on a cigar while doing difficult writing is preferable to running the risk of getting sidetracked by taking an unnecessary break.) Putting it into industrial engineering terminology, make sure you have a long enough production run to justify the setup time.

If you can't finish the project by working late, then it is usually better to leave it in the middle of a paragraph than to try and finish the particular section or thought. Finishing the thought the next day will be relatively easy, and this will serve to prime the pump for the next thought. I used to make the mistake of staying up until whatever hour was necessary to get a major section finished, only to find that it would take me all the next morning to stop resting on my laurels and to uncork my thoughts for the next section. Conversely, when I don't try so hard to come to a logical stopping place, I can usually continue the section without any difficulty the next morning and then launch right into the next section. (I can't take full credit for this approach; someone named Hemingway recommended it in a book called "A Movable Feast.")

4. Watch Out for Time-Wasting Verbosity

Not everybody has the uncoiling problems dealt with in the previous section. In fact, some people who can uncoil most of the time at the drop of a pencil encounter the opposite type of problem: How to avoid the verbosity that wastes their own time as well as that of the reader, so that they can make the most of their fluency as writers.

The first section in the 1966 "Efficient, Effective Writing" report[2] gave good advice on ways of recognizing and avoiding destructive verbosity. Although that section was aimed at making writing more informative, most of the suggestions can also lead to faster writing. For instance, the writer can usually save time by cutting down on passive verbs, abstract nouns, and prepositional phrases. (Obviously, it would have taken me longer to write the previous sentence had I said "Time can be saved by the writer if proper consideration is given to a reduction in the use of passive verbs, etc.")

Here are a few additional suggestions:

- Don't be legalistic in a nonlegal piece of writing. Lawyers have to be extremely careful to cover every possible contingency—hence they may feel justified in using strings of words that may differ only very slightly in meaning (e.g., null, void, of no legal force, etc.). But engineers are seldom justified in coming up with a phrase like "The *development, establishment,* and *implementation* of process-control *philosophies* and *policies* must take place at an *early* or *incipient* stage in a project." There just isn't enough difference between the italicized words to warrant using more than one of each; if you say "philosophies," 99 out of 100 readers will assume that this includes "policies."

- Don't waste time on excess hedging. For instance, when you say "Based on bench-scale experiments run at ten different temperatures, 300 F. produces the best yield," you have clearly indicated on what you base your conclusion, and there is no need to add hedge phrases such as ". . . 300 F. may tend to produce the best yields, assuming that these bench-scale results are freely applicable to commercial conditions. . . ." Putting it another way, readers generally realize that almost any technical, business or philosophical statement that can be made is subject to limitations and qualifications; if you insist on pointing out limitations that are either obvious or unimportant, you are wasting time (and probably producing dull writing). Particularly wasteful and deadly is the "triple hedge"—e.g., ". . . may, under some circumstances, tend to. . . ."

- Use more tables, illustrations and in-text listings to cut down on verbosity. . . . An item-by-item approach can result in tighter writing of all kinds, including the body of the report. (At the risk of appearing to disregard my own "hedging" caveat, I should point out that itemization can be carried to dull extremes, particularly once the triple sub-indentation stage is reached. But if you haven't been doing much itemizing, the technique can save you a lot of words in reducing generalities to specifics.)

- Consider leaving out some details altogether. Resist the temptation to tell the reader *everything* you know about the subject—just tell him what you think he needs to know. The latter is quite different from just telling him what you think he would like to hear—or from using a dual standard whereby you exclude all unfavorable details while including all those that are favorable. The memo or report that burdens the reader with *every* conceivable detail has not only taken the writer much more time than necessary, but suggests that the writer was unsure of himself because he left it to the reader to decide which of the details were significant. (If you are afraid that a short report won't adequately reflect the work that went into a particular study, you can always indicate the *type* of additional data that can be supplied on request.)

Of course, the classic example of detail elimination involves the man who got a letter from his landlord asking if he intended to vacate his apartment. The answer consisted of "Dear Sir: I remain, Yours Truly, Henry Smith."

Unfortunately, it's not always that easy to combine succinctness with politeness in handling one's correspondence, particularly when one is dictating it. Things that can waste the dictator's (and the reader's) time include:

- Marathon sentences. An occasional long sentence can supply useful variety, and may be needed in order to relate ideas to each other, but strings of runaway sentences impede efficient communication.

- Ditto for marathon paragraphs.

- Shotgun or overkill attacks on the topic, whereby the dictator, not being sure he has said what he really wanted to say, goes on to re-attack the topic in several other, equally roundabout, ways.

- Tendencies to throw in cliches and meaningless phrases just to keep the dictation process going. It is less wasteful to keep your secretary waiting for a minute while you find the right phrase than to dictate a phrase that adds nothing.

5. Save Time via the "Example" Technique

Most of us find the going slow when we write on an abstract, philosophic level for any length of time. True, the amount of such writing can be minimized by translating abstract concepts into dollars and cents, but this cannot always be done. For instance, if you are trying to change the attitudes of foremen towards some community or labor-relations problem, neither payout time nor discounted cash flow is going to be of much help to you. But this does not mean that your communications with the foremen must be entirely on an abstract philosophic level.

Good philosophy is hard to write. There are all sorts of pitfalls: failure to define terms, or to relate them to the reader's frame of mind, failure to avoid either oversimplification or obtuseness, etc. But fortunately, you can write about an abstract topic—e.g., a desired change in attitude—without staying on the abstract level for very long. The idea here is to translate the abstract into the specific by using analogies, miniature case histories (either actual or hypothetical), projections of what might happen if the status quo were maintained, etc.

Of course, this "example" technique is not limited to communications that deal with corporate philosophy but should also be used when generalities and abstract concepts crop up in technical writing. Here, a one-sentence "for instance" can often take the place of a much longer explanation; a liberal sprinkling of such sentences can keep the discussion on the ground, and can result in an easier-to-write yet more-informative communication than one in which all abstract technical concepts are explained or promoted in only theoretical terms.

6. Know Thyself, and Thy Writing

The difficulty in many articles dealing with improving your writing is their generality; they presuppose that all writers have the same problems. This report has tried to be more specific—for instance, by showing how *less* discipline can be a timesaver for the engineer who has trouble uncoiling, whereas *more* discipline can be an eventual timesaver for someone whose problem is verbosity or poor organization rather than lack of writing fluency.

Where do you fall within these two extremes? Should your prime emphasis be on boosting your writing output or on boosting its quality? If you have difficulty answering that question, you can get help quite readily.

For example, the 1966 "Efficient, Effective Writing" report[2] supplied some simple tests whereby you can evaluate the informative quality of your writing. If your score is low, perhaps your prime goal should be to make your writing more informative. At the beginning, this may reduce your page output because you will be spending more time on editing and rewriting. However, if you try to learn from your editing, you will find that output will eventually increase along with quality. This means spending a few minutes reviewing an edited draft to see what type of corrections are prevalent, and to think about ways of minimizing the need for these types of corrections in subsequent writing.

Discuss your writing with your boss. Some bosses are reluctant to initiate such a discussion because they have found that it takes almost as much tact to constructively criticize a subordinate's writing as it would to constructively criticize his wife or family. But if you initiate such a discussion . . . the chances are that overly defensive postures can be avoided, and that you and your boss will both gain a better insight into problem areas.

Ask your boss whether he thinks you are spending too much or too little time on writing. For instance, based on samples, would he settle for draftless dictation on some reports in order to give you more time for engineering?

If one of your writing problems is that interruptions are always breaking your train of thought, ask your boss about ways of getting more privacy, or about occasionally working at home to make headway on difficult writing chores.

In order to discuss other aspects of your writing, you may want to go over a sort of writing-inventory checklist, such as the one published in the *Harvard Business Review* article "What Do You Mean I Can't Write?"[3] This can be a good starting point in getting your supervisor's views on such matters as whether you sometimes present too many opinions and not enough supporting data (or vice versa), whether you tend to under- or overestimate his familiarity with your work, etc.

A concluding thought: The engineer who progresses in his company tends to do more writing every year. Eventually, he may also have to supervise the writing of subordinates; many of their reports and memos will go out over his signature and will reflect on the caliber of the work done under his supervision. Thus the engineer who becomes adept at fast, functional writing is in an enviable position—he can save a significant and increasing amount of time, establish his credentials as an efficient communicator, and eventually help his subordinates solve their own communication problems. We hope that the suggestions in various sections of this report will help point the way, and will let you apply the "work smarter, not harder" principle to your communicating.

Acknowledgement

Some of the ideas in this final section stem from various members of *Chemical Engineering*'s editorial staff, and also from Manny Meyers of Picatinny Arsenal, and Peter J. Rankin of Basford Inc.

References

1. See, for instance, "How to Write for *Chemical Engineering*," a booklet available from *Chemical Engineering*, 330 W. 42 St., New York City.
2. Johnson, Thomas P., How Well Do You Inform?, *Chem. Eng.*, Mar. 14, 1966 (Reprint No. 295).
3. Fielden, J., *Harvard Bus. Rev.*, May-June 1964, p. 147.

Using PAFEO Planning

JOHN KEENAN

A former technical writer for SmithKline, John Keenan is Professor of English at La Salle University in Philadelphia and co-author with Kevin J. Harty of *Writing for Business and Industry: Process and Product (Macmillan, 1987).*

Surveys tell us that "lack of clarity" is the most frequently cited weakness when executives evaluate their employees' writing. But since lack of clarity results from various bad habits, it is often used as a convenient catchall criticism. Pressed to explain what they meant by lack of clarity, readers would probably come up with comments such as these:

"I had to read the damn thing three times before I got what he was driving at. At least I *think* I got his point; I'm not sure."

"I couldn't follow her line of thought."

"I'm just too busy to wade through a lot of self-serving explanation and justification. If he has something to say, why didn't he just say it without all that buildup?"

Most unclear writing results from unclear thinking. But it is also true that habits of clear writing help one to think clearly. When a writer gets thoughts in order and defines the purpose and goal, what he wants to say may no longer be exactly the same as it was originally. Sometimes the writer may even decide it is better *not* to write. Whatever the case, the work done *before* the first draft in the prewriting process and *after* the draft in the revising process is often the difference between successful communication and time-wasting confusion. . . .

Think PAFEO

Some years ago I made up a nonsense word to help my students remember the important steps in constructing a piece of writing. It seemed to stick in their minds. In fact, I keep running into former students who can't remember my name, but remember PAFEO because it proved to be so useful. Here are the magic ingredients.

P stands for purpose
A stands for audience
F stands for format
E stands for evidence
O stands for organization

Put together, they spell PAFEO, and it means the world to me!

Purpose

Put the question to yourself, "Why am I writing this?" ("Because I have to," is not a sufficient answer.) This writing you're going to do must aim at accomplishing something; you must be seeking a particular response from your reader. Suppose, for example, you're being a good citizen and writing to your congressman on a matter of interest to you. Your letter may encompass several purposes. You are writing to inform him of your thinking and perhaps to persuade him to vote for or against a certain bill. In explaining your position, you may find it useful to narrate a personal experience or to describe a situation vividly enough to engage his emotions. Your letter may therefore include the four main kinds of writing—exposition, argument, narration, and description—but one of them is likely to be primary. Your other purposes would be subordinated to your effort to persuade the congressman to vote your way. So your precise purpose might be stated: "I am writing to Congressman Green to persuade him to vote for increased social security benefits provided by House Bill 5883."

Write it out in a sentence just that way. Pin it down. And make it as precise as you can. You will save yourself a good deal of grief in the writing process by getting as clear a focus as you can on your purpose. You'll know better what to include and what to omit. The many choices that combine to form the writing process will be made easier because you have taken the time and the thought to determine the exact reason you have for writing this communication.

When you're writing something longer than a letter, like a report, you can make things easier for yourself and your reader by making a clear statement of the central idea you're trying to develop. This is your thesis. To be most helpful, it must be a complete sentence, not just the subject of a sentence. "Disappointing sales" may be the subject you are writing about, but it is not a thesis. Stating it that way won't help you organize the information in your report. But if you really say something specific about "disappointing sales," you will have a thesis that will provide a framework for development. For example:

> Disappointing sales may be attributed to insufficient advertising, poor selection of merchandise, and inadequate staffing during peak shopping hours.

The frame for the rest of the report now exists. By the time you have finished explaining how each cause contributes to the result (disappointing sales), the report is finished. Not only finished, but clear; it follows an orderly pattern. The arguments, details, illustrations, statistics, or quotations are relevant because the thesis has given you a way of keeping your purpose clearly in focus.

Of course the ideal method is to get your purpose and your thesis down before you write a first draft, but I can tell you from experience that it doesn't always work that way. Sometimes the only way to capture a thesis statement is to sneak up on it by means of a meandering first draft. When you've finished that chore, read the whole thing over and try to ambush the thesis by saying, "OK, now just what am I trying to say?" Then *say it* as quickly and concisely as you can—out loud, so you can hear how it sounds. Then try to write it down in the most precise and concise way you can. Even if you don't capture the exact thesis statement you're looking for, there's a good chance that you will have clarified your purpose sufficiently to make your next revision better.

Audience

Most of the writing the average person does is aimed at a specific reader: the congressman, the boss, a business subordinate, a customer, a supplier. Having a limited audience can be an advantage. It enables the writer to analyze the reader and shape the writing so that it effectively achieves the purpose with that particular reader or group of readers.

Here are some questions that will help you communicate with the reader:

1. How much background do I need to give this reader, considering his or her position, attitude toward the subject, and experience with this subject?

2. What does the reader need to know, and how can I best give him or her this information?

3. How is my credibility with this reader? Must I build it gradually as I proceed, or can I assume that he or she will accept certain judgments based on my interpretations?

4. Is the reader likely to agree or disagree with my position? What tone would be most appropriate in view of this agreement or disagreement?

The last question, I think, is very important. It implies that the writer will try to see the reader's point of view, will bend every effort to look at the subject the way the reader will probably look at it. That isn't easy to do. Doing it takes both imagination and some understanding of psychology. But it is worth the considerable effort it involves; it is a gateway to true communication.

Let me briefly suggest a point here that is easily overlooked in the search for better techniques of communication. It is simply this: *better writing depends on better reading.* Technique isn't everything. One cannot learn to be imaginative and understanding in ten easy lessons, but reading imaginative literature— fiction, poetry, drama—is one way of developing the ability to put yourself in someone else's place so you can see how the problem looks from that person's angle. The writer who limits reading to his or her own technical field is building walls around the imagination. The unique value of imaginative literature is the escape that it allows from the prison of the self into the experiences and emotions of persons of different backgrounds. That ability to understand why a reader is likely to think and act in a certain way is constantly useful to the writer in the struggle to communicate.

Format

Having thought about your purpose and your audience, consider carefully the appropriate format for this particular communication you are writing. Of course the range of choice may be limited by company procedures, but even the usual business formats allow some room for the writer to use ingenuity and intelligence.

The key that unlocks this ingenuity is making the format as well as the words work toward achieving your purpose. You can call attention to important points by the way you arrange your material on the page.

Writers sometimes neglect this opportunity, turning the draft over to the typist without taking the trouble to plan the finished page. Remember the reader, his or her desk piled high with things to be read, and try to make your ideas as clear as possible on the page as the reader glances at it.

External signals such as headings, underlining, and numerals are ways of giving the reader a quick preview. Use them when they are appropriate to your material.

Don't be afraid of using white space as a way of drawing attention to key ideas.

To see how experts use format for clarity and emphasis, take a look at some of the sales letters all of us receive daily. Note how these persuasive messages draw the reader's attention to each advantage of the product. You may not want to go that far, but the principle of using the format to save the reader's time is worth your careful consideration.

Overburdened executives are always looking for shortcuts through the sea of paper. Many admit that they cannot possibly read every report or memo. They scan, they skip, they look for summaries. A good format identifies the main points quickly and gives an idea of the organizational structure and content. If the format looks logical and interesting, readers may be lured into spending more time on your ideas. You've taken the trouble to separate the important from the unimportant, thus saving them time. The clear format holds promise of a clear analysis, and what boss can be too busy for that?

Evidence

Unless you're an authority on your subject, your opinions carry only as much weight as the evidence you can marshal to support them. The more evidence you can collect before writing, the easier the writing task will be. Evidence consists of the facts and information you gather in three ways: (1) through careful observation, (2) through intelligent fieldwork (talking to the appropriate persons), and (3) through library research.

When you follow the evidence where it leads and form a hypothesis, you are using inductive reasoning, the scientific method. If your evidence is adequate, representative, and related to the issue, your conclusion must still be considered a probability, not a certainty, since you can never possess or weigh *all* the evidence. At some point you make the "inductive leap" and conclude that the weight of evidence points to a theory as a probability. The probability is likely to be strong if you are aware of the rules of evidence.

The Rules of Evidence

Rule 1.   Look at the Evidence and Follow Where It Leads.

The trick here is not to let your own bias seduce you into selecting only the evidence you agree with. If you aren't careful, you unconsciously start forcing the evidence to fit the design that seems to be emerging. When fact A and fact B both point toward the same conclusion, there is always the temptation to *make* fact C fit. Biographer Marchette Chute's warning is worth heeding: ". . . you will never succeed in getting at the truth if you think you know, ahead of time, what the truth ought to be."

A reliable generalization ought to be based on a number of verifiable, relevant facts—the more the better. Logicians tell us that evidence supporting a generalization must be (1) known or available, (2) sufficient, (3) relevant, and (4) representative. Let's see how these apply to the generalization, "Cigarette smoking is hazardous to your health."

The evidence accumulated in animal studies and in comparative studies of smokers and nonsmokers has been published in medical journals: it is therefore known and available. Is it sufficient? The government thinks so; the tobacco industry does not. Which is more likely to have a bias that might make it difficult to follow where the evidence leads?

Tobacco industry spokesmen argue that animal studies are not necessarily relevant to human beings and point to individuals of advanced age who have been smoking since childhood as living refutations of the supposed evidence. But the number of cases studied is now in the thousands, and studies have been done with representative samplings. The individuals who have smoked without apparent damage to their health are real enough, but can they be said to be numerous enough to be representative of the usual effects of tobacco on humans? "Proof" beyond doubt lies only in mathematics, but the evidence in this example is the kind on which a sound generalization can be based.

Rule 2.   Look for the Simplest Explanation that Accounts for All the Evidence.

When the lights go out, the sudden darkness might be taken as evidence of a power failure. But a quick investigation turns up other evidence that must be accounted for: the streetlights are still on; the refrigerator is still functioning. So a simpler explanation may exist, and a check of the circuit breakers or fuse box would be appropriate.

Rule 3.   Look at All Likely Alternatives.

Likely alternatives in the example just discussed would include such things as burned-out bulbs, loose plugs, and defective outlets.

Rule 4.   Beware of Absolute Statements.

In the complexity of the real world, it is seldom possible to marshal sufficient evidence to permit an absolute generalization. Be wary of writing general statements using words like *all, never* or *always.* Sometimes these words are implied rather than stated, as in this example:

> Jogging is good exercise for both men and women.

> [Because it is unqualified, the statement means *all* men and women. Since jogging is not good for people with certain health problems, this statement would be better if it said *most* or *many* men and women.]

Still, caution is always necessary. Induction has its limitations, and a hypothesis is best considered a probability subject to change on the basis of new evidence.

The other kind of reasoning we do is called deduction. Instead of starting with particulars and arriving at a generalization, deduction starts with a general premise or set of premises and works toward the conclusion necessarily implied by them. If the premise is true, it follows that the conclusion must be true. This logical relationship is called an inference. A fallacy is an erroneous or unjustified inference. When you are reasoning deductively, you can get into trouble if your premise is faulty or if the route from premise to conclusion contains a fallacy. Keep the following two basic principles in mind, and watch out for the common fallacies that can act as booby traps along the path from premise to conclusion.

Two Principles for Sound Deduction

1. The ideas must be true; that is, they must be based on facts that are known, sufficient, relevant, and representative.

2. The two ideas must have a strong logical connection.

If your inductive reasoning has been sound enough to take care of the first principle, let me warn you that the second is not so simple as it sounds. We have all been exposed to so much propaganda and advertising that distort this principle that we may have trouble recognizing the weak or illogical connection. Nothing is easier than to tumble into one of the commoner logic fallacies. As a matter of fact, no barroom argument would be complete without one of these bits of twisted logic.

Twisted Logic

Begging the question. Trying to prove a point by repeating it in different words.

> Women are the weaker sex because they are not as strong as men.

> Our company is more successful because we outsell the competition.

Non sequitur. The conclusion does not follow logically.

> I had my best sales year; the company's stock should be a big gainer this year.

> I was shortchanged at the supermarket yesterday. You can't trust these young cashiers at all.

Post hoc. Because an event happened first, it is presumed to be the cause of the second event.

> Elect the Democrats and you get war; elect the Republicans and you get a depression.

Oversimplification. Treating truth as an either-or proposition, without any degrees in between.

> Better dead than Red.

> America—love it or leave it.

> If we do not establish our sales leadership in New York, we might as well close up our East Coast outlets.

False analogy. Because of one or two similarities, two different things are assumed to be *entirely* similar.

> You can lead a horse to water but you can't make him drink; there is no sense in forcing kids to go to school.

Giving the Canal back to Panama would be like giving the Great Lakes back to the Indians.

Seen in raw form, as in the examples, these fallacies seem easy to avoid. Yet all of us fall into them with dismaying regularity. A writer must be on guard against them whenever he or she attempts to draw conclusions from data.

Organization

Experienced writers often use index cards when they collect and organize information. Cards can be easily arranged and rearranged. By arranging them in piles, you can create an organizational plan. Here's how you play the game.

1. You can write only one point on each card—one fact, one observation, one opinion, one statistic, one whatever.

2. Arrange the cards into piles, putting all closely related points together. All evidence related to marketing goes in one pile, all evidence related to product development goes in another pile, and so on.

3. Now you can move the piles around, putting them in sequence. What kind of sequence? Consider one of the following commonly used principles:

> **Chronological.** From past to present to future.
> Background, present status, prospects
> **Spatial.** By location.
> New England territory, Middle Atlantic, Southern
> **Logical.** Depends on the topic.
> Classification and division according to a consistent principle
> (divisions of a company classified according to function)
> Cause and effect (useful in troubleshooting manuals)
> **Problem-analysis-solution.** Description of problem, why it exists, what to do about it.
> **Order of importance.** From least important to most important or from most important to least important.

The choice of sequence will depend largely on the logic of the subject matter and the needs of your audience.

4. Go through each pile and arrange the cards in an understandable sequence. Which points need to precede others in order to present a clear picture?

5. That's it! You now have an outline that is both orderly and flexible. You can add, subtract, or rearrange whenever necessary.

Summary

Think PAFEO. Use this word to remind you to clarify your purpose and analyze your audience before you write. When you have a clear sense of purpose, create a thesis that will act as a frame for your ideas.

Choose a format for your communication that will help the reader identify the main points quickly.

Collect your evidence before you write by observing, interviewing, and doing library research. Use the index card system to help you organize your evidence. Keep in mind the rules of evidence before you draw conclusions. Be alert to the common logic fallacies that can easily undermine the deductive process.

Try the file card system as a way of organizing your material. Write one point on each card and then place closely related points together in a pile. Place the piles in sequence according to a principle of organization you select. Some useful organizing principles include: chronological, spatial, logical, problem-analysis-solution, and order of importance. The sequence you choose will depend on the logic of the subject matter and the needs of your audience.

The Writing Process

MICHAEL E. ADELSTEIN

Michael E. Adelstein is Professor of English at the University of Kentucky and coauthor with W. Keats Sparrow of *Business Communications* (Harcourt Brace Jovanovich, 1983).

The Writing Process

Their prevalent belief in the myths of genius, inspiration, and correctness prevents many people from writing effectively. If these individuals could realize that they can learn to write, that they cannot wait to be inspired, and that they must focus on other aspects besides correctness, then they can overcome many obstacles confronting them. But they should be aware that writing, like many other forms of work, is a process. To accomplish it well, people should plan on completing each one of its five stages. The time allocations may vary with the deadline, subject, and purpose, but the work schedule should generally follow this pattern:

1. Worrying—15%

2. Planning—10%

3. Writing—25%

4. Revising—45%

5. Proofreading—5%

Note that only 25% of the time should be spent in writing; the rest—75%—should be spent in getting ready for the task and perfecting the initial effort. Observe also that more time is spent in revising than in any other stage, including writing.

Stage One—Worrying (15%)

Worrying is a more appropriate term for the first operation than *thinking* because it suggests more precisely what you must do. When you receive a writing assignment, you must avoid blocking it out of your mind until you're ready to write; instead, allow it to simmer while you try to cook up some ideas. As you stew about the subject while brushing your teeth, taking a shower, getting dressed, walking to class, or preparing for bed, jot down any pertinent thoughts. You need only note them on scrap paper or the back of an envelope. But if you fail to write them down, you'll forget them.

Another way to relieve your worrying is to read about the subject or discuss it with friends. The chances are that others have wrestled with similar problems and written their ideas. Why not benefit from their experience? But if you think that there is nothing in print about the subject or a related one—either because your assignment is restricted, localized, or topical—then you should at least discuss it with friends.

Let's say, for example, that as a member of the student government on your campus, you've been asked to investigate the possibility of opening a student-operated bookstore to combat high textbook prices. During free hours, you might drop into the library to read about the retail book business and, if possible, about college bookstores. If your student government is affiliated with the National Student Association, you might write to it for information about policies and practices on other campuses. In addition, you might start talking about the problem to the manager of your college bookstore, owners of other bookstores in your community, student transfers from other schools, managers of college bookstores in nearby communities, and some of your professors. Because you might be concerned about the public-relations repercussions of a student book-store, you should propose the venture to college officials. At this point, you will have heard many different ideas. To discuss some of them, bring up the subject of a student bookstore with friends. As you talk, you will be clarifying and organizing your thoughts.

The same technique can be applied to less involved subjects, such as a description of an ideal summer job, or an explanation of a technical matter like input-output analysis. By worrying about the subject as you proceed through your daily routine, by striving to get ideas from books and people or both, and by clarifying your thoughts in conversation with friends, you will be ready for the next step. Remember: you can proceed only if you have some ideas. You must have something to write about.

Stage Two—Planning (10%)

Planning is another term for organizing or for the task that students dread so—*outlining*. You should already have had some experience with this process. Like many students, unfortunately, you may have learned only how to outline a paper after writing it. This practice is a waste of time. If you want to operate efficiently, then it follows that you will have to specialize in each of the writing stages in turn. When you force yourself simultaneously to conceive of ideas, to arrange them in logical order, and to express them in words, you cannot perform all of these complex activities as effectively as if you had concentrated on each one separately. By dividing the writing process into five stages, and by focusing on each one individually, the odds are that the result will be much better than you had thought possible. Of course you will hear about people who never plan their writing but who do well anyway, just as you may know someone who skis or plays golf well without having had a lesson. There are always some naturals who can flaunt the rules. But perhaps these people could have significantly improved their writing, golf, or skiing if they had received some formal instruction and proceeded in the prescribed manner.

An efficient person plans his work. Many executives take a few minutes before leaving the office or retiring at night to jot down problems to attend to the following day. Many vacationers list tasks to do before leaving home: stop the newspaper, turn down the refrigerator, inform the mailman, cut off the hot water, check the car, mail the mortgage payment, notify the police, and the like. Of course, you can go on vacation without planning—just as you can write without planning—but the chances are that the more carefully you organize, the better the results will be.

In writing, planning consists mainly in examining all your ideas, eliminating the irrelevant ones, and arranging the others in a clear, logical order. Whether you write a formal outline or merely jot down your ideas on scrap paper is up to you. The outline is for your benefit; follow the procedure that helps you the most. But realize that the harder you work on perfecting your outline, the easier the writing will be. As you write, therefore, you can concentrate on formulating sentences instead of also being concerned with thinking of ideas and trying to organize them. For the present, realize the importance of planning. . . .

Stage Three—Writing (25%)

When you know what you want to say and have planned how to say it, then you are ready to write. This third step in the writing process is self-explanatory. You need only dash away your thoughts, using pen, pencil, or typewriter, whichever you prefer. Let your mind flow along the outline. Don't pause to check spelling, worry about punctuation, or search for exact words. If new thoughts pop into your mind, as they often do, check them with your outline, and work them into your paper if they are relevant. Otherwise discard them. Keep going until either the end or fatigue halts you. And don't worry if you write slowly: many people do.

Stage Four—Revising (45%)

Few authors are so talented that they can express themselves clearly and effectively in a first draft. Most know that they must revise their papers extensively. So they roll up their sleeves and begin slashing away, cutting out excess verbiage, tearing into fuzzy sentences, stabbing at structural weaknesses, and knifing into obfuscation. Revision is painful: removing pet phrases and savory sentences is like getting rid of cherished possessions. Just as we dislike to discard old magazines, books, shoes, and clothes, so we hate to get rid of phrases and sentences. But no matter how distasteful the process may be, professional writers know that revising is crucial; it is usually the difference between a mediocre paper and an excellent one.

Few students revise their work well; they fail to realize the importance of this process, lack the necessary zeal, and are unaware of how to proceed. Once you understand why you seem to be naturally adverse to revision, you may overcome your resistance.

Because writing requires concentrated thought, it is about the most enervating work that humans perform. Consequently, upon completing a first draft, we are so relieved at having produced something that we tidy it up slightly, copy it quickly, and get rid of it immediately. After all, why bother with it anymore? But there's the rub. The experienced writer knows that he has to sweat through it again and again, looking for trouble, willing to rework cumbersome passages, and striving always to find a better word, a more felicitous phrase, and a smoother sentence. John Galbraith, for example, regularly writes five drafts, the last one reserved for inserting "that note of spontaneity" that ironically makes his work appear natural and effortless. The record for revision is probably held by Ernest Hemingway, who wrote the last page of *A Farewell to Arms* thirty-nine times before he was satisfied!

To revise effectively, you must not only change your attitude, but also your perspective. Usually we reread a paper from our own viewpoint, feeling proud of our accomplishment. We admire our cleverness, enjoy our graceful flights, and glow at our fanciful turns. How easy it is to delude ourselves! The experienced writer reads his draft objectively, looking at it from the standpoint of his reader. To accomplish this, he gets away from the paper for a while, usually leaving it until the following morning. You may not be able to budget your time this ideally, but you can put the paper aside while you visit a friend, grab a bite to eat, or phone someone. Unless you divorce yourself from the paper, you will probably be under its spell; that is, you will reread it with your mind rather than with your eyes. You will see only what you think is on the page instead of what is actually there. And you will not be able to transport yourself from your role of writer to that of critic.

Only by attacking your paper from the viewpoint of another person can you revise it effectively. You must be anxious to find fault and you must be honest with yourself. If you cannot or will not realize the weaknesses in your writing, then you cannot correct them. This textbook should open your eyes to many things that can go wrong, but above all you must *want* to find them. If you blind yourself to the bad, then your work will never be good. You must convince yourself that good writing depends on good rewriting. This point cannot be repeated too frequently or emphasized too much. Tolstoy revised *War and Peace*—one of the world's longest and greatest novels—five times. The brilliant French stylist Flaubert struggled for hours, even days, trying to perfect a single sentence. But question your professors about their own writing. Many—like me—revise papers three, four, or five times before submitting them for publication. You may not have this opportunity, your deadlines in school and business may not permit this luxury; but you can develop a respect for revision and you can devote more time and effort to this crucial stage in the writing process. . . .

Stage Five—Proofreading (5%)

Worrying, planning, writing, and revising are not sufficient. The final task, although not as taxing as the others, is just as vital. Proofreading is like a quick check in the mirror before leaving for a date. A sloppy appearance can spoil a favorable acceptance of you or your paper. If, through your fault or your typist's, words are missing or repeated, letters are transposed, or sentences juxtaposed, a reader may be perturbed enough to ignore or resist your ideas or information. Poor proofreading of an application letter can cost you a job. Such penalties may seem unfair, but we all react in this fashion. What would you think of a doctor with dirty hands? His carelessness would not only disgust you but would also raise questions about his professional competence. Similarly, carelessness in your writing antagonizes readers and raises questions in their minds about your competence. The merit of a person or paper should not depend on appearances, but frequently it does. Being aware of this possibility, you should keep yourself and your writing well groomed.

Poor proofreading results from failure to realize its importance, from inadequate time, and from improper effort. Unless you are convinced that scrutinizing your final copy is important, you cannot proofread effectively. If you realize the significance of this fifth step in the writing process, then you will not only have the incentive to work hard at proofreading but also will allow time for it in planning.

Like most things, proofreading takes time. We usually run out of time for things that we don't care about. But there's always time for what we enjoy or what is important to us. So with proofreading; lack of time is seldom a legitimate excuse for doing it badly.

But lack of technique is. To proofread well, you must forget the ideas in a paper and focus on words. Slow down your reading speed, stare hard at the black print, and search for trouble rather than trying to finish quickly. . . . Some professional proofreaders start with the last sentence and read backward to the first. Whatever technique you adopt, work painstakingly, so that a few careless errors will not spoil your efforts. If you realize the importance of proofreading, view it as one of the stages in the writing process, and labor at it conscientiously, your paper will reflect your care and concern. . . .

Each Stage Is Important

These then are the five stages in the writing process: worrying, planning, writing, revising, and proofreading. Each is vital. You need to become proficient at each of them, although, at some later point in your life, an editor or efficient secretary may relieve you of some proofreading chores. But in your career as a student and in your early business years, you will be on your own to guide your paper through the five stages. Since it is your paper, no one else will be as interested in it as you. It's your offspring—to nourish, to cherish, to coddle, to bring up, and finally, to turn over to someone else. You will be proud of it only if you have done your best throughout its growth and development.

The Direct Writing Process for Getting Words on Paper

PETER ELBOW

Peter Elbow teaches at the University of Massachusetts at Amherst. He is also the author of *Writing without Teachers* (Oxford, 1973), an innovative introduction to the writing process.

The direct writing process is most useful if you don't have much time or if you have plenty to say about your topic. It's a kind of let's-get-this-thing-over-with writing process. I think of it for tasks like memos, reports, somewhat difficult letters, or essays where I don't want to engage in much new thinking. It's also a good approach if you are inexperienced or nervous about writing because it is simple. . . .

Unfortunately, its most common use will be for those situations that aren't supposed to happen but do: when you have to write something you *don't* yet understand, but you also don't have much time. The direct writing process may not always lead to a satisfactory piece of writing when you are in this fix, but it's the best approach I know.

The process is very simple. Just divide your available time in half. The first half is for fast writing without worrying about organization, language, correctness, or precision. The second half is for revising.

Start off by thinking carefully about the audience (if there is one) and the purpose for this piece of writing. Doing so may help you figure out exactly what you need to say. But if it doesn't, then let yourself put them out of mind. You may find that you get the most benefit from ignoring your audience and purpose at this early stage of the writing process. . . .

In any event spend the first half of your time making yourself write down everything you can think of that might belong or pertain to your writing task: incidents that come to mind for your story, images for your poem, ideas and facts for your essay or report. Write fast. Don't waste any time or energy on how to organize it, what to start with, paragraphing, wording, spelling, grammar, or any other matters of presentation. Just get things down helter-skelter. If you can't find the right word just leave a blank. If you can't say it the way you want to say it, say it the wrong way. (If it makes you feel better, put a wavy line under those wrong bits to remind you to fix them.)[1]

I'm not saying you must never pause in this writing. No need to make this a frantic process. Sometimes it is very fruitful to pause and return in your mind to some productive feeling or idea that you've lost. But don't stop to worry or criticize or correct what you've already written.

While doing this helter-skelter writing, don't allow too much digression. Follow your pencil where it leads, but when you suddenly realize, "Hey, this has nothing to do with what I want to write about," just stop, drop the whole thing, skip a line or two, and get yourself back onto some aspect of the topic or theme.

Similarly, don't allow too much repetition. As you write quickly, you may sometimes find yourself coming back to something you've already treated. Perhaps you are saying it better or in a better context the second or third time. But once you realize you've done it before, stop and go on to something else.

When you are trying to put down everything quickly, it often happens that a new or tangentially related thought comes to mind while you are just in the middle of some train of thought. Sometimes two or three new thoughts crowd in on you. This can be confusing: you don't want to interrupt what you are on, but you fear you'll forget the intruding thoughts if you don't write them down. I've found it helpful to note them without spending much time on them. I stop right at the moment they arrive—wherever I am in my writing—and jot down a couple of words or phrases to remind me of them, and then I continue on with what I am writing. Sometimes I jot the reminder on a separate piece of paper. When I write at the typewriter I often just put the reminder in caps inside double parentheses ((LIKE THIS)) in the middle of my sentence. Or I simply start a new line
LIKE THIS
and then start another new line to continue my old train of thought. But sometimes the intruding idea seems so important or fragile that I really want to go to work on it right away so I don't lose it. If so, I drop what I'm engaged in and start working on the new item. I know I can later recapture the original thought because I've already written part of it. The important point here is that what you produce during this first half of the writing cycle can be very fragmented and incoherent without any damage at all.

There is a small detail about the physical process of writing down words that I have found important. Gradually I have learned not to stop and cross out something I've just written when I change my mind. I just leave it there and write my new word or phrase on a new line. So my page is likely to have lots of passages that look like

[1]An excerpt from a letter giving me feedback on an earlier draft: "I tried the direct writing process. Though it sounds simple enough, I . . . see now that in the past I've often interrupted the flow of writing by spending disproportionate time on spelling, punctuation, etc. I can spend hours on an opening paragraph stroking the words to death; then, if there's a deadline, have to rush through the remainder." (Joanne Turpin, 7/24/78.)

Many of my pages
Still I don't mean that you should stop and rewrite every passage till you are
happy with it.
This kind of appearance.

What is involved here is developing an increased tolerance for letting mistakes show. If you find yourself crumpling up your sheet of paper and throwing it
away and starting with a new one every time you change your mind, you are
really saying, "I must destroy all evidence of mistakes." Not quite so extreme is the
person who scribbles over every mistake so avidly that not even the tail of the "y"
is visible. Stopping to cross out mistakes doesn't just waste psychic energy, it
distracts you from full concentration on what you are trying to say.

What's more, I've found that leaving mistakes uncrossed out somehow
makes it easier for me to revise. When I cross out all my mistakes I end up with a
draft. And a draft is hard to revise because it is a complete whole. But when I leave
my first choices there littering my page along with some second and third choices,
I don't have a draft, I just have a succession of ingredients. Often it is easier to
whip that succession of ingredients into something usable than, as it were, to
undo that completed draft and turn it into a better draft. It turns out I can just
trundle through that pile of ingredients, slash out some words and sections,
rearrange some bits, and end up with something quite usable. And quite often I
discover in retrospect that my original "mistaken phrase" is really better than
what I replaced it with: more lively or closer to what I end up saying.

*   *   *

If you only have half an hour to write a memo, you have now forced yourself
in fifteen minutes to cram down every hunch, insight, and train of thought that
you think might belong in it. If you have only this evening to write a substantial
report or paper, it is now 10:30 P.M., you have used up two or two and a half hours
putting down as much as you can, and you only have two more hours to give to
this thing. You must stop your raw writing now, even if you feel frustrated at not
having written enough or figured out yet exactly what you mean to say. If you
started out with no real understanding of your topic, you certainly won't feel
satisfied with what is probably a complete mess at this point. You'll just have to
accept the fact that of course you will do a poor job compared to what you could
have done if you'd started yesterday. But what's more to the point now is to
recognize that you'll do an even crummier job if you steal any of your revising time
for more raw writing. Besides, you will have an opportunity during the revising
process to figure out what you want to say—what all these ingredients add up
to—and to add a few missing pieces. It's important to note that when I talk about
revising in this book I mean something much more substantial than just tidying up
your sentences.

So if your total time is half gone, stop now no matter how frustrated you are
and change to the revising process. That means changing gears into an entirely

different consciousness. You must transform yourself from a fast-and-loose-thinking person who is open to every whim and feeling into a ruthless, tough-minded, rigorously logical editor. Since you are working under time pressure, you will probably use quick revising or cut-and-paste revising. . . .

* * *

Direct writing and quick revising are probably good processes to start with if you have an especially hard time writing. They help you prove to yourself that you *can* get things written quickly and acceptably. The results may not be the very best you can do, but they work, they get you by. Once you've proved you can get the job done you will be more willing to use other processes for getting words down on paper and for revising—processes that make greater demands on your time and energy and emotions. And if writing is usually a great struggle, you have probably been thrown off balance many times by getting into too much chaos. The direct writing process is a way to allow a limited amount of chaos to occur in a very controlled fashion.

It's easiest to explain the direct writing process in terms of pragmatic writing: you are in a hurry, you know most of what you want to say, you aren't trying for much creativity or brilliance. But I also want to stress that the direct writing process can work well for very important pieces of writing and ones where you haven't yet worked out your thinking at all. But one condition is crucial: you must be confident that you'll have no trouble finding lots to say once you start writing. . . .

As I wrote many parts of this book, for example, I didn't have my thinking clear or worked out by any means, I couldn't have made an outline at gunpoint, and I cared deeply about the results. But I knew that there was lots of *stuff* there swirling around in my head ready to go down on paper. I used the direct process. I just wrote down everything that came to mind and went on to revise.

But if you want to use the direct writing process for important pieces of writing, you need plenty of time. You probably won't be able to get them the way you want them with just quick revising. You'll need thorough revising or revising with feedback. . . . For important writing I invariably spend more time revising than I do getting my thoughts down on paper the first time.

Main Steps in the Direct Writing Process

- If you have a deadline, divide your total available time: half for raw writing, half for revising.

- Bring to mind your audience and purpose in writing but then go on to ignore them if that helps your raw writing.

- Write down as quickly as you can everything you can think of that pertains to your topic or theme.

- Don't let yourself repeat or digress or get lost, but don't worry about the order of what you write, the wording, or about crossing out what you decide is wrong.

- Make sure you stop when your time is half gone and change to revising, even if you are not done.

- The direct writing process is most helpful when you don't have difficulty coming up with material or when you are working under a tight deadline.

The Word Processor and the Writing Process

**ANDREW FLUEGELMAN and
JEREMY JOAN HEWES**

Both Andrew Fluegelman and Jeremy
Joan Hewes have been members of the
editorial board of *PC* magazine. Each has
authored books on a variety of topics.

I deally, the writing process is a direct path from the mind to the page. And for this purpose, word processing [w/p] may be the best game in town. Never mind that the page isn't printed by the w/p system as it is being written; that's often an advantage. The important feature of w/p writing is that it is immediate—that it is, quite literally, fingertip thinking.

So far, no invention—electronic, mechanical, or otherwise—can match the powers of the human brain. But for writing, a word processor comes as close as any machine: the speed of recording letters, words, and pages is limited only by the speed and accuracy of a writer's fingers on the keys. So if you're reasonably agile on the keyboard, you can probably keep up with your brain most of the time.

Of course there are other stages in the writing process—most notably editing. . . . But the first stage has to be producing some text, whether it is a fractured assemblage of phrases or a coherent sequence of paragraphs. With the help of a word processor, you can make something polished and professional out of either one.

In this chapter, the suggestions and many of the tips could apply to writing with any set of tools. We've presented most of these thoughts in the context of w/p writing, however, so that you can adapt them to your own system, whether it's a fixture in your office or still a contemplated acquisition.

Before getting into styles and strategies, though, we'd like to offer a . . . bit of advice. . . . [I]t is: Be daring—be critical. Because you have such powerful tools at your command with word processing, you can take risks and try writing experiments that might be too tedious or time-consuming with a typewriter or pen and paper, and you can edit all that daring work with just a few keystrokes if the experiments go awry. So don't be timid; attempt miracles, and you're likely to find that occasionally they happen.

Writing Without Barriers

There are two kinds of barriers on that direct path from the mind to the page. The first is physical—the interference of a typewriter's noise and its tendency to seize up if the keys are struck too quickly, as well as the human body's limits in getting the words down in writing, whether on a keyboard or with a pen or pencil. . . . [A] word processor very nearly eliminates those physical barriers.

The second wall we writers run up against is psychological, and it's usually trickier than stuck keys or writer's cramp. At times we all must struggle with temptation or lethargy, and having the latest in word processing technology will not automatically drive these wolves away from the door. Yet this set of electronic tools can lessen the psychological burdens by making it easy to write and even easier to edit.

In short, because you know that you can write down unrelated thoughts and put them in order later or begin a sentence three different ways and wait to choose one until you edit the completed draft, you're free to compose and experiment as comfortably and endlessly as you wish. Computer myths to the contrary, the blank screen is somehow friendlier than the blank sheet of paper. Maybe this is because you can fill up the screen faster or because you never have to replace it with another page, or maybe it's because the words appear on the screen as if by magic. When you think about it, the electronic wizardry that puts letters on the screen is a study in miniature of what writing truly is—a mystery that you can participate in and even control.

Styles of Writing

Perhaps the simplest way to pursue this mystery is by writing from the hip, so to speak. This is what we call the Sprint—writing as quickly as possible, without worrying about smooth phrasing or dangling participles or optimal choice of vocabulary. As you put your thoughts into written form rapidly, you are generating a manuscript in much the same way that an artist makes a sketch; the important thing is to get the ideas down in quick, fluid strokes, and you can come back later to polish the rough edges and fill in the details.

• Sprint writing is often the most expedient way to create a draft or to get beyond a block. Because word processing gives you extensive tools for editing, you can forget about the organization of your chapter or the appropriateness of your characters' dialogue and give all your energy to discovering ideas and recording them swiftly.

When you write at a Sprint pace, you may find that the speed itself is thrilling and that it sparks new ideas to challenge your mind—and your fingers. In rare instances this combination of pace and concept can achieve a union of mind and machine, so that your thoughts seem to appear on the screen almost as you become aware of them. The prose that comes out of such a session may be far from perfect, but the experience is exhilarating and instructive.

Most writers Sprint some of the time, but few of us can sustain this pace indefinitely. The more likely scenario is a few paragraphs or pages of Sprinting, preceded and followed by the slower, more methodical approach to writing we call (mainly to keep the analogy going) the Stride.

This style of working is deliberate, and it is often aided by a plan, such as an outline or a page of notes. Speed is the obvious difference between Stride writing and Sprinting, but these two styles also usually diverge in tone and editorial quality. That is, because you are proceeding slowly, choosing the right word and the appropriate sentence structure as you go, the finished draft of a Stride piece is likely to require less revision and a good deal less cutting than one written in a Sprint.

These two approaches to writing share a common goal—to create a draft manuscript. Whether you're able to write this initial text at a fast clip, more slowly, or at a varying pace, you've generated a fistful of pages that are ready to be edited. (Rarely, if ever, are drafts complete and perfect; all writing can benefit from your own careful editing and additional scrutiny by another experienced editor.) When you're writing a draft, you may do some minor editing as you go along, but it's wise to stick to the primary objective of completing a given chapter or section of text and make editing a separate stage in the creative process.

At certain times still another style of writing is appropriate. This is what we call Reworking-in-Progress, because it combines the stages of creating draft text and editing that work. (We were tempted to call this style the Foxtrot, to suggest that this writing style is like a dance that moves back and forth and sideways and still gets you somewhere, but we concluded that our pedal analogy had gone far enough.) Predictably, this write-and-edit method is usually quite slow, and for most writers it's an acquired skill.

• Reworking-in-Progress may be the most efficient way to write short pieces or to meet a regular schedule, such as producing a weekly column. In these situations, a looming deadline can make separate draft-edit-revise stages too risky; you may finish the draft on time and be tempted—or compelled—to hand in unedited work because you can't get an extension, or you may take time to edit and tarnish your credibility by being late. So the most propitious use of a tight writing schedule could be to polish as you work, drafting a sentence or paragraph and then editing it—honing the phrases, weighing each word, and writing transitions that make the parts flow together.

Of course all of these writing styles are general themes, subject to much individual variation. Most writers develop a personal way of working, which may combine elements of each writing style or may be a fairly pure version of one style. The most important consideration is not that you use one style or another, but that you find the approach that works best for you.

• Discovering the most effective writing style is one task for which word processing seems tailor-made. Even if you are comfortable with the work style you've developed, try some experiments with Sprint, Stride, and Reworking-in-Progress when you're not laboring against a deadline. Besides introducing alternative writing styles that could come in handy if the old reliable method deserts you someday, this foray into the unfamiliar may lead to a more efficient way of writing—and it will certainly give you the full tour of word processing.

W/P Features and Writing Styles

Like each writer, each word processing program goes about its work in a slightly different way. We can't anticipate all of these variations, but we've tried to cover the most common versions of each feature in the context of our three writing styles. As you'll note, our discussion here applies only to word processing features, such as inserting text, that have a direct bearing on one or more of the approaches to creating initial drafts. . . .

Inserting text is probably the most variable w/p feature involved in writing drafts. In fact, the ease or difficulty with which you can insert a word or several sentences into the text will affect your writing efficiency and perhaps even determine the writing style you choose. Consequently, you will be able to make the best use of your w/p system (or any you are contemplating) if you become familiar with the way it handles the insertion of letters, words, and longer sections of text.

For Sprint writing, you'll want a clean slate, so the ability to insert characters or words is not especially important. When you're trying to direct your thoughts to your fingertips as quickly as possible, you needn't be concerned with typos or word choice—the entire focus of your attention is on what you're thinking and writing, rather than how well it is expressed.

For Stride writing or Reworking-in-Progress, however, inserting short or long portions of text can be important. In both of these writing styles, working with the Insert feature on is preferable if your word processor handles this task smoothly. Unfortunately, all w/p programs do not make inserting text a simple matter.

Many word processors insert text by accepting whatever is typed at the cursor position and moving over all text following the cursor. So if you want to add an 'r' to 'gatitude', you would simply place the cursor in the correct spot and hit the 'r', and 'atitude' would step aside. This method works particularly well for short insertions, such as a letter, word, or phrase, but it may be slow or distracting if you want to add several lines or more to the text. Depending on how quickly your system pushes the existing text over and down as you're adding new text, you may find that the program pauses frequently to make these adjustments, giving you a message on the screen that says 'WAIT', or something similar. In addition, you may be distracted by the constant movement of all the text beside and below the words you're inserting.

• To avoid these problems, you can give yourself a partially clean slate by inserting several Returns (or blank lines) at the point where you plan to add new text. You can insert just one empty line, which is very helpful in letting you see the new phrases without having them run into the existing text, or you can add enough Returns to send the old text off the screen altogether. When you've finished the insertion, of course, you'll have to delete those blank lines to close up the text.

Some w/p programs automatically insert several blank lines when you turn on the Insert feature. This is desirable for adding long passages, but it can be bothersome if you only want to insert a letter or word. You have to be sure to position the cursor at the correct spot before you turn on Insert, and you won't see the finished results of your addition until you turn Insert off and the blank space is closed up (again, automatically). So with this type of program you may need to turn Insert on and off several times if you miscalculate the location of a change or if you subsequently decide to add something more.

Another group of word processing features can affect production of a draft or a piece that you edit in progress. These are the formatting and printing commands, which are primarily concerned with the printed manuscript but may also determine some aspects of the on-screen appearance of your work. The form of these commands varies among systems, but most programs allow you to imbed some or all of the format and print directives in the electronic files that contain your writing.

Because writing the draft and editing it are separate stages in both Sprint and Stride styles, you can probably ignore most of the formatting and printing commands when writing in either of these styles. The simplest way to write drafts is probably to use the default format and print settings that are automatically in effect when you begin writing. If you customarily change one or more of the defaults, you may want to override those default settings by entering the appropriate imbedded commands at the beginning of your file.

For the most part, however, you don't have to worry about the final format for the manuscript, because you will be editing and very likely Reforming much of the text as you revise it. Also, when you have completed the editing stage, you may find that you have to change the page margins or the type size in order to make the manuscript meet an editor's specifications for length.

Unlike draft writing, the Reworking-in-Progress style aims to avoid a separate editing stage. For this approach, you may want to make most of your formatting decisions when you're ready to start writing. You can then put all the necessary imbedded commands at the beginning of the file and—unless you change your mind—you'll be ready to print the finished product without further ado.

When you're writing in any of the three basic styles, you may want to go back and read from the beginning of your work to see what ground you've covered so far. Often, however, you won't want to read the entire piece; you may read a few paragraphs, get your bearings, and then go to the end of the draft to resume writing. Two fundamental cursor movement commands do this easily; they are usually called Cursor to Beginning of File and Cursor to End of File, or something similar.

The various other features that govern cursor movement are likewise helpful as you're writing, particularly in the Reworking-in-Progress style. For example, if you think of a better word or spot a typo on the top right corner of the screen and the cursor is at the bottom left, you can move the cursor to the top, then to the right side, make your change, then move the cursor back to the left and to its original position with a few deft keystrokes.

Scrolling is also useful for editing as you write; for example, if you want to go back a few paragraphs and edit the text you've just written, you can scroll by screenfuls until you find the passages to be revised. Similarly, if you know a specific word that you want to change but don't know its location, you can use the Search features to find and replace it, although you'll encounter every instance of that word in your text if you've used it more than once.

• All of the word processing features that allow you to move around in the text—in essence, to shuffle your electronic pages—are conveniences that let you review your work and possibly change it. These features are most appropriate to editing the drafts you have already written, however. With the exception of the Reworking-in-Progress style, you will probably be more successful at creating a draft if you concentrate on keeping the writing going, rather than on making changes in the text you've already generated. In short, unless you are unusually skilled at first-draft-perfect writing (and few of us are), your work will benefit most from going through separate drafting and editing stages.

• One more reminder about using a crucial word processing routine: Be sure to save your work often, no matter which writing style you use. When the creative juices are flowing and you're getting the words onto the screen in a steady stream, be sure to pause long enough to save the work every fifteen to twenty minutes, or each time you fill the screen with new text. Even if you're proceeding slowly, perhaps going back over the same page or two to perfect your work, don't let more than a quarter hour pass without saving the text on disk.

Building Confidence

Regardless of how experienced and productive we writers are, there will be times when we just can't find the right words—or any words at all. Those are the moments when we seriously wonder whether we'll ever have another thought or fashion another sentence, though a few hours later we can usually look back and laugh at our temporary panic. Somehow we manage to finish the assignment or meet the deadline, even if we spend almost as much time worrying as we do writing.

There are strategies to avoid some of that worry, however, and to bolster our confidence that the right words will indeed materialize. And at least some of these measures are ideally suited to writing with a word processor.

For example, you can keep all the drafts, partial paragraphs, and false starts you make on a project and easily integrate some of that work into a later version by using the program's Block Move features. If the writing is going slowly and you are trying one phrase and then another to find the words that seem right, you can work with the Insert feature turned on and keep all of your attempts on the screen until you decide which phrases to use and which to erase.

• The Insert feature is especially useful for sentences that you start over two or three times; if you have one opening phrase and want to try another, you can simply move the cursor back to the beginning of the sentence and write the new introductory phrase in front of the old one. If you want some blank space around the new words to distinguish them from the text already on the screen, you can hit the space bar several times or insert a Return before typing the new phrase, so that you can easily read and judge your latest attempt.

• In some instances the screen's 24 lines are not a large enough window on your text. For example, if you have a number of drafts and sections of text that you've saved but can't decide how to knit together, try printing out each individual piece of text on a separate page. Then you can read the pages and shuffle them until you determine the proper content and order of the sections. Once you've made this decision, you can go back to the electronic files and use the word processor's cut-and-paste abilities to create the manuscript. (You may still want to keep the unused bits of text in a separate file, in case you have an opportunity to include them in some other part of your work.)

One of the chief advantages of w/p writing is that you can have clean printed pages as often as you wish. This can be a real psychological boost, particularly if you've been struggling with a project. You can print out the work you've done so far, and just seeing the finished, professional-looking pages could be the catalyst you need to complete the job. At the very least, you'll probably be surprised at how much you've accomplished.

Similarly, there's a real difference between working with those tidy pages and the old typewriter products that have strikeovers and words inserted between lines and notes in the margin. Even though you're likely to make the same kinds of changes in your electronic pages, you can do that work on the screen and always have clean copy for the next editing stage. This opportunity to read your work straight through, without the visual interruption of handwritten insertions or messy corrections, can be a significant contribution to both your confidence and your ability to assess and improve your writing.

Clearing the Hurdles

As one observer has noted, writing is always easy, except for three times: when you're getting started, when you've got to keep going, and when you're trying to finish. In fact, writing is hard work, and it is prey to the same hazards as any job— at times your energy lags, your insight fails, and you'd rather be doing anything else. These moments are inevitable in a writer's life; the first step in conquering them is to realize that such lapses are natural, temporary, and universal. Then you can meet them head on without shaking the confidence that you've developed through your writing achievements.

The strategies that follow are useful for getting over the temporary hurdles that crop up in your work. Not all of these ideas will appeal to every writer, nor are these methods limited to w/p writing. Like the basic styles of writing, however, we've presented these suggestions in the context of word processing whenever appropriate.

• Writing generates ideas. One strategy for getting started is definitely enhanced by the word processor's speed and relative quiet. If you are staring at the blank screen and can't think of a way to begin an article or section of text, simply put down whatever comes into your mind (a process that goes faster with the w/p keyboard than with any other writing instrument). One of your random thoughts will very likely be the opening you need, and even if these jottings aren't "keepers," the process of writing will generate new ideas. When you see these new thoughts on the screen, they will trigger still more connections in your mind, and chances are you'll find that you are writing the piece as you continue to think with the keys.

Of course these random thoughts should be somehow related to the assigned topic, but keeping your mind as free and open to ideas as possible is preferable to stewing over the subject (and therefore staring at the screen instead of writing). By using this technique, you can keep assembling thoughts until you work around to the topic at hand, even if it's by way of a long and windy road of prose. And if the place where your on-screen thinking intersects with the assigned topic doesn't happen to be the beginning of the piece, don't worry—just keep that writing rhythm alive and come back later to knock off an introduction.

• The beginning is not always the best start. This is another strategy for getting past what many writers find most difficult—fashioning those first few words that will grab readers and crystallize the topic. If you have trouble finding those opening lines, skip them and begin with a part of the subject that is concrete and familiar. What often happens when you explain the key concepts and details of your topic is that a beginning image or analogy pops into your mind as you're writing or reading this latter part of the work. Granted, sometimes you have a great title or opening line that dictates how the rest of the article will proceed, but more often the beginning can just as easily take its cue from the main body of your text.

Of course the word processor can make writing the introduction when you're halfway through the piece an easy procedure. When the right opening words occur to you, even as you're working on another section of the text, you can get them down quickly, mark them as a block, and transfer this new writing to the beginning of your text. You then can return to the place where you left off or continue to expand the opening section that you've just moved to its intended location.

• An outline can be a sight for sore eyes. Even with the versatile editing features of a word processor, which let you bring a file of notes to the screen quickly and easily, a written copy of your outline or list of topics is invaluable. For example, you may already keep a paper holder (one of those metal or plastic triangular gadgets that display pages to be typed) near your keyboard; this is a logical place to put a page of notes or a printout of the outline you've created as an electronic file. In addition to providing an alternative to looking at the screen constantly (thereby helping to avoid possible eyestrain or headache from too much screen exposure), the printed notes can be a stimulant for your mind.

Another useful tactic is to keep some notepaper near the keyboard—index cards, perhaps, or larger sheets—so that you can scribble a phrase or idea that you want to use later. This suggestion may sound vaguely subversive in a book about word processing, but there are times when it's bothersome to interrupt the work on screen to make a note, mark it as a block, and send it to another file. Besides, that note has to be retrieved to act as a reminder when you're working on the later section of text, so on some occasions a stash of notes that fit neatly on some part of your keyboard or monitor can be a source of quick inspiration.

• The screen can take a role in your mind's dialogue. Writing is quite often a product of the internal conversations that writers hear. If these sorts of split-personality dialogues are characteristic of your work at times, take advantage of the quick keyboard and let the silent screen play a role. For example, you might consult your notes and find a reference that you don't understand; your on-screen conversation might go like this: "Why did I put 'Roosevelt connection' in my notes? Was it Teddy or FDR or maybe Eleanor?" Then search your mental library for everything you know about the Roosevelts, and write it down. You can do this speedily with the processor, and you'll have a page or two of notes to pore over, instead of just a series of thoughts that flashed through your brain and disappeared.

By asking your internal questions on the screen, you're recording them for future reference and triggering more ideas by virtue of seeing your thoughts in writing. In addition, this technique could be ideal for getting the characters in a story to come alive. Once you give them some tentative dialogue on the screen, they may take over your mind—and possibly your fingertips—and do most of the work from then on.

• A letter is worth a thousand words. Sometimes you know everything you want to say, you have a detailed outline, and the piece seems as if it should write itself—but it doesn't. That's when the letter-writing technique can save you: assemble your notes, study the outline, and put everything you know about the subject in a letter to a friend. Depending on how "real" you want to make this process, you could write an actual letter, complete with salutation, small talk, and some explanation of what you're doing. When you're finished, you could use the various Delete and Search functions to remove the personal comments, or you could even print the complete letter and send it to the intended recipient.

The letter-writing strategy is quite valuable for several kinds of writing projects. One of the most difficult types of writing is an "attitude" piece, in which you discuss your views on some pithy topic. Quite often you also discover what you believe about that subject—and the world in general—as you write. But finding a confident, expressive voice for this kind of writing is usually the hardest part of the job, and that's precisely the direct way you're likely to speak in a letter to someone you know.

Another excellent forum for the letter-writing strategy is an assignment that requires you to explain complex, technical information in layperson's language. For example, if you're writing an article about heart surgery for a general-interest magazine, you have to define medical terms, discuss anatomy, and present the causes and consequences with even-handed precision and without confusion or condescension. The problem of finding the right tone for this article might be readily solved if you choose a person whom you know and hold that friend or acquaintance in your mind as you write. When this process works well, you're really having a mental conversation with someone familiar, instead of trying to write for an unknown audience and guess at what they should know and how you should tell it.

Your choice of the person to whom you direct such a letter is important, of course. If you want your article to be chatty and even intimate, pick a close friend as your mental correspondent; if your article should be more formal, choose someone you respect but can speak openly with, such as a professional colleague. Often the best candidates for your mental missives are people to whom you actually do write occasionally, because you've already established this process of conversing with them in your mind.

• It's easier to loosen the reins than to tighten them. This may not sound like a writing strategy, but it is; the reins in this example are writers' attitudes toward a particular project or toward writing in general. Sometimes our "mental muscles" become too tight and we get bound up in our work, taking every word and phrase more seriously than the project merits. These are the times when deep breathing helps—both the physical variety and some mental equivalent. To achieve this mental exchange of air, try coaching yourself to care a bit less about this particular job, if only as an experiment. If you can sit back and wing it, your hastily expressed thoughts could make the points you're after, and you can use your command of language and style to polish the work at the editing stage.

This is not to suggest that you should lower your writing standards or become even slightly cynical about your work. Yet if the effort of writing becomes your focus, instead of the expression of ideas, your writing may seem forced and unconnected, and your progress at filling the pages (or simply the screen) may be painfully slow. Oddly enough, this is a time when easing up a bit can make the work go more smoothly, in the same way that relaxing your arm muscles when carrying a heavy suitcase can make the load seem lighter.

One way to loosen up your approach is to rediscover the fun of writing. The vast majority of writers have chosen this pursuit because they enjoy the work; when the pressure is heavy, though, the fun is easy to forget. If you can recall the times when writing gave you a sense of pleasure and accomplishment, you'll be relaxing those mental muscles as you reminisce. You might also reread some of the work you most enjoyed, which could further loosen the writing reins and let you return to the current project with a refreshed spirit.

• A trip away from the keyboard can move you ahead in your work. Just as the mental muscles need stretching, so do the bodily ones. It's wise to change positions often when writing, to avoid stiff muscles or headaches, and ideally you should move away from the keyboard and screen for ten minutes of every hour. Although such frequent breaks may not be practical, you can relax your muscles and stimulate circulation by doing some exercise at regular intervals. For calisthenic purposes, doing some isometrics at your desk and some flexing and stretching movements away from the desk two or three times each workday will help keep your body as limber as your imagination.

• Reading other writers' work nourishes your own. One of the most important contributions writers can make to their work is reading. The flow of words and ideas into our minds is vital to a flexibility of style and a breadth of knowledge for all of us. Although reading can't replace ''live'' contacts, especially good conversation, a major part of our mental nourishment should be in written form—so that we experience the medium that is also our work.

There is really no substitute for the stimulation that reading good writing can provide. It's a rejuvenation of our writing energies, a replenishing of the stores of vocabulary and expression. In short, writers are almost always inspired by reading quality work by our peers, and we are often moved to respond in kind.

Though reading continually is necessary nourishment for all writers, a good book near the word processor can be an antidote for an occasional block or an overdose of technology. If you are stymied by a particular passage or assignment, or your machine is misbehaving, take a break by turning away from the keyboard and screen, preferably putting your feet up, and opening that safety-valve book. A few minutes—or an hour—of reading could be the catalyst for your flow of words, and perhaps also the needed rest period for a balky machine.

• When in doubt, change tools. One final strategy to vary the rhythm of your work is to leave the word processor and spend half an hour or more writing the way you used to—with a typewriter or pen and paper. Just the change in writing mechanics could get you over a hurdle in the project, or at least allow you to view the work from a different perspective. And if you make the temporary switch because you've tired of the keyboard and screen, a short stint of labor-intensive writing the old way could send you back to your system with a new appreciation for its power and efficiency.

All of these writing styles and strategies are designed to help you get your thoughts into words quickly and gracefully. You can think of the keyboard as an extension of your fingers and the screen as an endless page or many-chambered notebook. Whatever images you invent for these writing tools (or whatever names you may call them at times), word processing makes it easy for you to write drafts, take chances, say anything you please in every way you like, and—when you're finished—it will reward you with a bulging pile of pages on which to hone your editing skills.

Transforming Writer-Based Prose into Reader-Based Prose

LINDA FLOWER

Linda Flower is Professor of English at Carnegie-Mellon University and a nationally recognized authority on the teaching of writing.

Good writers know how to transform writer-based prose (which works well for them) into reader-based prose (which works for their readers as well). Writing is inevitably a somewhat egocentric enterprise. We naturally tend to talk to ourselves when composing. As a result, we often need self-conscious strategies for trying to talk to our reader.

Strategy 1 Set Up a Shared Goal

The first strategy for adapting a paper to a reader is to create a shared goal. Try to find a reason for writing your paper and a reason for reading it that both you and your reader share. (Remember that your desire to convey information will not necessarily be met by your reader's desire to receive it.) Then organize your ideas and your arguments around this common goal. You will need to consider the knowledge, attitudes, and needs of your reader. . . .

A shared goal can be a powerful tool for persuasion. To illustrate, try this exercise:

> You have just been commissioned to write a short booklet on how to preserve older homes and buildings, which the City Historical Society wants to distribute throughout a historical section of the city in an effort to encourage preservation. Most of your readers will simply be residents and local business people. How are you going to get them, first, to read this booklet and, second, to use some of its suggestions?

Take several minutes to think about this problem, then write an opening paragraph for the booklet that includes a shared goal.

To test the effectiveness of your paragraph, consider the following two points about shared goals:

TRANSFORMING WRITER-BASED PROSE INTO READER-BASED PROSE By Linda Flower. Excerpted from *Problem-Solving Strategies for Writing*, Second Edition, by Linda Flower, copyright © 1985 by Harcourt Brace Jovanovich, Inc. Reprinted by permission of the publisher.

1. A shared goal can *motivate your audience* to read and remember what you have to say. Does your paragraph suggest that the booklet will solve some problem your reader faces or achieve some end he or she really cares about? An appeal to vague goals or a wishy-washy generalization such as "our heritage" is unlikely to keep the reader interested. Use your knowledge to fill some need your reader really has.

In a professional situation think of it this way: Your reader has ten letters and five reports on her desk this morning. Your opening statement with its shared goal should tell her why she would want to read your report first and read it carefully.

2. A shared goal can *increase comprehension*. People understand and retain information best when they can fit it into a framework they already know. For example, the context of "home repair" and "do-it-yourself" would be familiar and maybe attractive to your readers. In contrast, if you defined the goal as "architectural renovation" or "techniques of historical landmark preservation" you would make sense to members of the historical society but would have missed your primary audience, the local readers. They would probably find that context not only unfamiliar but somewhat intimidating.

Offer your readers a shared goal—one for which they already have a framework—that helps them turn your message into something meaningful to them.

Here are examples of three different introductory paragraphs written for this booklet. After reading each one, consider how you would evaluate its power to motivate and aid comprehension. Then read the reaction of another reader, which follows each paragraph.

1. This booklet will help you create civic pride and preserve our city's heritage. In addition you will be helping the Historical Society to grow and extend its influence over the city.
A reader's response:
I suppose civic pride is a good thing, but I'm not sure I'd want to help create it. This paragraph makes me feel a little suspicious. What does the Historical Society want from me? I'll bet this is going to be a booklet about raising money so they can put up city monuments.

2. This booklet is concerned with civic restoration and maintenance projects in designated historical areas. It discusses the methods and materials approved by the City Historical Society and City Board of Engineers.
A reader's response:
I guess this is some booklet for city planners or the people who want to set up museums. "Methods and materials" must refer to all those rules and regulations that city contractors have to follow. I wouldn't want to get mixed up with all that if I were doing improvements on my own home.

3. If you own an older home or historical building, there are a number of ways you can preserve its beauty and historical value. At the same time you can increase its market value and decrease its maintenance costs. This

booklet will show you five major ways to improve your building and give you step-by-step procedures for how to do this. Please read the booklet over and see which of the suggestions might be useful to you.
A reader's response:
This might be a good idea. I don't know if I'd want to buy the whole package, but I think I'll read it over. What is it—five things I could do? I might find something useful I could try out. I'm particularly concerned about the maintenance costs. Maybe I can find something here on insulation.

Note that in the final example the writer not only has identified shared goals but has given the reader a sort of mental map for reading and understanding the rest of the booklet.

Sometimes a shared goal is something as intangible as intellectual curiosity. But it is the writer's job, in whatever field, to recognize goals or needs that his reader might have and to try to fulfill them. . . . A good shared goal will motivate your reader by providing a context for understanding your ideas and a reason for acting on them.

Strategy 2   Develop a Reader-Based Structure

Most of us intend to write reader-based prose, to communicate with our reader. But for various reasons, people often end up writing writer-based prose, or talking to themselves. For example, the following excerpts are from letters written by students applying for summer jobs. They had been asked to include some personal background and experience.

Do some detective work on these paragraphs and try to describe the hidden logic that you think is organizing each one. Compare the paragraph to some other way you could write it. Why did the writers choose to include the particular facts they did, and why did they organize them in these particular ways?

Terry F.:
      I was born in Wichita, Kansas, on December 4, 1962. After four years there my family moved to Topeka, Kansas, where I attended kindergarten. The next year my family moved to Rose Hill, Iowa. I went to first grade there and my family moved again. I started second grade in Butler, Pennsylvania, and finished it in Pittsburgh, Pennsylvania, where I still live today. . . . I took the college curriculum in high school, which included English, history, science, French, and mathematics, and am currently a college sophomore.
      I would like this job for two reasons. First, I could use the money for school next year. Second, the experience would be very helpful. It would help me get a job in that specific area when I graduate.

Katherine P.:
      As a freshman I worked as a clerk in a student-managed store, Argus. . . . I became acquainted with the university personnel manager and was offered the position of Argus personnel manager for the semester beginning August, 1979. I accepted and held the job until December of 1979, when a managerial position

was eliminated. With managerial staff reduced to two people, responsibilities were adjusted and I was offered the position of purchasing agent. Again I accepted.

Notice that in these examples there is a logic organizing each paragraph, but it is the logic of a story, based on the writer's own memories and, in Terry's case, personal needs. The needs of the reader have not been considered. This is writer-based prose—writing that may seem quite clear and organized to the writer but is not yet adequately designed for the reader. In each case, the potential employer probably wanted to know how the applicant's background and experience could fit his or her needs. But neither paragraph was organized around that goal.

Why do people write to themselves when they are ostensibly writing to a reader? . . . [I]t is usually because they have simply forgotten to consider the reader.

There is another very good reason adults write writer-based prose. If you are working on a difficult paper, it is often easier to discover what you know first and worry about designing it for a reader later. . . .

Note, however, that in draft form, writer-based prose can have a real use. Since this type of writing comes naturally to us, it can be an efficient strategy for exploring a topic and outwitting our nemesis, short-term memory. If a writer's material is complicated or confusing, he may initially have to concentrate all his attention on generating and organizing his own knowledge. He might simply be too preoccupied to simultaneously imagine another person's point of view and adapt to it. The reader has to wait. But you don't want to make the reader wait forever.

You can usually recognize writer-based prose by one or more of these features:

1. An *egocentric focus* on the writer

2. A *narrative organization* focused on the writer's own discovery process

3. A *survey structure* organized, like a textbook, around the writer's information

There are times, of course, when a narrative structure is exactly right—if, for example, your goal is to tell a story or describe an event. And a survey of what you know can be a reasonable way to organize a background report or survey. But in most expository and persuasive writing, the writer needs to reorganize his or her knowledge around a problem, a thesis, or the reader's needs. Writer-based prose just hasn't been reorganized yet. . . .

Creating Reader-Based Prose

In the best of all possible worlds we would all write reader-based prose from the beginning. It is theoretically much more efficient to generate and organize your ideas in light of the reader in the first place. But sometimes that is hard to do. Take the assignment "Write about the physics of wind resistance for a model airplane builder." For a physics teacher this would be a trivial problem. But for someone ten years out of Physics 101, the first task would be remembering whatever they knew about wind resistance or friction at all. Adapting that knowledge to the reader would just have to wait.

In general, write for your reader whenever you can, but recognize that many times a first draft is going to be more writer-based than you may want it to be. Even though the draft may not work well for your reader, it can represent a great deal of work for you and be the groundwork for an effective paper. The more complex your problem and the more difficult your material, the more you will need to transform your writer-based prose to reader-based prose. This is not an overly difficult step in the writing process, but many writers simply neglect to take it.

In order to transform your paper to more reader-based prose, there are four major things you can do . . . :

1. Organize your paper around a problem, a thesis, or a purpose you share with the reader—not around your own discovery process or the topic itself.

2. With a goal or thesis as the top . . . organize your ideas in a hierarchy. Distinguish between your major and minor ideas and make the relationship between them explicit to the reader. You can use this technique to organize not only an entire paper but sections and paragraphs.

3. If you are hoping that your reader will draw certain conclusions from your paper, or even from a portion of it, make those conclusions explicit. If you expect him or her to go away with a few main ideas, don't leave the work of drawing inferences and forming concepts up to your reader. He or she might just draw a different set of conclusions.

4. Finally, once you have created concepts and organized your ideas in a hierarchy focused on your reader and your goals, use cues—which we will discuss shortly—to make that organization vivid and clear to the reader.

Strategy 3   Give Your Reader Cues

Part of your contract with a reader, if you seriously want to communicate, is to guide him or her through your prose. You need to set up cues that help the reader see what is coming and how it will be organized. This means, first of all, creating expectations and fulfilling them so that when your point arrives, your reader will have a well-anchored hook to hang it on. . . . In addition, you want the reader to know which points are major, which are minor, and how they are related to one another. By using various kinds of cues and signposts, you can guide the reader to build an accurate mental tree of your discussion.

Readers, of course, come to your prose with built-in expectations about where these cues will be. For example, they expect to find

1. the most important points of a discussion stated at the beginning and summarized in some way at the end.

2. a topic sentence that tells them what they will learn from a paragraph.

3. the writer's key words in grammatically important places such as the subject, verb, and object positions.

It is to your advantage to fulfill these expectations whenever you can.

Writers have a number of tools and techniques they can use to *preview* their meaning, *summarize* it, and *guide* the reader. Figure [1] lists some of the most common. Check this list against the last paper you wrote. How many of these tools did you take advantage of?

The conventions of format on a page also work as familiar cues to the reader. Figure [2] shows a typical format for papers and reports. . . .

Strategy 4   **Develop a Persuasive Argument**

People often write because they want to make something happen: They want the reader to do something or at least to see things their way. But sometimes

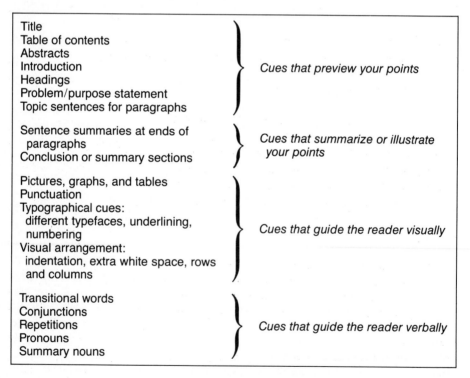

Figure [1] Cues for the Reader

THIS IS A TITLE: THE SUBTITLE QUALIFIES IT

The first sentence in this paragraph is a topic sentence, which announces the topic and previews the argument or point of the paragraph. The remainder of the paragraph often previews the rest of the paper, introducing the main points to be covered.

THIS IS A MAJOR HEADING

Major headings are placed flush left, often set in caps, and, in typewritten manuscript, usually underlined. In print they are often set in boldface type. Ideally a reader should be able to see the shape of your discussion simply by reading the title and major headings. Make the wording of major headings grammatically parallel, if you can, as the major and minor headings are in this example.

This Is a Minor Heading

Unlike a major heading it is indented and typed in capital and lowercase letters. It should be clearly and logically related to the major heading that precedes it.

> The fact that this passage is indented says it is either a long quotation or an example. The additional space around it and the single spacing signal that it is a different kind of text, and let readers adjust their reading speed and expectations.

Figure [2] Common Format for Typewritten Paper

expressing a point of view isn't enough, because it conflicts with the way the reader *already* sees things. We are faced with the same old problem of communication: Your image of something and your reader's are not the same. What kinds of arguments can you use that will make him or her see things *your* way? In this section we will look at the nature of arguments and at one type, the Rogerian argument, that can help you persuade another person to see things differently.

Winning an Argument Versus Persuading a Listener

When people think of arguments they usually think of winning them. And the time-honored method of winning an argument is by force ("You agree or I'll shoot.") or, in its more familiar form, by authority ("This is right because I [your mother, father, teacher, sergeant, boss] say it is."). The problem with force or authority is that, short of brainwashing, it often changes people's behavior but not their minds.

A second familiar form of argument is debate. Yet many people who learn to debate in high school discover that in the real world their debate strategies can indeed prove their point—but lose the argument. Debate is an argumentative contest: Person A is pitted against person B, and the winner is decided by an impartial judge. But in the real world, person A is trying not to impress a judge but to *convince* person B. The goal of such an argument is not to win points but to affect your listener, to change his or her image of your subject in some significant way. And, as you remember, that image may be a large, complex network of ideas, associations, and attitudes. The goal of communication is to find a common ground and create a shared image, but debate typically polarizes a discussion by pitting one image against the other.

Let us look for a moment at the possible outcomes of an argument or discussion in which the two parties have firmly held but differing images. Ann has decided to take a year off to work and travel before she finishes college and settles on a career. Her parents immediately oppose the idea. To them, this plan conveys an image of "dropping out" and wasting a year, with the possibility that Ann might not return to school. Furthermore, they have saved money to help put her through school and see this prospect as an indication that she doesn't value their plans, hopes, and efforts for her.

For Ann, on the other hand, taking a year off means getting time and experience that would enable her to take better advantage of college. She hopes it will help her decide what sort of work she wants to do, but more importantly she sees it as a chance to develop on her own for a while. In her mind, the goal of going to college isn't getting a degree but figuring out what things you want to learn more about.

Clearly Ann and her parents have very different images of taking a year off. Assume you are Ann in this situation. What are the possible outcomes of an argument you might have with your parents?

One outcome, and usually the least likely one, is that you will totally reconstruct your listeners' image so they see the issue just as you do. You simply replace their perspective with yours. Reconstruction can no doubt happen if your audience has an undeveloped image of the subject or sees you as a great authority, but argument strategies that set out to reconstruct someone else's ideas completely—to *win* the point—are usually ill-founded and unrealistic. They are more likely to polarize people than to persuade them.

A second alternative is to modify someone else's image, to add to or clarify it. You do this when you clarify an issue (for example, taking a year off is not the same as "dropping out") or when you add new information (Ann's college even has a special program for this and might give her some course credit for work experience). As a writer this is clearly the most reasonable effect you can aim for. In doing so you respect the other person's point of view while striving to modify those features you can reasonably affect.

The third possible outcome of an argument may be the most common: no change. Think for a minute of how many speeches, lectures, classes, sermons, and discussions you have sat through in your life and how many of those had no discernible effect on your thinking. If we think of an argument as debate in which a "good" argument inevitably wins, we forget that it is possible for even a "correct" argument to have absolutely no effect on our listener.

To sum up, the goal of an argument is to modify the image of your listener— and that this is not the same as simply presenting your own image. A successful argument is a reader-based act. It considers attitudes and images the reader already holds.

However, a great roadblock stands in the way of modifying a listener's image. Many people perceive any change in their image of things as a threat to their own security and stability. People's images are part of themselves, and a part of how they have made sense of the world. To ask them to change their image in any significant way can make people anxious and resistant to change. When this happens, communication simply stops.

Arguments that polarize issues often create just this situation. The more the speaker argues, the more firmly the listener clings to his own position. And instead of listening, the listener spends his time thinking up counter-arguments to protect his own position and image. So the critical question for the writer is this: How can I persuade my reader to listen to my position and maybe even modify his or her image without creating this sense of threat that stops communication?

Rogerian Argument

Rogerian argument, developed in part from the work of Carl Rogers, is an argument strategy designed not to win but to increase communication in both directions. It is based on the fact that if people feel they are understood—that their position is honestly recognized and respected—they may cease to feel a sense of threat. Once the threat is removed, listening is no longer an act of self-defense, and people feel they can afford to truly listen to and consider other ways of seeing things.

The goal of an argument, then, is to induce your reader at least to consider your position and the possibility of modifying his or her own. One way to make this happen is to demonstrate an understanding of your listener's position *first*. That means trying to see the issue from his or her point of view. For face-to-face discussions, Carl Rogers suggested this rule of thumb: Before you present your position and argue for your way of seeing things, you must be able to describe your listener's position back to your listener in such a way that he or she *agrees* with your version of it. In other words, you are demonstrating that you not only care about your listener's perspective but care enough to actively try (and keep trying) to understand it. So Ann in our example would have begun the discussion with her parents by exploring with them their response to her leaving college and the reasons behind their feelings.

What does this mean for writers who don't have the luxury of a face-to-face discussion? First, you can use the introduction to your paper, including your shared goal, to demonstrate to your reader a thorough understanding of his or her problems and goals. This is your chance to look at the question from your reader's point of view and show how your message is relevant to them.

Secondly, try to avoid categorizing people and issues. This puts people into camps, polarizes the argument, and stops communication. For example, Ann may well have felt that her parents were being old-fashioned and conventional to resist her idea, but establishing that point would have done little to change their minds. A Rogerian argument, by contrast, would begin by acknowledging the parents' plans and hopes for her and recognizing the element of truth in their fear of her "dropping out." They know that, despite good intentions, many people don't come back to college. In taking a Rogerian approach, Ann might also begin to understand the issues more clearly herself. One of the hidden strengths of a Rogerian argument is that, besides increasing one's power to persuade, it also opens up communication and may even end up persuading the persuader. It increases the possibility of genuine communication and change for both the speaker and listener.

The first draft of Ann's letter started like this:

Dear Mom and Dad,

    I wish you would try to see my point of view and not be so conventional. Things are different from when you went to school. And you must realize I am old enough to make my own decisions, even if you disagree. There are a number of good reasons why this is the best decision I could make. First, . . .

Although this letter created a "strong" argument, it was also likely to stop communication and unlikely to persuade. Here is the letter Ann eventually wrote to her parents, which tries to take an open Rogerian approach to the problem.

Dear Mom and Dad,

As I told you the other night on the phone, I want to consider taking a year off from college to work and be on my own for a while. I've been thinking over what you said because this is an important decision and, like you, I want to do what will be best in the long run, not just what seems attractive now. I think some of your objections make a lot of sense. After all the effort you've put into helping me get through college, it would be terrible to just "drop out" or never find a real career that I could be committed to.

I know you're also wondering if I recognize what an opportunity I have and are probably worrying if I'm just going to let it slip through my fingers. Well, in a way I'm worried about that too. Here I am working hard, but I don't really know where I want to go or why. It's time for me to specialize and I can't decide what to do. And it's that opportunity I'm afraid of losing. I feel I need some time off and some experience so I can make a better decision and really take advantage of my last year here.

But there's still the question of whether I would be dropping out. The college actually has a program for people who want to take a year off, and they even encourage you to enter it if you have some idea of what you'd be doing. So, as far as the school is concerned, I'd be in a well-established leave of absence program. But the fact is, people do drop out. They don't always come back. What would a whole year away from school do to me? You're right, I can't really be sure. But I think my reasons are good ones, and I'm working on a plan that would let me earn credit while I work and come back to school with a clearer sense of where I want to go. Can you offer me any more suggestions on ways I could plan ahead?

Love,
ANN

2

PROBLEMS WITH LANGUAGE

In Lewis Carroll's *Through the Looking Glass*, Alice has the following exchange with Humpty Dumpty:

> "When *I* use a word," Humpty Dumpty said, in a rather scornful tone, "it means just what I choose it to mean—nothing more nor less."
> "The question is," said Alice, "whether you *can* make words mean so many different things."

When you read technical and business documents, you may suspect that Humpty Dumpty has been promoted to project manager—or even company president.

It is not always clear why business and technical writers get themselves into problems with language. At times, they mistakenly assume their readers will know what they are talking about, or that their goal is to impress rather than inform their readers. At other times, they simply imitate their superiors or model their documents after those in the files, as if the filing cabinet were a repository for sacred writings handed down from on high.

To solve problems with language, you must remember your readers and then be guided by only two principles:

- write everything as clearly, straightforwardly, and simply as possible;

- write in a form with which you would be comfortable speaking.

These principles will help you avoid problems with jargon, gobbledygook, legalese, and sexist language. They will also serve as a guide in selecting the style appropriate to different writing situations.

Jargon is simply technical language unique to a profession or occupation. It becomes a problem only when you use it in writing to an audience without the background necessary to understand it. A systems engineer writing to another systems engineer could rightly assume that the following passage would make sense.

> If you are using a CONFIG.SYS file to modify version 2.0 of the Personal Computer DOS, you may want to create a CONFIG.SYS file to use with this program instead of the AUTOEXEC.BAT file.

Unfortunately, this passage comes from an introductory computer manual.

Jargon in the extreme becomes gobbledygook, mindless gibberish akin to doubletalk and characterized by pretentiousness. For example, the host of a television game show tells contestants who are losing that they are in "a deficit situation"; ordinary No. 2 pencils become, in the requisitions of some bureaucrats, "writing implements, standard issue"; politicians wary of angering voters call tax increases "revenue enhancements"; "Turn out the lights when you leave" becomes "Illumination is required to be extinguished upon vacation of the premises."

Gobbledygook also includes words and phrases that writers mistakenly think sound the way business and technical writing should sound. They may be in vogue or out of date, but either way, they have unfortunately come to be accepted by some unskilled writers as good professional writing practices. People no longer meet for discussions—they "interface," and every issue about which they interface has "parameters." Some of these same people see nothing wrong with beginning their letters with "Per yours of the twelfth, we are pleased to advise that" and go on to refer to data "hereunder discussed" or "above referenced."

Legalese is an over-reliance on legal terminology—or legal *sounding* terminology—when Plain English will serve both the reader and the writer as well. The Commerce Department, under the leadership of its late secretary, Malcolm Baldridge, has been a leading force in the battle against legalese. In *How Plain English Works* (Washington, DC: Government Printing Office, 1984), the department's Office of Consumer Affairs presents twelve case studies showing how business organizations have successfully simplified consumer documents. As the introduction to this publication points out, such efforts benefit a company in a number of ways:

> When a company simplifies its language, it builds business and saves time and money. It streamlines its procedures, eliminates unnecessary forms, and reduces customer complaints. Its employees, as well as its customers, get a better grasp of how the company does business. This increases productivity and customer satisfaction (p. v).

Sexist language is linguistic discrimination usually, although not exclusively, against women. Just as all managers are not men, so all secretaries are not women. Common sense and fairness can help you avoid sexism in your writing. You need to be careful that you do not exclude readers based on sex and that you do treat members of both sexes equally.

The five selections that follow address further the issues raised in these introductory comments. In a now classic piece, Stuart Chase sends up the linguistic overkill that is all too common in the writing of government officials, lawyers, and academics. William Zinsser follows with an essay that suggests it is possible for you to write for the world of work and still sound like a human being.

John S. Fielden then provides a detailed discussion of style:

> that choice of words, sentences, and paragraph format which by virtue of being appropriate to the situation and to the power positions of both writer and reader produces the desired reaction and result (p. 85).

Fielden discusses six styles appropriate for business communication.

Using Fielden's definition of style, we can see legalese as style gone haywire. The antidote to legalese is Plain English. Alan Siegel provides a brief history of the Plain English movement in his account of the work his company has done in helping clients reduce legalese in functional documents.

William C. Paxson concludes Part Two by providing five easy-to-follow rules for avoiding sexism in your written business and technical communication.

Gobbledygook

STUART CHASE

Stuart Chase worked for many years as a consultant to various government agencies; his other books include *The Tyranny of Words* (1938) and *Democracy Under Pressure* (1945).

 aid Franklin Roosevelt, in one of his early presidential speeches: "I see one-third of a nation ill-housed, ill-clad, ill-nourished." Translated into standard bureaucratic prose his statement would read:

> It is evident that a substantial number of persons within the Continental boundaries of the United States have inadequate financial resources with which to purchase the products of agricultural communities and industrial establishments. It would appear that for a considerable segment of the population, possibly as much as 33.3333* of the total, there are inadequate housing facilities, and an equally significant proportion is deprived of the proper types of clothing and nutriment.
> *Not carried beyond four places.

This rousing satire on gobbledygook—or talk among the bureaucrats—is adapted from a report[1] prepared by the Federal Security Agency in an attempt to break out of the verbal squirrel cage. "Gobbledygook" was coined by an exasperated Congressman, Maury Maverick of Texas, and means using two, or three, or ten words in the place of one, or using a five-syllable word where a single syllable would suffice. Maverick was censuring the forbidding prose of executive departments in Washington, but the term has now spread to windy and pretentious language in general.

"Gobbledygook" itself is a good example of the way a language grows. There was no word for the event before Maverick's invention; one had to say: "You know, that terrible, involved, polysyllabic language those government people use down in Washington." Now one word takes the place of a dozen.

A British member of Parliament, A. P. Herbert, also exasperated with bureaucratic jargon, translated Nelson's immortal phrase, "England expects every man to do his duty":

[1] This and succeeding quotations from F.S.A. report by special permission of the author, Milton Hall.

England anticipates that, as regards the current emergency, personnel will face up to the issues, and exercise appropriately the functions allocated to their respective occupational groups.

A New Zealand official made the following report after surveying a plot of ground for an athletic field:[2]

It is obvious from the difference in elevation with relation to the short depth of the property that the contour is such as to preclude any reasonable developmental potential for active recreation.

Seems the plot was too steep.

An office manager sent this memo to his chief:

Verbal contact with Mr. Blank regarding the attached notification of promotion has elicited the attached representation intimating that he prefers to decline the assignment.

Seems Mr. Blank didn't want the job.

A doctor testified at an English trial that one of the parties was suffering from "circumorbital haematoma."

Seems the party had a black eye.

In August 1952 the U.S. Department of Agriculture put out a pamphlet entitled: "Cultural and Pathogenic Variability in Single-Condial and Hyphaltip Isolates of Hemlin-Thosporium Turcicum Pass."

Seems it was about corn leaf disease.

On reaching the top of the Finsteraarhorn in 1845, M. Dollfus-Ausset, when he got his breath, exclaimed:

The soul communes in the infinite with those icy peaks which seem to have their roots in the bowels of eternity.

Seems he enjoyed the view.

A government department announced:

Voucherable expenditures necessary to provide adequate dental treatment required as adjunct to medical treatment being rendered a pay patient in in-patient status may be incurred as required at the expense of the Public Health Service.

Seems you can charge your dentist bill to the Public Health Service. Or can you?

[2]This item and the next two are from the piece on gobbledygook by W. E. Farbstein, New York Times, March 29, 1953.

Legal Talk

Gobbledygook not only flourishes in government bureaus but grows wild and lush in the law, the universities, and sometimes among the literati. Mr. Micawber was a master of gobbledygook, which he hoped would improve his fortunes. It is almost always found in offices too big for face-to-face talk. Gobbledygook can be defined as squandering words, packing a message with excess baggage and so introducing semantic "noise." Or it can be scrambling words in a message so that meaning does not come through. The directions on cans, bottles, and packages for putting the contents to use are often a good illustration. Gobbledygook must not be confused with double talk, however, for the intentions of the sender are usually honest.

I offer you a round fruit and say, "Have an orange." Not so an expert in legal phraseology, as parodied by editors of *Labor*:

> I hereby give and convey to you, all and singular, my estate and interests, right, title, claim and advantages of and in said orange, together with all rind, juice, pulp and pits, and all rights and advantages therein . . . anything herein-before or hereinafter or in any other deed or deeds, instrument or instruments of whatever nature or kind whatsoever, to the contrary, in any wise, notwithstanding.

The state of Ohio, after five years of work, has redrafted its legal code in modern English, eliminating 4,500 sections and doubtless a blizzard of "where-ases" and "hereinafters." Legal terms of necessity must be closely tied to their referents, but the early solons tried to do this the hard way, by adding synonyms. They hoped to trap the physical event in a net of words, but instead they created a mumbo-jumbo beyond the power of the layman, and even many a lawyer, to translate. Legal talk is studded with tautologies, such as "cease and desist," "give and convey," "irrelevant, incompetent, and immaterial." Furthermore, legal jargon is a dead language; it is not spoken and it is not growing. An official of one of the big insurance companies calls their branch of it "bafflegab." Here is a sample from his collection.[3]

> One-half to his mother, if living, if not to his father, and one-half to his mother-in-law, if living, if not to his mother, if living, if not to his father. Thereafter payment is to be made in a single sum to his brothers. On the one-half payable to his mother, if living, if not to his father, he does not bring in his mother-in-law as the next payee to receive, although on the one-half to his mother-in-law, he does bring in the mother or father.

You apply for an insurance policy, pass the tests, and instead of a straightforward "here is your policy," you receive something like this:

> This policy is issued in consideration of the application therefor, copy of which application is attached hereto and made part hereof, and of the payment for said insurance on the life of the above-named insured.

[3]Interview with Clifford B. Reeves by Sylvia F. Porter, New York *Evening Post*, March 14, 1952.

Academic Talk

The pedagogues may be less repetitious than the lawyers, but many use even longer words. It is a symbol of their calling to prefer Greek and Latin derivatives to Anglo-Saxon. Thus instead of saying: "I like short clear words," many a professor would think it more seemly to say: "I prefer an abbreviated phraseology, distinguished for its lucidity." Your professor is sometimes right, the longer word may carry the meaning better—but not because it is long. Allen Upward in his book *The New Word* warmly advocates Anglo-Saxon English as against what he calls "Mediterranean" English, with its polysyllables built up like a skyscraper.

Professional pedagogy, still alternating between the Middle Ages and modern science, can produce what Henshaw Ward once called the most repellent prose known to man. It takes an iron will to read as much as a page of it. Here is a sample of what is known in some quarters as "pedageese":

> Realization has grown that the curriculum or the experiences of learners change and improve only as those who are most directly involved examine their goals, improve their understandings and increase their skill in performing the tasks necessary to reach newly defined goals. This places the focus upon teacher, lay citizen and learner as partners in curricular improvement and as the individuals who must change, if there is to be curriculum change.

I think there is an idea concealed here somewhere. I think it means: "If we are going to change the curriculum, teacher, parent, and student must all help." The reader is invited to get out his semantic decoder and check on my translation. Observe there is no technical language in this gem of pedageese, beyond possibly the word "curriculum." It is just a simple idea heavily oververbalized.

In another kind of academic talk the author may display his learning to conceal a lack of ideas. A bright instructor, for instance, in need of prestige may select a common sense proposition for the subject of a learned monograph—say, "Modern cities are hard to live in" and adorn it with imposing polysyllables: "Urban existence in the perpendicular declivities of megalopolis . . ." et cetera. He coins some new terms to transfix the reader—"mega-decibel" or "strato-cosmopolis"—and works them vigorously. He is careful to add a page or two of differential equations to show the "scatter." And then he publishes, with 147 footnotes and a bibliography to knock your eye out. If the authorities are dozing, it can be worth an associate professorship.

While we are on the campus, however, we must not forget that the technical language of the natural sciences and some terms in the social sciences, forbidding as they may sound to the layman, are quite necessary. Without them, specialists could not communicate what they find. Trouble arises when experts expect the uninitiated to understand the words; when they tell the jury, for instance, that the defendant is suffering from "circumorbital haematoma."

Here are two authentic quotations. Which was written by a distinguished modern author, and which by a patient in a mental hospital? You will find the answer at the end of the [selection].

1. Have just been to supper. Did not knowing what the woodchuck sent me here. How when the blue blue blue on the said anyone can do it that tries. Such is the presidential candidate.

2. No history of a family to close with those and close. Never shall he be alone to be alone to be alone to be alone to be alone to lend a hand and leave it left and wasted.

Reducing the Gobble

As government and business offices grow larger, the need for doing something about gobbledygook increases. Fortunately the biggest office in the world is working hard to reduce it. The Federal Security Agency in Washington,[4] with nearly 100 million clients on its books, began analyzing its communication lines some years ago, with gratifying results. Surveys find trouble in three main areas: correspondence with clients about their social security problems, office memos, official reports.

Clarity and brevity, as well as common humanity, are urgently needed in this vast establishment which deals with disability, old age, and unemployment. The surveys found instead many cases of long-windedness, foggy meanings, clichés, and singsong phrases, and gross neglect of the reader's point of view. Rather than talking to a real person, the writer was talking to himself. "We often write like a man walking on stilts."

Here is a typical case of long-windedness:

> *Gobbledygook as found:* "We are wondering if sufficient time has passed so that you are in a position to indicate whether favorable action may now be taken on our recommendation for the reclassification of Mrs. Blank, junior clerk-stenographer, CAF 2, to assistant clerk-stenographer, CAF 3?"
> *Suggested improvement:* "Have you yet been able to act on our recommendation to reclassify Mrs. Blank?"

Another case:

> Although the Central Efficiency Rating Committee recognizes that there are many desirable changes that could be made in the present efficiency rating system in order to make it more realistic and more workable than it now is, this committee is of the opinion that no further change should be made in the present system during the current year. Because of conditions prevailing throughout the country and the resultant turnover in personnel, and difficulty in administering the Federal programs, further mechanical improvement in the present rating system would require staff retraining and other administrative expense which would seem best withheld until the official termination of hostilities, and until restoration of regular operations.

The F.S.A. invites us to squeeze the gobbledygook out of this statement. Here is my attempt:

[4]Now the Department of Health and Human Services.

> The Central Efficiency Rating Committee recognizes that desirable changes could be made in the present system. We believe, however, that no change should be attempted until the war is over.

This cuts the statement from 111 to 30 words, about one-quarter of the original, but perhaps the reader can do still better. What of importance have I left out?

Sometimes in a book which I am reading for information—not for literary pleasure—I run a pencil through the surplus words. Often I can cut a section to half its length with an improvement in clarity. Magazines like *The Reader's Digest* have reduced this process to an art. Are long-windedness and obscurity a cultural lag from the days when writing was reserved for priests and cloistered scholars? The more words and the deeper the mystery, the greater their prestige and the firmer the hold on their jobs. And the better the candidate's chance today to have his doctoral thesis accepted.

The F.S.A. surveys found that a great deal of writing was obscure although not necessarily prolix. Here is a letter sent to more than 100,000 inquirers, a classic example of murky prose. To clarify it, one needs to *add* words, not cut them:

> In order to be fully insured, an individual must have earned $50 or more in covered employment for as many quarters of coverage as half the calendar quarters elapsing between 1936 and the quarter in which he reaches age 65 or dies, whichever first occurs.

Probably no one without the technical jargon of the office could translate this: nevertheless, it was sent out to drive clients mad for seven years. One poor fellow wrote back: "I am no longer in covered employment. I have an outside job now."

Many words and phrases in officialese seem to come out automatically, as if from lower centers of the brain. In this standardized prose people never *get jobs*, they "secure employment"; *before* and *after* become "prior to" and "subsequent to"; one does not *do*, one "performs"; nobody *knows* a thing, he is "fully cognizant"; one never *says*, he "indicates." A great favorite at present is "implement." Some charming boners occur in this talking-in-one's-sleep. For instance:

> The problem of extending coverage to all employees, regardless of size, is not as simple as surface appearances indicate.
> Though the proportions of all males and females in ages 16–45 are essentially the same . . .
> Dairy cattle, usually and commonly embraced in dairying . . .

In its manual to employees, the F.S.A. suggests the following:

INSTEAD OF	USE
give consideration to	consider
make inquiry regarding	inquire
is of the opinion	believes
comes into conflict with	conflicts
information which is of a confidential nature	confidential information

Professional or office gobbledygook often arises from using the passive rather than the active voice. Instead of looking you in the eye, as it were, and writing "This act requires . . ." the office worker looks out of the window and writes: "It is required by this statute that . . ." When the bureau chief says, "We expect Congress to cut your budget," the message is only too clear; but usually he says, "It is expected that the departmental budget estimates will be reduced by Congress."

> GOBBLED: "All letters prepared for the signature of the Administrator will be single spaced."
> UNGOBBLED: "Single space all letters for the Administrator." (Thus cutting 13 words to 7.)

Only People Can Read

The F.S.A. surveys pick up the point . . . that human communication involves a listener as well as a speaker. Only people can read, though a lot of writing seems to be addressed to beings in outer space. To whom are you talking? The sender of the officialese message often forgets the chap on the other end of the line.

A woman with two small children wrote the F.S.A. asking what she should do about payments, as her husband had lost his memory. "If he never gets able to work," she said, "and stays in an institution would I be able to draw any benefits? . . . I don't know how I am going to live and raise my children since he is disable to work. Please give me some information. . . ."

To this human appeal, she received a shattering blast of gobbledygook, beginning, "State unemployment compensation laws do not provide any benefits for sick or disabled individuals . . . in order to qualify an individual must have a certain number of quarters of coverage . . ." et cetera, et cetera. Certainly if the writer had been thinking about the poor woman he would not have dragged in unessential material about old-age insurance. If he had pictured a mother without means to care for her children, he would have told her where she might get help—from the local office which handles aid to dependent children, for instance.

Gobbledygook of this kind would largely evaporate if we thought of our messages as two way—in the above case, if we pictured ourselves talking on the doorstep of a shabby house to a woman with two children tugging at her skirts, who in her distress does not know which way to turn.

Results of the Survey

The F.S.A. survey showed that office documents could be cut 20 to 50 percent, with an improvement in clarity and a great saving to taxpayers in paper and payrolls.

A handbook was prepared and distributed to key officials.[5] They read it,

5By Milton Hall.

thought about it, and presently began calling section meetings to discuss gobbledygook. More booklets were ordered, and the local output of documents
began to improve. A Correspondence Review Section was established as a kind
of laboratory to test murky messages. A supervisor could send up samples for
analysis and suggestions. The handbook is now used for training new members;
and many employees keep it on their desks along with the dictionary. Outside the
Bureau some 25,000 copies have been sold (at 20 cents each) to individuals,
governments, business firms, all over the world. It is now used officially in the
Veterans Administration and in the Department of Agriculture.

The handbook makes clear the enormous amount of gobbledygook which
automatically spreads in any large office, together with ways and means to keep it
under control. I would guess that at least half of all the words circulating around
the bureaus of the world are "irrelevant, incompetent, and immaterial"—to use a
favorite legalism; or are just plain "unnecessary"—to ungobble it.

My favorite story of removing the gobble from gobbledygook concerns the
Bureau of Standards at Washington. I have told it before but perhaps the reader
will forgive the repetition. A New York plumber wrote the Bureau that he had
found hydrochloric acid fine for cleaning drains, and was it harmless? Washington
replied: "The efficacy of hydrochloric acid is indisputable, but the chlorine residue
is incompatible with metallic permanence."

The plumber wrote back that he was mighty glad the Bureau agreed with
him. The Bureau replied with a note of alarm: "We cannot assume responsibility
for the production of toxic and noxious residues with hydrochloric acid, and
suggest that you use an alternate procedure." The plumber was happy to learn
that the Bureau still agreed with him.

Whereupon Washington exploded: "Don't use hydrochloric acid; it eats hell
out of the pipes!"

Note: The second quotation on page 72 comes from Gertrude Stein's *Lucy Church Amiably.*

Writing in Your Job

WILLIAM ZINSSER

William Zinsser is the author of nine books
and a former columnist, editor, and critic for
Life, the *New York Herald Tribune*, and the
New York Times. He is now Executive Editor of the Book-of-the-Month Club.

Most people work for institutions—businesses and banks, insurance
firms and law firms, government agencies, school systems, nonprofit
organizations and various other entities. Many of them are executives
whose writing goes out to the public: the corporation president addressing his
stockholders, the bank manager explaining a change in procedure, the school
principal writing a newsletter to parents. Whoever they are, they are so uncom-
fortable or fearful that their sentences lack all humanity—and so do their institutions. In fact, it is hard to imagine that these are real places where real men and
women come to work every morning.

But just because people work for an institution they don't have to write like
one. Institutions can be warmed up. Administrators and executives can be turned
into human beings. Information can be imparted clearly and without pompous
verbosity. It's a question of remembering that readers identify with people, not
with abstractions like ''profitability,'' or with Latinate nouns like ''utilization'' and
''implementation,'' or with passive-verb constructions in which nobody can be
visualized doing something (''pre-feasibility studies are in the paperwork stage'').

Nowhere has the point been made better than in George Orwell's ''translation'' into modern bureaucratic fuzz of this famous verse from Ecclesiastes:

> I returned and saw under the sun, that the race is not to the swift, nor the
> battle to the strong, neither yet bread to the wise, nor yet riches to men of
> understanding, nor yet favor to men of skill; but time and chance happeneth to
> them all.

Orwell's version goes:

> Objective consideration of contemporary phenomena compels the con-
> clusion that success or failure in competitive activities exhibits no tendency to be
> commensurate with innate capacity, but that a considerable element of the
> unpredictable must invariably be taken into account.

Gone are the short words and vivid images from everyday life—the race and the battle, the bread and the riches—and in their place have waddled the long and flabby nouns of generalized meaning. Gone is any sense of what one person did ("I returned") or what he realized ("saw") about one of life's central mysteries: the capriciousness of fate.

I'll use school principals as my first example here, not because they are the worst offenders (they aren't), but because I happen to have such an example. My points are intended, however, for all the big and small executives in all the organizations where language has lost its humanity and nobody quite knows what the people in charge are trying to say.

My encounter with the principals began when I got a call from Ernest B. Fleishman, superintendent of schools in Greenwich, Conn. "We'd like you to come and 'dejargonize' us," he said. "We don't think we can teach students to write unless all of us at the top of the school system clean up our own writing." He said he would send me some typical materials that had originated within the system. His idea was for me to analyze the writing and then conduct a workshop.

What appealed to me was the willingness of Dr. Fleishman and his colleagues to make themselves vulnerable. We decided on a date, and soon a fat envelope arrived. It contained various internal memos and a number of mimeographed newsletters that had been mailed to parents by the sixteen elementary, junior and senior high schools ("A Message from the Principal").

The newsletters had a cheery and informal look. Obviously the system was making an effort to communicate warmly with its families. But even at first glance certain chilly phrases caught my eye—"prioritized evaluative procedures," "modified departmentalized schedule"—and one principal promised that his school would provide "enhanced positive learning environments." Just as obviously the system wasn't communicating as warmly as it thought it was.

I studied the principals' material and divided it into good and bad examples. On the appointed morning in Greenwich I found forty principals, directors and curriculum coordinators assembled and eager to learn. I said that I could only applaud them for submitting to a process that so threatened their identity. In the national clamor over why Johnny can't write, Dr. Fleishman was the first adult in my experience who admitted that youth has no monopoly on verbal sludge and that the problem must also be attacked at the top.

I told the principals that as parents we want to think of the men and women who run our children's schools as people not unlike ourselves. We are suspicious of pretentiousness, of all the fad words that the social scientists have coined to avoid the horrid necessity of making themselves clear to ordinary mortals. I urged them to be natural. How we write and how we talk is how we define ourselves.

I asked them to listen to how they were defining themselves to the community. I had made forty copies of certain bad examples, changing the names of the schools and principals. I explained that I would read some of the examples aloud. Later we would see if they could turn what they had written into plain English. This was my first example:

Dear Parent:

We have established a special phone communication system to provide additional opportunities for parent input. During this year we will give added emphasis to the goal of communication and utilize a variety of means to accomplish this goal. Your inputs, from the unique position as a parent, will help us to plan and implement an educational plan that meets the needs of your child. An open dialogue, feedback and sharing of information between parents and teachers will enable us to work with your child in the most effective manner.

DR. GEORGE B. JONES
Principal

That is the kind of communication I don't want to receive, unique though my parent inputs might be. I'd like to be told that the school is going to make it easier for me to telephone the teachers and that they hope I'll call often to discuss how my children are getting along. Instead the parent gets junk: "special phone communication system," "added emphasis to the goal of communication," "plan and implement an educational plan." As for "open dialogue, feedback and sharing of information," they are three ways of saying the same thing.

Dr. Jones is clearly a man who means well, and his plan is one that we all want: a chance to pick up the phone and tell the principal what a great kid Johnny is despite that unfortunate incident in the playground last Tuesday. But Dr. Jones doesn't sound like a person I want to call. In fact, he doesn't sound like a person. His message could have been tapped out by a computer. He is squandering a rich resource: himself.

Another example that I chose was a "Principal's Greeting" sent to parents at the start of the year. It consisted of two paragraphs that were very different:

Fundamentally, Foster is a good school. Pupils who require help in certain subjects or study skills areas are receiving special attention. In the second year ahead we seek to provide enhanced positive learning environments. Children, and staff, must work in an atmosphere that is conducive to learning. Wide varieties of instructional materials are needed. Careful attention to individual abilities and learning styles is required. Co-operation between school and home is extremely important to the learning process. All of us should be aware of desired educational objectives for every child.

Keep informed about what is planned for our children this year and let us know about your own questions and about any special needs your child may have. I have met many of you in the first few weeks. Please continue to stop in to introduce yourself or to talk about Foster. I look forward to a very productive year for all of us.

DR. RAY B. DAWSON
Principal

In the second paragraph I'm being greeted by a person; in the first I'm hearing from an educator. I like the real Dr. Dawson of Paragraph 2. He talks in warm and comfortable phrases: "Keep informed," "Let us know," "I have met," "Please continue," "I look forward."

By contrast, Educator Dawson of Paragraph 1 never uses "I" or even suggests a sense of "I." He falls back on the jargon of his profession, where he feels safe, not stopping to notice that he really isn't telling the parent anything. What are "study skills areas" and how do they differ from "subjects"? What are "enhanced positive learning environments" and how do they differ from "an atmosphere that is conducive to learning"? What are "wide varieties of instructional materials": pencils, textbooks, filmstrips? What exactly are "learning styles"? What "educational objectives" are "desired," and who desires them?

The second paragraph, in short, is warm and personal; the other is pedantic and vague. This was a pattern that I found repeatedly. Whenever the principals wrote to notify the parents of some human detail they wrote with humanity:

> It seems that traffic is beginning to pile up again in front of the school. If you can possibly do so, please come to the rear of the school for your child at the end of the day.

> I would appreciate it if you would speak with your children about their behavior in the cafeteria. Many of you would be totally dismayed if you could observe the manners of your children while they are eating. Check occasionally to see if they owe money for lunch. Sometimes children are very slow in repaying.

But when the educators wrote to explain how they proposed to do their educating, they vanished without a trace:

> In this document you will find the program goals and objectives that have been identified and prioritized. Evaluative procedures for the objectives were also established based on acceptable criteria.

> Prior to the implementation of the above practice, students were given very little exposure to multiple choice questions. It is felt that the use of practice questions correlated to the unit that a student is presently studying has had an extremely positive effect as the test scores confirm.

After I had read various good and bad examples, the principals began to hear the difference between their true selves and their educator selves. The problem was how to close the gap. I recited my articles of faith: humanity, clarity, simplicity, vitality. I explained about using active verbs and avoiding windy nouns. I told them not to use the private vocabulary of education as a crutch. There is almost no specialized subject that can't be made accessible in good English.

These were all basic tenets, but the principals wrote them down as if they had never heard them before—and maybe they hadn't, or at least not for many years. Perhaps this is why bureaucratic prose becomes so turgid, whatever the bureaucracy. Once an administrator rises to a certain level, nobody ever points out to him again the beauty of a short declarative sentence, or shows him how his writing has become swollen with ornate generalizations.

Finally our workshop got down to work. I distributed my forty copies and asked the principals to rewrite the more knotty sentences. It was a grim moment. They had met the enemy for the first time. They scribbled on their pads and scratched out what they had scribbled. Some didn't write anything. Some crumpled their paper. They began, in fact, to look like writers. An awful silence hung over the room, broken only by the crossing out of sentences and the crumpling of paper. They began to sound like writers.

As the day went on, they slowly relaxed. They began to write in the first person and to use active verbs. For a while they still couldn't loose their grip on long words and vague nouns ("parent communication response"). But gradually their sentences became human. When I asked them to tackle "Evaluative procedures for the objectives were established based on acceptable criteria," one of them wrote: "At the end of the year we will evaluate our progress." Another wrote: "We will see how well we have succeeded."

That's the kind of plain talk that a parent wants. It's also what the stockholder wants from his corporation, what the customer wants from his bank, what the widow wants from the government office that is handling her social security. There is a yearning for human contact and a resentment of bombast. Any institution that won't take the trouble in its writing to be both clear and personal will lose friends, customers and money. Let me put it another way for business executives: a shortfall will be experienced in anticipated profitability.

Still, plain talk will not be easily achieved in corporate America. Too much vanity is on the line. Executives at every level are prisoners of the notion that a simple style reflects a simple mind. Actually a simple style is the result of hard work and hard thinking; a muddy style reflects a muddy thinker or a person too lazy to organize his thoughts.

I learned about corporate America by venturing out into it, after Greenwich, to conduct similar workshops for several of the country's biggest corporations, which also asked to be dejargonized. I worked with men and women who produce the vast amounts of written material that these huge companies generate for internal and external consumption.

The internal material consists of house organs and newsletters—daily, weekly and monthly—that are written to tell employees what is happening at their "facility" and to give them a sense of belonging. The external material includes the glossy magazines that go to the public, the speeches that are delivered by the president, and releases that are sent to the press. I found almost all of it lacking in human juices and much of it impenetrable.

Typical of the sentences in the newsletters were these:

> Included was the Configuration Requirements Processing (CRP) delivery
> containing the first complete process-control tables that will be used to specify

software requirements by mission and the Software Checkout (SWCO) confidence tape for validating the real-time Mission Control application programs.

Announced concurrently with the above enhancements were changes to the System Support Program, a program product which operates in conjunction with the NCP. Among the additional functional enhancements are dynamic reconfiguration and inter-systems communications.

There is no joy for the writer in such work, and certainly none for the reader. It is language out of *Star Trek*, and if I were an employee I would not be cheered—or informed—by these efforts to raise my morale. In fact, I would soon stop reading them, just as I soon learned not to try to decipher the internal memos that circulate through Yale. Life is too short for such dreary mental gymnastics.

I told the corporate writers that they had to find the people behind these fine scientific achievements. "Go to the engineer who created the system," I said, "or to the technicians who assembled it, and get them to tell you in their own words how the idea came to them, or how they put it together, and how it will be used." The way to warm up an institution is to locate the missing "I." He or she is the most interesting part of any story.

The writers explained that they often did interview the engineer but couldn't get him to talk English. They showed me some typical quotations in their newsletters that proved the point all too well. The engineers spoke in an arcane language studded with acronyms ("Sub-system support is available only with VSAG or TNA").

I said that the writers had to keep going back to the engineer until he finally made himself intelligible. They said that the engineer didn't *want* to be made intelligible: if he spoke too simply he would look like a jerk to his peers. I said that their responsibility was to the facts and to the reader, not to the vanity of the engineer. I urged them to believe in themselves as writers and not to relinquish control. They replied that this was easier said than done in hierarchical corporations where approval is required at various higher levels. I sensed an undercurrent of fear: do things the company way and don't risk your job trying to make the company human.

But I found that high executives were equally victimized by the syndrome of sounding important. One corporation, for instance, had a monthly newsletter to enable "management" to share its concerns with middle managers and lower employees. Prominent in every issue was a message of exhortation from the division vice-president, whom I'll call Vernon B. Smith. Judging by his monthly message, he was a pompous ass, saying nothing and saying it in inflated verbiage.

When I mentioned this, the writers said that Vernon B. Smith was actually a diffident man and a good executive with a good mind. They pointed out that he doesn't write the message himself; it's written for him. I said that Vernon B. Smith was being done a disservice—that the writers should go to him every month (with a tape recorder, if necessary) and stay there until he talked about his concerns in the same language that he would use when he got home and talked to Mrs. Vernon B. Smith.

What I realized—by extension—was that most executives in America don't write what appears over their signature or what they say in their speeches. They have surrendered the qualities that make them unique. If they and their institutions seem cold and pretentious it is because they acquiesce in the process of being pumped up and dried out. Preoccupied with their complex equipment, they forget that words are among the most powerful of all tools—for good and bad.

If you work for an institution, whatever your job, whatever your level, be yourself when you write. You will stand out as a real person among the robots, and your example might even persuade Vernon B. Smith to write his own stuff.

"What Do You Mean You Don't Like My Style?"

JOHN S. FIELDEN

John S. Fielden is University Professor of Management at the University of Alabama.

I n large corporations all over the country, people are playing a game of paddleball—with drafts of letters instead of balls. Volley after volley goes back and forth between those who sign the letters and those who actually write them. It's a game nobody likes, but it continues, and we pay for it. The workday has no extra time for such unproductiveness. What causes this round robin of revision?

Typos? Factual misstatements? Poor format? No. *Style* does. Ask yourself how often you hear statements like these:

- "It takes new assistants about a year to learn my style. Until they do, I have no choice but to bounce letters back for revision. I won't sign a letter if it doesn't sound like me."

- "I find it difficult, almost impossible, to write letters for my boss's signature. The boss's style is different from mine."

In companies where managers primarily write their own letters, confusion about style also reigns. Someone sends out a letter and hears later that the reaction was not at all the one desired. It is reported that the reader doesn't like the writer's "tone." A colleague looks over a copy of the letter and says, "No wonder the reader doesn't like this letter. You shouldn't have said things the way you did. You used the wrong style for a letter like this." "Style?" the writer says. "What's wrong with my style?" "I don't know" is the response. "I just don't like the way you said things."

Everybody talks about style, but almost nobody understands the meaning of the word in the business environment. And this lack of understanding hurts both those who write letters for another's signature and those who write for themselves. Neither knows where to turn for help. Strunk and White's marvelous book

The Elements of Style devotes only a few pages to a discussion of style, and that concerns only literary style.[1] Books like the Chicago *Manual of Style*[2] seem to define style as all the technical points they cover, from abbreviations and capitalizations to footnotes and bibliographies. And dictionary definitions are usually too vague to be helpful.

Even such a general definition as this offers scant help, although perhaps it comes closest to how business people use the word:

> Style is "the way something is said or done, as distinguished from its substance."[3]

Managers signing drafts written by subordinates, and the subordinates themselves, already know that they have trouble agreeing on "the way things should be said." What, for instance, is meant by "way"? In trying to find that way, both managers and subordinates are chasing a will-o'-the-wisp. There *is* no magical way, no perfect, universal way of writing things that will fend off criticism of style. There is no one style of writing in business that is appropriate in all situations and for all readers, even though managers and subordinates usually talk and behave as if there were.

But why all the confusion? Isn't style really the way we say things? Certainly it is. Then writing style must be made up of the particular words we select to express our ideas and the types of sentences and paragraphs we put together to convey those ideas. What else could it be? Writing has no tone of voice or body gesture to impart additional meanings. In written communication, tone comes from what a reader reads into the words and sentences used.

Words express more than *denotations*, the definitions found in dictionaries. They also carry *connotations*. In the feelings and images associated with each word lies the capacity a writing style has for producing an emotional reaction in a reader. And in that capacity lies the tone of a piece of writing. Style is largely a matter of tone. The writer uses a style; the reader infers a communication's tone. Tone comes from what a reader reads into the words and sentences a writer uses.

In the business environment, tone is especially important. Business writing is not literary writing. Literary artists use unique styles to "express" themselves to a general audience. Business people write to particular persons in particular situations, not so much to express themselves as to accomplish particular purposes, "to get a job done." If a reader doesn't like a novelist's tone, nothing much can happen to the writer short of failing to sell some books. In the business situation, however, an offensive style may not only prevent a sale but may also turn away a customer, work against a promotion, or even cost you a job.

[1] William Strunk, Jr. and E. B. White, *The Elements of Style* (New York: Macmillan, 1979).

[2] *A Manual of Style* (Chicago: University of Chicago Press, 1969).

[3] *The American Heritage Dictionary of the English Language* (Boston: American Heritage and Houghton Mifflin, 1969).

While style can be distinguished from substance, it cannot be divorced from substance. In business writing, style cannot be divorced from the circumstances under which something is written or from the likes, dislikes, position, and power of the reader.

A workable definition of style in business writing would be something like this:

Style is that choice of words, sentences, and paragraph format which by virtue of being appropriate to the situation and to the power positions of both writer and reader produces the desired reaction and result.

Which Style Is Yours?

Let's take a case and see what we can learn from it. Assume that you are an executive in a very large information-processing company. You receive the following letter:

Mr.(Ms.) Leslie J. Cash
XYZ Corporation
Main Street
Anytown, U.S.A.

Dear Leslie:
As you know, I respect your professional opinion highly. The advice your people have given us at ABC Corporation as we have moved into a comprehensive information system over the past three years has been very helpful. I'm writing to you now, however, in my role as chairman of the executive committee of the trustees of our hospital. We at Community General Hospital have decided to establish a skilled volunteer data processing evaluation team to assess proposals to automate our hospital's information flow.

I have suggested your name to my committee. I know you could get real satisfaction from helping your community as a member of this evaluation team. Please say yes. I look forward to being able to count on your advice. Let me hear from you soon.

Frank J. Scalpel
Chairman
Executive Committee
Community General Hospital
Anytown, U.S.A.

If you accepted the appointment mentioned in this letter, you would have a conflict of interest. You are an executive at XYZ, Inc. You know that XYZ will submit a proposal to install a comprehensive information system for the hospital. Mr. Scalpel is the vice president of finance at ABC Corp., a very good customer of yours. You know him well since you have worked with him on community programs as well as in the business world.

I can think of four typical responses to Scalpel's letter. Each says essentially the same thing, but each is written in a different business style:

Response 1

Mr. Frank J. Scalpel
Chairman, Executive Committee
Community General Hospital
Anytown, U.S.A.

Dear Frank,
As you realize, this litigious age often makes it necessary for large companies to take stringent measures not only to avoid conflicts of interest on the part of their employees but also to preclude even the very suggestion of conflict. And, since my company intends to submit a proposal with reference to automating the hospital's information flow, it would not appear seemly for me to be part of an evaluation team assessing competitors' proposals. Even if I were to excuse myself from consideration of the XYZ proposal, I would still be vulnerable to charges that I gave short shrift to competitors' offerings.

If there is any other way that I can serve the committee that will not raise this conflict-of-interest specter, you know that I would find it pleasurable to be of service, as always.

Sincerely,

Response 2

Dear Frank,
Your comments relative to your respect for my professional opinion are most appreciated. Moreover, your invitation to serve on the hospital's data processing evaluation team is received with gratitude, albeit with some concern.

The evaluation team must be composed of persons free of alliance with any of the vendors submitting proposals. For that reason, it is felt that my services on the team could be construed as a conflict of interest.

Perhaps help can be given in some other way. Again, please be assured that your invitation has been appreciated.

Sincerely,

Response 3

Dear Frank,
Thank you for suggesting my name as a possible member of your data processing evaluation team. I wish I could serve, but I cannot.

XYZ intends, naturally, to submit a proposal to automate the hospital's information flow. You can see the position of conflict I would be in if I were on the evaluation team.

Just let me know of any other way I can be of help. You know I would be more than willing. Thanks again for the invitation.

Cordially,

Response 4

Dear Frank,
Thanks for the kind words and the invitation. Sure wish I could say yes. Can't, though.

XYZ intends to submit a sure-fire proposal on automating the hospital's information. Shouldn't be judge and advocate at the same time!

Any other way I can help, Frank—just ask. Thanks again.

Cordially,

What Do You Think of These Letters?

Which letter has the style you like best? Check off the response you prefer.

Response	1	2	3	4
	☐	☐	☐	☐

Which letter has the style resembling the one you customarily use? Again, check off your choice.

Response	1	2	3	4
	☐	☐	☐	☐

Which terms best describe the style of each letter? Check the appropriate boxes.

Response 1	☐ Colorful ☐ Dull	☐ Passive ☐ Forceful	☐ Personal ☐ Impersonal
Response 2	☐ Colorful ☐ Dull	☐ Passive ☐ Forceful	☐ Personal ☐ Impersonal

Response 3	☐ Colorful ☐ Dull	☐ Passive ☐ Forceful	☐ Personal ☐ Impersonal
Response 4	☐ Colorful ☐ Dull	☐ Passive ☐ Forceful	☐ Personal ☐ Impersonal

Let's Compare Reactions

Now that you've given your reactions, let's compare them with some of mine.

Response 1 seems cold, impersonal, complex. Most business people would, I think, react somewhat negatively to this style because it seems to push the reader away from the writer. Its word choice has a cerebral quality that, while flattering to the reader's intelligence, also parades the writer's.

Response 2 is fairly cool, quite impersonal, and somewhat complex. Readers' reactions will probably be neither strongly positive nor strongly negative. This style of writing is "blah" because it is heavily passive. Instead of saying "I appreciate your comments," it says "Your comments are most appreciated"; instead of "I think that my services could be construed as a conflict of interest," it says "It is felt that my services could be construed . . ." The use of the passive voice subordinates writers modestly to the back of sentences or causes them to disappear.

This is the impersonal, passive style of writing that many with engineering, mathematics, or scientific backgrounds feel most comfortable using. It is harmless, but it is certainly not colorful; nor is it forceful or interesting.

Response 3 illustrates the style of writing that most high-level executives use. It is simple; it is personal; it is warm without being syrupy; it is forceful, like a firm handshake. Almost everybody in business likes this style, although lower-level managers often find themselves afraid to write so forthrightly (and, as a result, often find themselves retreating into the styles of responses 1 and 2—the style of 1 to make themselves look "smart" to superiors and the style of 2 to appear unbossy and fairly impersonal). Persons who find response 2 congenial may feel a bit dubious about the appropriateness of response 3. (Although I have no way of proving this judgment, I would guess that more readers in high positions—perhaps more owner-managers—would like response 3 than would readers who are still in lower positions.)

Response 4 goes beyond being forceful; it is annoyingly self-confident and breezy. It is colorful and conversational to an extreme, and it is so intensely personal and warm that many business people would be offended, even if they were very close acquaintances of Frank Scalpel's. "It sounds like an advertising person's chitchat," some would probably say.

Strategy Is Part of Style

As you compared your responses with mine, did you say, "What difference does it make which style *I* like or which most resembles *my* customary style? What matters is which style will go over best with Mr. Scalpel in this situation"? If you did, we're getting somewhere.

Earlier, when we defined business writing style, some may have wanted to add, "And that style should sound like me." This was left out for a good reason. Circumstances not only alter cases; they alter the "you" that it is wise for your style to project. Sometimes it's wise to be forceful; at other times it's suicidal. Sometimes being sprightly and colorful is appropriate; at other times it's ludicrous. There are times to be personal and times to be impersonal.

Not understanding this matter of style and tone is why the big corporation game of paddleball between managers and subordinates goes on and on. The subordinate tries to imitate the boss's style, but in actuality—unless the boss is extremely insensitive—he or she has no single style for all circumstances and for all readers. What usually happens is that after several tries, the subordinate writes a letter that the boss signs. "Aha!" the subordinate says. "So that's what the boss wants!" And then the subordinate tries to use that style for all situations and readers. Later, the superior begins rejecting drafts written in the very style he or she professed liking before. Both parties throw up their hands.

This volleying is foolish and wasteful. Both superior and subordinate have to recognize that in business writing, style cannot be considered apart from the given situation or from the person to whom the writing is directed. Expert writers select the style that fits a particular reader and the type of writing situation with which they are faced. In business, people often face the following writing situations:

Positive situations.
Saying yes or conveying good news.

Situations where some action is asked of the reader.
Giving orders or persuading someone to do as requested.

Information-conveying situations.
Giving the price of ten widgets, for example.

Negative situations.
Saying no or relaying bad news.

In each of these situations, the choice of style is of strategic importance.

In positive situations, a writer can relax on all fronts. Readers are usually so pleased to hear the good news that they pay little attention to anything else. Yet it is possible for someone to communicate good news in such a cold, impersonal, roundabout, and almost begrudging way that the reader becomes upset.

Action-request situations involve a form of bargaining. In a situation where the writer holds all the power, he or she can use a forceful commanding style. When the writer holds no power over the reader, though, actions have to be asked for and the reader persuaded, not ordered. In such cases, a forceful style will not be suitable at all.

In information-conveying situations, getting the message across forcefully and straightforwardly is best. Such situations are not usually charged emotionally.

In negative situations, diplomacy becomes very important. The right style depends on the relative positions of the person saying no and the person being told no.

For instance, if you were Leslie Cash, the person in the example at the beginning of the article whom Frank Scalpel was inviting to serve on a hospital's evaluation team, you would be in a situation of having to say no to a very important customer of your company. You would also be in a doubly sensitive situation because it is unlikely that Mr. Scalpel would fail to recognize that he is asking you to enter a conflict-of-interest situation. He is probably asking you *anyway*. Therefore, you would not only have to tell him no, but you would have to avoid telling him that he has asked you to do something that is highly unethical. In this instance, you would be faced with communicating two negative messages at once or else not giving Scalpel any sensible reason for refusing to serve.

Suit Your Style to the Situation

Now that we've thought about the strategic implications of style, let's go back to look at each of the responses to Scalpel's request and ask ourselves which is best.

Do we *want* to be personal and warm? Usually yes. But in this situation? Do we want to communicate clearly and directly and forcefully? Usually yes. But here? Do we want to appear as if we're brushing aside the conflict, as the third response does? Or do we want to approach that issue long-windedly, as in the first response, or passively, as in the second? What is the strategically appropriate style?

In the abstract, we have no way of knowing which of these responses will go over best with Mr. Scalpel. The choice is a matter of judgment in a concrete situation. Judging the situation accurately is what separates successful from unsuccessful executive communicators.

Looking at the situation with strategy in mind, we note that in the first response, the writer draws back from being close, knowing that it is necessary to reject not only one but two of the reader's requests. By using legalistic phraseology and Latinate vocabulary, the writer lowers the personal nature of the communication and transforms it into a formal statement. It gives an abstract, textbooklike response that removes the tone of personal rejection.

The very fact that response 1 is difficult to read and dull in impact may be a strategic asset in this type of negative situation. But if in this situation a subordinate presented response 1 to you for your signature, would it be appropriate for you to reject it because it is not written in the style *you* happen to *like* best in the abstract—say, the style of response 3?

Now let's look at response 2. Again, we see that a lack of personal warmth may be quite appropriate to the situation at hand. Almost immediately, the letter draws back into impersonality. And by using the passive constantly, the writer avoids the need to say "I must say no." Furthermore, the term *construed* reinforces the passive in the second paragraph. This term is a very weak but possibly a strategically wise way of implying that *some* persons (*other* people, not the writer) could interpret Scalpel's request as an invitation to participate in an improper action. Now we can see that, instead of seeming dull and lacking in personal warmth as it did in the abstract, response 2 may be the type of letter we would be wise to send out, that is, when we have taken the whole situation into careful consideration and not just our personal likes and dislikes.

The third response, and to even greater extent the fourth, have styles that are strategically inappropriate for this situation. In fact, Scalpel might well regard the colorful style of the fourth response as highly offensive. Both responses directly and forcefully point out the obvious conflict, but by being so direct each runs the risk of subtly offending him. (The third response is "you can see the position of conflict I'd be in if I were on the evaluation team," and the fourth is "Shouldn't be judge and advocate at the same time!") We could make a pretty strong argument that the direct, forceful, candid style of the third response and the breezy, warm, colorful, intensely personal "advertising" style of the fourth response may both prove ineffectual in a delicate, negative situation such as this.

What Effect Do You Want?

At this point, readers may say, "All right. I'm convinced. I need to adjust my style to what is appropriate in each situation. And I also need to give directions to others to let them know how to adjust their styles. But I haven't the foggiest notion of how to do either!" Some suggestions for varying your writing style follow. I am not implying that a communication must be written in one style only. A letter to be read aloud at a colleague's retirement party, for instance, may call not only for a warm, personal style but for colorfulness as well. A long analytic report may require a passive, impersonal style, but the persuasive cover letter may call for recommendations being presented in a very forceful style.

For a Forceful Style

This style is usually appropriate only in situations where the writer has the power, such as in action requests in the form of orders or when you are saying no firmly but politely to a subordinate.

- Use the active voice. Have your sentences do something to people and to objects, not just lie there having things done to them; have them give orders: "Correct this error immediately" (you-understood is the subject) instead of "A correction should be made" (which leaves the reader wondering, made by whom).

- Step up front and be counted:
  "I have decided not to recommend you for promotion" instead of "Unfortunately, a positive recommendation for your promotion is not forthcoming."

- Do not beat around the bush or act like a politician. If something needs to be said, say it directly.

- Write most of your sentences in subject-verb-object order. Do not weaken them by putting namby-pamby phrases before the subject:
  "I have decided to fund your project" instead of "After much deliberation and weighing of the pros and cons, I have decided to fund your project."

- Do not weaken sentences by relegating the point or the action to a subordinate clause:
  If your point is that your company has won a contract, say, "Acme won the contract, although the bidding was intense and highly competitive," not "Although Acme won the contract, the bidding was intense and highly competitive."

- Adopt a tone of confidence and surety about what you say by avoiding weasel words like:
  "Possibly," "maybe," "perhaps."
  "It could be concluded that . . . ."
  "Some might conclude that . . . ."

For a Passive Style

This style is often appropriate in negative situations and in situations where the writer is in a lower position than the reader.

- Avoid the imperative—never give an order:
  Say "A more effective and time-conserving presentation of ideas should be devised before our next meeting" as opposed to "Do a better job of presenting your ideas at our next meeting. Respect my time and get right to the point."

- Use the passive voice heavily because it subordinates the subject to the end of the sentence or buries the subject entirely. The passive is especially handy when you are in a low-power position and need to convey negative information to a reader who is in a higher position (an important customer, for instance):
  Say "Valuable resources are being wasted" instead of "Valuable resources are being wasted by your company" or, even worse, "You are wasting valuable resources."

- Avoid taking responsibility for negative statements by attributing them to faceless, impersonal "others":
  Say "It is more than possible that several objections to your proposed plans might be raised by some observers" or "Several objections might be raised by those hostile to your plans" instead of "I have several objections to your plans."

- Use weasel words, especially if the reader is in a high-power position and will not like what you are saying.

- Use long sentences and heavy paragraphs to slow down the reader's comprehension of sensitive or negative information.

For a Personal Style

This style is usually appropriate in good-news and persuasive action-request situations.

- Use the active voice, which puts you, as the writer, at the front of sentences:
  "Thank you very much for your comments" or "I appreciated your comments" instead of "Your comments were very much appreciated by me" or the even more impersonal "Your comments were very much appreciated."

- Use persons' names (first names, when appropriate) instead of referring to them by title:
  "Bill James attended the meeting" instead of "Acme's director attended the meeting."

- Use personal pronouns—especially "you" and "I"—when you are saying positive things:
  "I so much appreciate the work you've done" as opposed to "The work you've done is appreciated."

- Use short sentences that capture the rhythm of ordinary conversation:
  "I discussed your proposal with Frank. He's all for it!" as opposed to "This is to inform you that your proposal was taken up at Friday's meeting and that it was regarded with favor."

- Use contractions ("can't," "won't," "shouldn't") to sound informal and conversational.

- Direct questions to the reader:
  "Just ask yourself, how would your company like to save $10,000?"

- Interject positive personal thoughts and references that will make the reader know that this letter is really to him or her and not some type of form letter sent to just anyone.

For an Impersonal Style

This style is usually appropriate in negative and information-conveying situations. It's always appropriate in technical and scientific writing and usually when you are writing to technical readers.

- Avoid using persons' names, especially first names. Refer to people, if at all, by title or job description:

"I would like to know what you think of this plan" instead of "What do you think of this, Herb?"

"Our vice president of finance" or "the finance department," not "Ms. Jones."

- Avoid using personal pronouns, especially "you" and "I" ("we" may be all right because the corporate we is faceless and impersonal):
  "The logistics are difficult, and the idea may not work" instead of "I think you have planned things so that the logistics are difficult and your idea may not work." "We wonder if the idea will work" rather than "I don't think the idea will work."

- Use the passive voice to make yourself conveniently disappear when desirable:
  "An error in the calculations has been made" instead of "I think your calculations are wrong."

- Make some of your sentences complex and some paragraphs long; avoid the brisk, direct, simple-sentence style of conversation.

For a Colorful Style

Sometimes a lively style is appropriate in good-news situations. It is most commonly found in the highly persuasive writing of advertisements and sales letters.

- Insert some adjectives and adverbs:
  Instead of "This proposal will save corporate resources," write "This (hard-hitting) (productivity-building) (money-saving) proposal will (easily) (surely) (quickly) (immediately) save our (hard-earned) (increasingly scarce) (carefully guarded) corporate resources."

- If appropriate, use a metaphor (A is B) or a simile (A is like B) to make a point:
  "Truly this program is a *miracle* of logical design." "Our solution strikes at the very *root* of Acme's problems." "This program is like *magic* in its ability to . . . ."

For a Less Colorful Style

By avoiding adjectives, adverbs, metaphors, and figures of speech, you can make your style less colorful. Such a style is appropriate for ordinary business writing and also results from:

- Blending the impersonal style with the passive style.

- Employing words that remove any semblance of wit, liveliness, and vigor from the writing.

Please bear in mind that these six styles are not mutually exclusive. There is some overlap. A passive style is usually far more impersonal than personal and also not very colorful. A forceful style is likely to be more personal than impersonal, and a colorful style is likely to be fairly forceful. Nevertheless, these styles are distinct enough to justify talking about them. If we fail to make such distinctions, style becomes a catchall term that means nothing specific. Even if not precise, these distinctions enable us to talk about style and its elements and to learn to write appropriately for each situation.

Discuss Needs First

What conclusions can we draw from this discussion? Simply that, whether you write your own letters or have to manage the writing of subordinates, to be an effective communicator, you must realize that:

1. Each style has an impact on the reader.

2. Style communicates to readers almost as much as the content of a message.

3. Style cannot be isolated from a situation.

4. Generalizing about which style is the best in all situations is impossible.

5. Style must be altered to suit the circumstances.

6. Style must be discussed sensibly in the work situation.

These conclusions will be of obvious help to managers who write their own letters. But what help will these conclusions be to managers who direct assistants in the writing of letters? In many instances, writing assignments go directly to subordinates for handling. Often, manager and assistant have no chance to discuss style strategy together. In such cases, rather than merely submitting a response for a signature, the subordinate would be wise to append a note: e.g., "This is a very sensitive situation, I think. Therefore, I deliberately drew back into a largely impersonal and passive style." At least, the boss will not jump to the conclusion that the assistant has written a letter of low impact by accident.

When they do route writing assignments to assistants, superiors could save much valuable time and prevent mutual distress if they told the subordinates what style seemed strategically wise in each situation. Playing guessing games also wastes money.

And if, as is often the case, neither superior nor subordinate has a clear sense of what style is best, the two can agree to draft a response in one style first, and if that doesn't sound right, to adjust the style appropriately.

Those who write their own letters can try drafting several responses to tough but important situations, each in a different style. It's wise to sleep on them and then decide which sounds best.

Whether you write for yourself or for someone else, it is extremely unlikely that in difficult situations a first draft will be signed by you or anyone else. Only the amateur expects writing perfection on the first try. By learning to control your style and to engineer the tone of your communications, you can make your writing effective.

* * *

Such Stuff as Style Is Made On

To Frank A. Nichols, Secretary,
Concord Free Trade Club

Hartford, March 1885
Dear Sir:

I am in receipt of your favor of the 24th inst., conveying the gratifying intelligence that I have been made an honorary member of the Free Trade Club of Concord, Massachusetts, and I desire to express to the Club, through you, my grateful sense of the high compliment thus paid me.

It does look as if Massachusetts were in a fair way to embarrass me with kindnesses this year. In the first place a Massachusetts Judge has just decided in open court that a Boston publisher may sell not only his own property in a free and unfettered way, but may also as freely sell property which does not belong to him but to me—property which he has not bought and which I have not sold. Under this ruling I am now advertising that judge's homestead for sale; and if I make as good a sum out of it as I expect I shall go on and sell the rest of his property.

In the next place, a committee of the public library of your town has condemned and excommunicated my last book [*Adventures of Huckleberry Finn*], and doubled its sale. This generous action of theirs must necessarily benefit me in one or two additional ways. For instance, it will deter other libraries from buying the book and you are doubtless aware that one book in a public library prevents the sale of a sure ten and a possible hundred of its mates. And secondly it will cause the purchasers of the book to read it, out of curiosity, instead of merely intending to do so after the usual way of the world and library committees; and then they will discover, to my great advantage and their own indignant disappointment, that there is nothing objectionable in the book, after all.

And finally, the Free Trade Club of Concord comes forward and adds to the splendid burden of obligations already conferred upon me by the Commonwealth of Massachusetts, an honorary membership which is more worth than all the rest since it endorses me as worthy to associate with certain gentlemen whom even the moral icebergs of the Concord library committee are bound to respect.

May the great Commonwealth of Massachusetts endure forever, is the heartfelt prayer of one who, long a recipient of her mere general good will, is proud to realize that he is at last become her pet. . . .

Your obliged servant
S. L. Clemens

To the Gas Company

Hartford, February 1, 1891
Dear Sirs:

Some day you will move me almost to the verge of irritation by your chuckle-headed Goddamned fashion of shutting your Goddamned gas off without giving any notice to your Goddamned parishioners. Several times you have come within an ace of smothering half of this household in their beds and blowing up the other half by this idiotic, not to say criminal, custom of yours. And it has happened again to-day. Haven't you a telephone?

Ys
S L Clemens

The Plain English Revolution

ALAN SIEGEL

Alan Siegel, a leading consultant in the Plain English movement, is the Chairman and Chief Executive Officer of Siegel & Gale, a New York firm specializing in language simplification.

LOUIS XVI: C'est une grande révolte?

DUC DE LA ROCHEFOUCAULD–LIANCOURT: Non, Sire, c'est une grande révolution. (When the news arrived at Versailles of the Fall of the Bastille, 1789)

Three-and-a-half years ago I wrote an article . . . on the movement away from legalese toward forms and documents that can be understood by ordinary citizens.* At that time, the movement consisted of isolated revolts against legalistic gobbledygook and bureaucratese. A handful of business documents—mainly insurance policies and loan notes—had been simplified by forward-looking companies. In government, the scattered advocates of clear communication shared the lament of Alfred Kahn, then head of the Civil Aeronautics Board: "There's nothing I can do but cry. I feel so lonely and futile."

Now the plain language movement is becoming a revolution. . . . But the Bastille has not fallen, yet. Part of the legal community remains resistant to change. Some supposed practitioners of Plain English have confused simplicity with simplemindedness. And the greatest obstacle has yet to be fully overcome—a misunderstanding of what Plain English is all about.

That misunderstanding was dramatized when New Jersey's Plain English Bill, passed by the legislature, expired in February 1980, through a pocket veto by Gov. Brendan Byrne, who said: ". . . although regulating the protection of consumers is a worthy goal, legislating the style of a society's prose is another thing."†

But the movement has nothing to do with "legislating the style of a society's prose." We are not trying to turn English into one-syllable words, or to translate

---

*"To lift the curse of legalese—Simplify, Simplify," *Across the Board,* June 1977.

†Rewritten and reintroduced in June, the Bill was passed again. This time Gov. Byrne signed it (on October 10th), out of deference to its "unusually large" number of sponsors—65 of the Assembly's 80 members.

THE PLAIN ENGLISH REVOLUTION   By Alan Siegel. From *Across the Board* (February, 1981) reprinted by permission of *Across the Board* and its publisher, The Conference Board, 845 Third Avenue, New York, New York 10022. Also reprinted with the permission of Alan Siegel, Chairman and Chief Executive Officer, Siegel & Gale, Inc.

Saul Bellow into baby-talk. We are not even trying to do away with professional jargon, though that is a tempting target. Let lawyers talk to lawyers, or accountants to accountants, as they please. So long as they understand one another, that is just fine.

Well, what is the Plain English movement all about? *Its aim is to make functional documents function, whether they are put out by business or by government. If a consumer is expected to abide by a formal document—an insurance policy, a mortgage, a lease, a warranty, a tax form—then the consumer should be able to understand the document.* Carl Felsenfeld, vice president and counsel for Citicorp N.A., expresses the concept in legal terms: "There is growing dissatisfaction with contracts where consumers merely 'sign here' and can't, under any reputable system of contract law, be deemed to have agreed to all the printed verbiage." In social terms, I would say that people are learning a new right: the right to understand.

It's been argued that the fault lies with consumers, or with the educational system that does not train them to cope with legalese, or accounting, or insurance terminology. But that argument is neither reasonable nor realistic. In fact, documents meant for consumers have been made much more difficult than they really need to be. Redressing the balance—making sure that the documents consumers are expected to understand are made understandable—is a matter of simple fairness, and simple efficiency. In the long run it's in the interests of business as well as the consumer.

Five years of experience have proved that consumer contracts and forms of all kinds can be made much more understandable without sacrificing legal effectiveness. The very first plain language loan note, which I helped write for Citibank of New York, was introduced in 1975. Since then, Citicorp counsel Felsenfeld notes, "We've lost no money and there has been no litigation as a result of simplification."

That loan note remains a good example of just what plain language means. Among other things:

- A personal tone was used throughout—"I" and "me" rather than "the undersigned" or "Borrower," "you" and "yours" rather than "the Bank."

- Language was radically simplified. For example, "To repay my loan, I promise to pay you . . ." instead of "For value received, the undersigned (jointly and severally) hereby promise(s) to pay . . ."

- When unfamiliar terms couldn't be eliminated, we added explanatory phrases. For instance, " . . . if this loan is refinanced—that is, replaced by a new note—you [the bank] will refund the unearned finance charge, figured by the rule of 78—a commonly used formula for figuring rebates on installment loans."

- We shortened the sentences wherever possible and even used contractions ("I'll pay this sum . . ."). To enhance clarity, we chose active instead of passive verb forms where possible.

- Improvements in design included the use of larger (12-point) type printed in green on light brown stock. Compared with the previously intimidating format, this visually appealing approach suggests immediately that the document is supposed to be read.

The Citibank note taught us a fundamental lesson about simplifying language. Consumer contracts have traditionally been adapted from mercantile contracts, which feature verbose protective clauses accumulated over the years in an effort to cover all possible contingencies. Many of these provisions have no practical value in the consumer marketplace. So the first task in simplifying a document is not rewriting it in Plain English, but identifying clauses taken from commercial contracts that can be eliminated from the consumer contract without jeopardizing its validity. The secret to doing this lies in analyzing actual business experience to see which provisions are really being used.

In the case of the Citibank note, the provisions describing the lender's protections in case of default proved to be the biggest challenge. The traditional note listed a string of contingencies more than 180 words long:

Before

In the event of default in the payment of this or any other Obligation or the performance or observance of any term or covenant contained herein or in any note or other contract or agreement evidencing or relating to any Obligation or any Collateral on the Borrower's part to be performed or observed; or the undersigned Borrower shall die; or any of the undersigned become insolvent or make an assignment for the benefit of creditors; or a petition shall be filed by or against any of the undersigned under any provision of the Bankruptcy Act; or any money, securities or property of the undersigned now or hereafter on deposit with or in the possession or under the control of the Bank shall be attached or become subject to distraint proceedings or any order of process of any court; or the Bank shall deem itself to be insecure, then and in any such event, the Bank shall have the right (at its option), without demand or notice of any kind, to declare all or any part of the Obligations to be immediately due and payable. . . .

But analysis of Citibank's business experience disclosed that the typical consumer loan transaction needs only one event of default—failure to pay. With one additional protection added, the following replaced all the fine print above:

After

Default   I'll be in default—
1. If I don't pay an installment on time, or
2. If any other creditor tries by legal process to take any money of mine in your possession.

A number of insurance companies, whose product, after all, is words on paper, continue to get good marks for simplification. The Massachusetts Savings Bank Life Insurance (SBLI) Whole Life Policy used to begin like this:

IN CONSIDERATION OF THE APPLICATION for this policy (copy attached hereto) which is the basis of and a part of this contract and of the payment of an annual premium as hereinafter specified for the basic policy as of the Date of Issue as specified herein and on the anniversary of such date in each year during the continuance of this contract until premiums have been paid for the number of years indicated in the POLICY SPECIFICATIONS or until the prior death of the Insured . . .

By contrast, the cover of their simplified policy begins with this message:

Please take the time to read your SBLI policy carefully. Your SBLI representative will be glad to answer any questions. You may return this policy within ten days after receiving it. Deliver it to any SBLI agency. We'll promptly refund all premiums paid for it.

The insurer's promise to pay the consumer used to be phrased in these forbidding terms:

The Bank Hereby Agrees upon Surrender of this Policy to Pay the Face Amount Specified Above, less any indebtedness on or secured hereunder . . . upon receipt of due proof of the Insured's death to the beneficiary named in the Application herefor or to such other beneficiary as may be entitled thereto under the provisions hereof, or if no such beneficiary survives the Insured, then to the Owner or to the estate of the Owner.

In Plain English, policyholders can understand what they are buying:

We will pay the face amount when we receive proof of the Insured's death. We will pay the named Beneficiary. If no Beneficiary survives the Insured, we'll pay the Owner of this policy, or the Owner's estate.

Any amount owed to us under this policy will be deducted. We'll refund any premiums paid beyond the month of death.

Perhaps the most ambitious simplification program so far has been that undertaken by the St. Paul Fire and Marine Insurance Company, of St. Paul, Minnesota. In 1975 they became one of the first large insurers to begin simplifying their policies. As a pilot project, the company produced an easy-to-read "personal liability catastrophe policy" that used personalized examples in colloquial English:

Before

a. Automobile and Watercraft Liability:
1. any Relative with respect to (i) an Automobile owned by the Named Insured or a Relative, or (ii) a Non-owned Automobile, provided his actual operation or (if he is not operating) the other actual use thereof is with the permission of the owner and is within the scope of such permission, or

2. any person while using an Automobile or Watercraft, owned by, loaned or hired for use in behalf of the Named Insured and any person or organization legally responsible for the use thereof is within the scope of such permission.

After

We'll also cover any person or organization legally responsible for the use of a car, if it's used by you or with your permission. But again, the use has to be for the intended purpose.

You loan your station wagon to a teacher to drive a group of children to the zoo. She and the school are covered by this policy if she actually drives to the zoo, but not if she lets the children off at the zoo and drives to her parents' farm 30 miles away.

By 1978, St. Paul had reduced the number of policy forms in its commercial business package from 366 to 150. Plans now call for most of its commercial insurance policies to be rewritten and reprinted in a more readable format by 1982. The company has appointed a Manager of Forms Simplification, with his own staff and a detailed style manual, to oversee the effort.

The financial field is a particularly promising new area for Plain English efforts. A case in point: Sanford C. Bernstein & Co. is a New York broker-dealer advising clients on investments as well as trading for them. It is subject to regulation under the Federal Securities Exchange Act of 1934 and the Investment Advisers Act of 1940, as well as regulation by the New York Stock Exchange, the National Association of Securities Dealers, the Board of Governors of the Federal Reserve System, and state securities laws in various jurisdictions in which it does business or has clients. These various regulations extend to every aspect of the firm's business, from the content of advertising and soliciting materials to client reports, statements, and the consents that must be obtained before the firm can effect certain types of transaction on clients' behalf. Nonetheless, the firm was able to replace jargon with plain English, while satisfying legal and technical requirements.

Before

It is the express intention of the undersigned to create an estate or account as joint tenants with rights of survivorship and not as tenants in common. In the event of the death of either of the undersigned, the entire interest in the joint account shall be vested in the survivor or survivors on the same terms and conditions as theretofore held, without in any manner releasing the decedent's estate from the liability provided for in the next preceding paragraph.

After

Other signers share your interest equally. If one of you dies, the account will continue and the other people who've signed the agreement will own the entire interest in it.

Plain Language Scorecard

• Thirty-four states have laws or regulations setting standards for clear language in insurance policies. In 1978, New York became the first state to require that business contracts "primarily for personal, family, or household purposes" be plainly written in everyday language. Since then, New Jersey, Maine, Connecticut, and Hawaii have passed similar laws requiring consumer contracts to be understandable to the public, and a score of other states are considering such laws.

• Hundreds of corporations across the country are simplifying their documents—employee benefit manuals, brokerage account agreements, trusts, the notes to financial statements, customer correspondence, billing statements, and internal communications, ranging from corporate policy manuals to the humble memo.

• President Carter, following up a promise for "regulations in plain English for a change," issued two unprecedented Executive Orders to Federal agencies telling them to simplify paperwork and eliminate gobbledy-gook from regulations. Agencies that have started to do so include the Environmental Protection Agency and the Department of Health and Human Services (formerly HEW). The Civil Aeronautics Board, where Alfred Kahn started a push for Plain English, is rewriting the notices it requires to be posted at airline counters and printed on the backs of tickets. The Federal Acquisition Regulation Project (FARP), in the Office of Federal Procurement Policy (Department of Management and Budget), offers great potential: FARP is rewriting and recodifying the massive Federal regulations on procurement of goods and services.

• Major law firms, such as Shearman & Sterling in New York, have launched programs to train their young lawyers in clear legal drafting.

• The Internal Revenue Service committed over one million dollars in an all-out effort to simplify the Federal income tax forms. Simplified prototypes were presented to the Congress in November.

• The 1978 Amendments to the Constitution of the State of Hawaii include a provision that, "Insofar as practicable, all governmental writing meant for the public . . . should be plainly worded, avoiding the use of technical terms."

• On April 15, 1980, Gov. Hugh Carey of New York issued an Executive Order directing all state agencies to write their forms and regulations in plain language.

• Last fall, New York City's Department of Consumer Affairs proposed simplified language for more than 40 of its regulations covering deceptive and unconscionable business practices.

• The prestigious Practising Law Institute held a program and published a course book on "Drafting Documents in Plain Language." Another such program is planned for 1981.

• A lobbying group for the movement, Plain Talk, Inc., has been established in Washington, D.C.

• The National Institute for Education, a Federal research agency, has funded the Document Design Project, which is being run by the American Institutes of Research in conjunction with Siegel & Gale and Carnegie-Mellon University. The project's purpose is to study and encourage the use of simplified public documents.

—A.S.

Where obscure terms could not be eliminated, the new forms explain them. The meaning of the term "clearing agents," for instance, is described in this way:

> *Clearing agents.* We can use other broker/dealers as clearing agents to execute transactions, to hold securities in custody on your behalf and to perform other routine procedures in connection with your account. These clearing agents will act at our direction, and they won't have any part in investment decisions.

Especially complex ideas are not only explained but accompanied by illustrative examples:

> *Buying on margin.* In managing your account, we may buy securities on margin. This means that we'll loan you part of the cost of the securities and charge you interest on the loan. By buying on margin, we can purchase more securities on your behalf than we could using only the cash and securities actually available in your account at the time. Because it increases the amount we can invest on your behalf, buying on margin can increase the return on your investment. However, it can also increase the amount of loss on your account.

> Example: Assume that the value of A Manufacturing Corp. stock in your portfolio has increased from $5,000 to $10,000. Because of changed market conditions, we decide to sell it and buy Z Industries common stock for your portfolio. If, for instance, the margin requirement is 50%, in theory we could purchase $20,000 worth of Z Industries stock for your account by using the $10,000 proceeds from the sale of your A Manufacturing stock and loaning you the additional $10,000.

In government, the promise—and difficulty—of the Plain English movement is illustrated by the case of the Food Stamp program. That program, begun in 1961, was substantially revised by the Food Stamp Act of 1977. As a result, the forms that had been used by the states were made obsolete. There was a bewildering variety of these forms to begin with. Wisconsin's, for instance, was 37 pages long. To help the states design simple, client-oriented forms reflecting the changes in the law, the Food and Nutrition Service (FNS) of the Department of Agriculture commissioned my firm to come up with new forms to offer to the states as models.

Our approach is illustrated by the new titles we gave our forms:

OLD	NEW
Notice of Expiration	Continuing Your Food Stamps
Notice of Eligibility, Denial or Pending Status	Action Taken on Your Food Stamp Case
Tax Dependency Form	Student Tax Report

Significantly, the new forms ran into a special kind of opposition. First, we discovered that not all state governments agreed that the forms should *help*

Plain Research Is Needed

The writing of Plain English documents is still a developing field. Researchers have discovered that the reader's comprehension has as much to do with what is inside his or her head as it has to do with what is on the printed page. Diagnostic research can help clarify what information must be explained at greater length.

A study conducted by law professor Jeffrey Davis, described in *Virginia Law Review* 63: No. 6, 1977, provides an excellent example. Davis prepared a simplified installment purchase contract for a refrigerator, showed it to shoppers from various backgrounds, and then asked them questions about its contents. The contract included this definition of default: "I will be in default if I fail to pay an installment on time or if I sell or fail to take proper care of the collateral." Yet most of the readers—even the well educated—failed to understand that they would be in default if they carelessly damaged the refrigerator. They persisted in the common but mistaken belief that they could not be in default if they made all their payments on time.

—A.S.

---

people to use the program, as the law intended. Food Stamp recipients are seen as one measure of a state's poverty, so some officials were reluctant to "encourage" their use by simplifying the paperwork. Some states had actually sought to discourage applicants by using forms that needlessly demanded embarrassing information, such as whether the applicant was a drug user or had a criminal record. Some state officials also felt that the language of the new forms, which included words such as "please," "thank you," and "sincerely," was too nice to people wanting money from the government.

Second, we found that state caseworkers themselves often appeared threatened by new, simplified forms. Some felt that their authority was being undermined. For example, people whose applications for food stamps are turned down or who are cut off are allowed by law to request a fair hearing. We embodied this feature of the law in the forms themselves: letters bearing bad news to Food Stamp clients included a perforated tear-off portion that could be sent back to appeal the decision. Some caseworkers objected heatedly: they felt the tear-offs would cast doubts on their competence and would generate "unnecessary" hearings, increasing their already heavy work load.

After more than two years, the objections seem to have been overcome. Our model forms are used now by about half the states, and one FNS official commented earlier this year: "I've never heard a critical comment about the forms themselves." In fact, as in other simplifications projects, researchers got a strong impression that staff objections had as much to do with the fact the forms were new and unfamiliar as with their style or content.

Earlier in this piece I mentioned that some Plain English efforts have confused simplicity with simplemindedness. A major source of this confusion is the quick-

and-dirty "readability formula" that equates clarity with short words and sentences. Here is a rider to a health insurance policy obviously written to such a formula. It is both uncommunicative and insulting to the reader's intelligence.

THE DRUG SPECIAL ENDORSEMENT

The DRUG SPECIAL is a small Endorsement. It goes with your [name of company] Contract. It depends on that other Contract to say who's covered. It is added coverage, with big extra benefits.

The DRUG SPECIAL gives you special help in paying for DRUGS . . .

Some attempts at simplification produce a kind of black humor. One life insurance company offers a "simplified" policy requiring that, "The Insured must die while this policy is in force." In a grisly parody that might be called "Dick and Jane Become Underwriters," the policy continues:

The Insured's death may be caused by accidental Bodily Injury. If so the Beneficiary may be paid an additional amount. It will be equal to the Face Amount. Three things must all happen. (1) Death must have been caused by Accidental Bodily Injury. Not by sickness. Not by anything else. . . .

Another misuse of the movement is the way some lawyers are cynically using "simplified" language, notably in apartment leases, to misinform consumers and to mislead them by playing on their ignorance. The nation's first plain language law went into effect in New York State in November 1978. One year later, the State Consumer Protection Board found that most revised lease forms "force tenants to surrender nearly every right they have under law." Rosemary S. Pooler, the board's executive director, referring to the lease prepared by the New York City Bar Association, commented: "It is ironic that tenants were in some respects better off with the 'legalese' of the 1965 lease since the . . . 'plain language' lease seems to have taken almost every opportunity to resolve legal issues in favor of landlords, sometimes at the expense of existing statutory and decisional law."

To illustrate her point, Mrs. Pooler gave, among others, the following examples:

RENT PAYMENT PROVISION

Pre-plain language version (1965):
"The tenant will pay the rent as herein provided."

Plain language version (1978):
"Tenant will pay the rent without any deductions, even if permitted by law."

The new document flies in the face of New York State's Multiple Dwelling Law (Sec. 302-a); Real Property Law (Sec. 235-2); Real Property Actions and Proceedings (Sec. 756 and Article 7-A); and several recent court decisions, all of which give tenants the right to reduce or withhold rent under certain circumstances—for instance, when there are serious building code violations.

ASSIGNMENT AND SUBLETTING

Pre-plain language version (1965):
"(Tenant) will not assign this lease or underlet the leased premises or any part thereof without the landlord's written consent, which landlord agrees not to withhold unreasonably."

Plain language version (1978):
"Tenant shall not assign this lease or enter into a sublease unless it is allowed by a law of the State of New York."

Since 1975, New York's Real Property Law (Sec. 226-b) has given tenants the right to request their landlord's permission to sublet or assign their lease. If the landlord withholds permission unreasonably, he must let the tenant break the lease. The 1965 version is a better statement of existing law than the plain language version, which implies that subletting is allowed by state law only in very special situations.

INSTALLATION OF LOCKS, CHAINS, ETC.

Pre-plain language version (1965):
None.

Plain language version (1978):
"Tenant will not, without landlord's written approval: . . . 3. Put in any locks or chain guards or change any lock-cylinders on the doors of the Apartment."

But New York State's Multiple Dwelling Law (Sec. 51-c) gives tenants of multiple dwellings the right to install additional locks without the landlord's permission, provided that the landlord who requests a key is given one.

Though many lawyers have seen the light, some of them—and their corporate clients—misguidedly try to protect themselves by insisting on too-precise standards for compliance. Such traditionalists do not like the Plain English laws that have been passed in New York, Maine, and Hawaii. Those laws simply require that each document for a residential lease or for a loan, property or services of less than $50,000 for personal, family or household purposes be:

1. Written in a clear and coherent manner using words with common everyday meanings;

2. Appropriately divided and captioned by its various sections.

Ironically, some lawyers and executives who are quick to decry regulatory minutiae in other areas object to this general approach to plain language legislation. They yearn for the false security of the simplistic "readability formula" approach,

---

Safe English

The New York Times (Aug. 31, 1980) reported the first case under the Plain English law on contracts:

"The New York State Attorney General was puzzled by this sentence.

'The liability of the bank is expressly limited to the exercise of ordinary diligence and care to prevent the opening of the within-mentioned safe deposit box during the within-mentioned term, or any extension or renewal thereof, by any person other than the lessee or his duly authorized representative and failure to exercise such diligence or care shall not be inferable from any alleged loss, absence or disappearance of any of its contents, nor shall the bank be liable for permitting a co-lessee or an attorney in fact of the lessee to have access to and remove the contents of said safe deposit box after the lessee's death or disability and before the bank has written knowledge of such death or disability.'

"Saying, 'I defy anyone, lawyer or lay person, to understand or explain what that means,' Attorney General Robert Abrams sued the Lincoln Savings Bank in New York City . . . demanding that it simplify a customer agreement on safe-deposit boxes.

"The case is settled . . . The former 121-word sentence now says: 'Our liability with respect to property deposited in the box is limited to ordinary care by our employees in the performance of their duties in preventing the opening of the box during the term of the lease by anyone other than you, persons authorized by you or persons authorized by the law.'"

---

which ignores less easily quantified elements such as grammar, logic, and organization. They fear that without an exact definition of "clear, coherent, everyday language," compliance will elude them. Lawyers such as Wilbur H. Friedman, chairman of the New York County Lawyers' Association Special Committee on Consumer Agreements, direfully predicted that New York's law would create "upheaval" among businesses and an "absolutely staggering" burden on the courts.

But these fears were unfounded: there has been no flood of lawsuits. The arguments of the technically minded still have their appeal, however, as demonstrated by Connecticut's plain language law. It lists two alternate sets of criteria for plain language, with nine and eleven different tests respectively, including these:

1. The average number of words per sentence is less than twenty-two; and

2. No sentence in the contract exceeds fifty words; and

3. The average number of words per paragraph is less than seventy-five; and

4. No paragraph in the contract exceeds one hundred fifty words; and

5. The average number of syllables per word is less than 1.55; and . . .

Cookbook detail like this only guarantees that the spirit of plain language legislation will be lost in attempts to follow it to the letter: the clarity of a sentence becomes less important than seeing that it has "less than 1.55" syllables per word. And what would happen to interstate commerce if one of Connecticut's neighbors were to require less than 20 words per sentence instead of 22, or 160 words per paragraph instead of 150?

Keeping plain language laws simple, like the law in New York State, is essential. The courts should be left free to judge particular cases according to a general standard, as they do now with the concept of the "reasonable man." Lawyers who hang back, in favor of the traditional approach to legal language, should remember the traditional result: as Harold Laski put it, in every revolution the lawyers lead the way to the guillotine.

Nondiscriminatory Writing

WILLIAM C. PAXSON

William C. Paxson is an editor and writer who lives in Sacramento, California. His articles have covered a wide variety of topics, including air pollution, electronics, travel, and school administration.

L anguage shapes thought. If language didn't shape thought, words like *propaganda* and *publicity* wouldn't be in dictionaries. If language didn't shape thought, politicians wouldn't be elected. If language didn't shape thought, Hitler would never have gotten out of the beer halls.

In shaping thought, language has the power to reinforce and perpetuate ethnic, racial, or sexual discrimination. Language used in this manner works against attempts to achieve equal opportunity in education, housing, and jobs; and equal opportunity is a national philosophy supported by law.

Discrimination in writing can be traced in part to the myths and stereotypes that have become associated with certain groups. This association has produced a form of folklore in which Italians are swarthy, Chinese are smiling and serene, blacks are athletic and shuffling, Mexicans are lazy, Spaniards are passionate, and native American Indians are proud and stoic.

Another form of folklore leads to discrimination on the basis of sex. This form stresses the concepts of male superiority and female inferiority. In this particular folklore, all positions of leadership are held by men, and all low-status occupations and activities are performed by women.

It would take [an article longer] than this one to trace the source of such attitudes. Still, we cannot deny their existence, and they do find their way into writing. A personnel report that evaluates Mary Smith as "a well-groomed black clerk" implies that other blacks are not well-groomed. An ad for a manager that reads "he is required to monitor production and he must act decisively" carries with it the message that only a man can handle the job.

In reality, attitudes such as these deny the fact that all sorts of personal attributes can be found in all groups and individuals. Therefore—don't label. All Asians are not inscrutable. All Anglo-Saxons are not poised and prim. All Scots are not thrifty. Many elderly people detest being called *senior citizens*. There is no such person as a *typical teenager*. All women are not weak and flighty, and all men are not strong, logical thinkers. A man's wife is not his *little woman*, and females in college are not *coeds*; they are students.

Another cause of discrimination in writing is found in the noun *man* and the pronouns *he, him,* and *his.* These traditionally have been used to apply to both men and women. Thus, we see statements like "Man works to protect nature"; "The manager is a busy person, and he needs the essential details of a report quickly"; and "An employee is encouraged to express his opinions about morale."

Granted, the writers of sentences such as these may not mean to exclude women. Still, the words literally say "men only," and the writing can be judged as discriminatory.

What is needed is a neutral noun or pronoun that applies equally to both sexes. The English language does not have such a word, but other alternatives are to:

1. Use the male pronouns *he, him,* and *his* when discussing a specific man only and not to lump everybody together regardless of sex.

2. When discussing people without regard to sex, use the genderless *one*, words such as *person* or *individual,* or the second person *you, your,* or *yours.* Thus, "his position in the organization" becomes "one's position"; "this person's position"; or "your position."

You can also neuter prose with *the* in certain situations. As an example, instead of writing of an engineer using "his test meter" write "the test meter."

In some instances, plurals work out. Thus "a man's opportunity is unlimited" becomes "their opportunity is unlimited" or "these people have unlimited opportunity."

Still another method is to write *he* or *she* instead of just *he* when both sexes are being referred to. When this is done, "he must have the appropriate technical ability" becomes "he or she must have the appropriate technical ability." Alternating between *he* and *she* is not limited to single phrases but can be done from sentence to sentence, paragraph to paragraph, or chapter to chapter.

But using *he* or *she* consistently in a short publication or alternating between genders in the parts of a longer publication poses problems a writer must be aware of. First, the frequent use of *or* is a weakness in style. Second, the frequent use of *he* or *she* or *his* or *her* bounces the reader back and forth, and the bouncing is tiring. If you can use some of the other methods suggested here, your writing will be stronger and show more polish.

Also, remember that language is first a spoken tool and then a written one. What sounds good usually reads that way. Therefore, if we are going to preserve the strength of our language we will have to avoid unpronounceable combinations such as *he/she* or *s/he.* How does one pronounce those crisply? Try it out loud: "he slant she," "he or she," "he and she"; or "ess slant he," "she he"? Which is right? What is meant? What does it *sound like?*

3. To further reduce discrimination in writing, use nonsexual titles and references:

INSTEAD OF	WRITE
man-made	synthetic, artificial
manpower	workers, workforce
man-hours	working hours, staff hours
gentlemen's agreement	informal agreement
you and your wife	you and your spouse
chairman	chair
businessman	executive, entrepreneur
foreman	supervisor
salesman	sales agent

4. When using names and courtesy titles, refer to men and women equally:

INSTEAD OF	WRITE
Roger Smith and Miss Jones	Roger Smith and Sarah Jones
Mr. Smith and Sarah Jones	Mr. Smith and Miss Jones
Roger and Jones	Roger and Sarah

Along these same lines, if you are writing to a woman and if you don't know if she is a *Miss* or *Mrs.*, use *Ms. Ms.* is generally accepted as being the female equivalent of *Mr.* The rule is to address women by the same standards as one addresses men.

5. Lastly, don't get carried away. *Host* and *hostess* are usable; *adulterer* and *adulteress* are specific and correct; and *leading lady* and *leading man* are bonafide titles.

Also, don't write *Black* unless you are willing to give whites equal uppercase time.

And if you are writing to an addressee whose gender is unknown, your options are: *To whom it may concern, Dear Sales Director, Dear XYZ Company, Dear Sir or Madam*, or perhaps no salutation at all. In any event, a term like *Dear Gentlepeople* is strictly a last resort. A writer in an organization where I worked did that once and got this reply: "Dear Sir. In an oil field, there are no gentlepeople."

3

BUSINESS AND TECHNICAL CORRESPONDENCE

Business and technical correspondence takes two forms: the letter and the memo. In general, you write letters to people outside your company. No matter what their goals, your letters present an opportunity to put your best professional foot forward. Your letters can be advertisements for yourself, for your department or division, and for your company.

Memos are the most frequently used form of internal written communication. Primarily memos provide a record of decisions made and actions taken within your company.

Letters and memos can announce or reaffirm policies; they can confirm decisions and conversations; they can send or request information. Some letters and memos are routine; others concern pressing issues. In either case, they require careful writing.

Given the volume of correspondence many companies produce, you may be tempted to use short cuts when you write letters or memos. For example, you may look for form responses or for copies of previous—but not necessarily good examples of—similar correspondence. In looking for short cuts, however, you are courting danger.

There is nothing wrong with form letters or memos, as long as such correspondence is appropriate to the given writing situation. A form letter reminding your customers of bills past due or a form memo transmitting attached data is often an effective and time-efficient way to communicate—provided such letters and memos are, in the words of Linda Flower (pp. 53–63), "reader-based," and they avoid the problems with language discussed in Part Two of this anthology.

The danger with form letters and memos is that they can become a crutch that you depend on even in situations in which they are inappropriate. Such misuse of form letters and memos can create new problems for you. You might have to send a follow-up letter or memo to fix what you tried to do in the first piece of correspondence. Or worse, you might have to send *several* follow-up messages.

Again, a process approach to business and technical correspondence will help you determine when form letters and memos are appropriate, and when something more original is required. The careful use of the writing process should also make follow-ups unnecessary.

The selections that follow take a decidedly process-oriented approach to business and technical correspondence. Malcolm Forbes writes from the dual perspective of a harried reader and of a writer. Forbes, like everyone else in the world of work, is a busy person who is impatient with correspondence that wastes his time. David V. Lewis expands on Forbes' advice on how to write to people effectively by offering suggestions on how to use correspondence to sell yourself to readers.

Writers for the Royal Bank of Canada agree with Lewis, arguing that *all* letters can be letters that sell. They suggest you use formulas for your correspondence to achieve this goal. Of course, when your purpose is to say "no," you face special difficulties. As Allan A. Glatthorn next suggests, you can say *no* in your letters and still keep or make friends.

You can adapt the principles contained in these first four essays to memos as well as to letters. The final two selections in Part Three address memo writing in particular. Harold K. Mintz offers a formula for writing better memos, while Marvin H. Swift shows how the writing process can help a manager rework and rethink a routine memo to produce a clear and effective message.

How to Write a Business Letter

MALCOLM FORBES

Malcolm Forbes is President and Editor-in-Chief of *Forbes Magazine*.

 good business letter can get you a job interview.

Get you off the hook.

Or get you money.

It's totally asinine to blow your chances of getting *whatever* you want—with a business letter that turns people off instead of turning them on.

The best place to learn to write is in school. If you're still there, pick your teachers' brains.

If not, big deal. I learned to ride a motorcycle at 50 and fly balloons at 52. It's never too late to learn.

Over 10,000 business letters come across my desk every year. They seem to fall into three categories: stultifying if not stupid, mundane (most of them), and first rate (rare). Here's the approach I've found that separates the winners from the losers (most of it's just good common sense)—it starts *before* you write your letter:

Know What You Want

If you don't, write it down—in one sentence. "I want to get an interview within the next two weeks." That simple. List the major points you want to get across—it'll keep you on course.

If you're *answering* a letter, check the points that need answering and keep the letter in front of you while you write. This way you won't forget anything— *that* would cause another round of letters.

And for goodness' sake, answer promptly if you're going to answer at all. Don't sit on a letter—*that* invites the person on the other end to sit on whatever you want from *him*.

Plunge Right In

Call him by name—not "Dear Sir, Madam, or Ms." "Dear Mr. Chrisanthopoulos"—and be sure to spell it right. That'll get him (thus, you) off to a good start.

HOW TO WRITE A BUSINESS LETTER   By Malcolm Forbes. Reprinted by permission of International Paper Company.

(Usually, you can get his name just by phoning his company—or from a business directory in your nearest library.)

Tell what your letter is about in the first paragraph. One or two sentences. Don't keep your reader guessing or he might file your letter away—even before he finishes it.

In the round file.

If you're answering a letter, refer to the date it was written. So the reader won't waste time hunting for it.

People who read business letters are as human as thee and me. Reading a letter shouldn't be a chore—*reward* the reader for the time he gives you.

Write So He'll Enjoy It

Write the entire letter from his point of view—what's in it for *him*? Beat him to the draw—surprise him by answering the questions and objections he might have.

Be positive—he'll be more receptive to what you have to say.

Be nice. Contrary to the cliché, genuinely nice guys most often finish first or very near it. I admit it's not easy when you've got a gripe. To be agreeable while disagreeing—that's an art.

Be natural—write the way you talk. Imagine him sitting in front of you—what would you *say* to him?

Business jargon too often is cold, stiff, unnatural.

Suppose I came up to you and said, "I acknowledge receipt of your letter and I beg to thank you." You'd think, "Huh? You're putting me on."

The acid test—read your letter *out loud* when you're done. You might get a shock—but you'll know for sure if it sounds natural.

Don't be cute or flippant. The reader won't take you seriously. This doesn't mean you've got to be dull. You prefer your letter to knock 'em dead rather than bore 'em to death.

Three points to remember:

Have a sense of humor. That's refreshing *anywhere*—a nice surprise in a business letter.

Be specific. If I tell you there's a new fuel that could save gasoline, you might not believe me. But suppose I tell you this:

"Gasohol"—10% alcohol, 90% gasoline—works as well as straight gasoline. Since you can make alcohol from grain or corn stalks, wood or wood waste, coal—even garbage, it's worth some real follow-through.

Now you've got something to sink your teeth into.

Lean heavier on nouns and verbs, lighter on adjectives. Use the active voice instead of the passive. Your writing will have more guts.

Which of these is stronger? Active voice: "I kicked out my money manager." Or, passive voice: "My money manager was kicked out by me." (By the way, neither is true. My son, Malcolm Jr., manages most Forbes money—he's a brilliant moneyman.)

Give It the Best You've Got

When you don't want something enough to make *the* effort, making *an* effort is a waste.

Make your letter look appetizing—or you'll strike out before you even get to bat. Type it—on good-quality 8½" × 11" stationery. Keep it neat. And use paragraphing that makes it easier to read.

Keep your letter short—to one page, if possible. Keep your paragraphs short. After all, who's going to benefit if your letter is quick and easy to read?

You.

For emphasis, underline important words. And sometimes indent sentences as well as paragraphs.

Like this. See how well it works? (But save it for something special.)

Make it perfect. No typos, no misspellings, no factual errors. If you're sloppy and let mistakes slip by, the person reading your letter will think you don't know better or don't care. Do you?

Be crystal clear. You won't get what you're after if your reader doesn't get the message.

Use good English. If you're still in school, take all the English and writing courses you can. The way you write and speak can really help—or *hurt*.

If you're not in school (even if you are), get the little 71-page gem by Strunk & White, *Elements of Style*. It's in paperback. It's fun to read and loaded with tips on good English and good writing.

Don't put on airs. Pretense invariably impresses only the pretender.

Don't exaggerate. Even once. Your reader will suspect everything else you write.

Distinguish opinions from facts. Your opinions may be the best in the world. But they're not gospel. You owe it to your reader to let him know which is which. He'll appreciate it and he'll admire you. The dumbest people I know are those who Know It All.

Be honest. It'll get you further in the long run. If you're not, you won't rest easy until you're found out. (The latter, not speaking from experience.)

Edit ruthlessly. Somebody ~~has~~ said that words are ~~a lot~~ like inflated money— the more ~~of them that~~ you use, the less each one ~~of them~~ is worth. ~~Right on.~~ Go through your entire letter ~~just~~ as many times as it takes. ~~Search out and~~ Annihilate all unnecessary words, ~~and~~ sentences—even ~~entire~~ paragraphs.

Sum It Up and Get Out

The last paragraph should tell the reader exactly what you want *him* to do—or what *you're* going to do. Short and sweet. "May I have an appointment? Next Monday, the 16th, I'll call your secretary to see when it'll be most convenient for you."

Close with something simple like, "Sincerely." And for heaven's sake sign legibly. The biggest ego trip I know is a completely illegible signature.

Good luck.

I hope you get what you're after.

Sincerely,

Malcolm S. Forbes

Making Your Correspondence Get Results

DAVID V. LEWIS

David V. Lewis is an in-house consultant
with Western Company of North America
in Fort Worth, Texas, where he is involved
in sales and management training.

If you turn out an average of five letters a day, you'll produce nearly twice as many words during the year as the typical professional writer.

These letters reflect *your* attitude—and obviously your organization's—toward customers. Realizing this, many progressive organizations train key people in the art of writing readable, results-getting letters. For example, the New York Life Insurance Company produces more than a million letters a year and uses its correspondence as a public relations tool.

"Anyone who writes a letter for New York Life holds a key position in our organization," says Nathan Kelne, vice president of the company. "By the letters our people write, they help determine how the public feels toward our company, and toward the life insurance business as a whole. Since they are instrumental in shaping the personality of the company, they are in a very real sense public relations writers."

For example, before New York Life launched its companywide letter-writing courses, here's how one of its executives tried to explain to a beneficiary the way the death claim was to be paid on a $3,000 policy:

> The monthly income per $1,000 under option 10 years certain is $7.93 per $1,000 total face amount of insurance, which total is $3,000.

Fortunately, the beneficiary was able to cut through the jargon. He replied:

> As I understand your letter, you seem to be saying that I should receive a monthly check for the amount of $23.79 for at least 10 years.

But another policyholder's response to a similarly bewildering letter is more typical:

Please tell me what you want me to do, and I'll be glad to do it.

Some universally proven principles that can help you sell yourself and your company to the public will now be examined.

Write for Him, Not to Him

General Foods is an organization that believes strongly in creating a favorable image through its correspondence. The public relations people came across this letter signed by a marketing executive and ready for mailing:

Dear Sir:

Enclosed please find a questionnaire which we are sending to all our retail contacts in this state.

Will you please answer this as soon as possible? It's very important that we have an immediate reply. We're delaying final plans for our retail sales program in this area until we get answers to the questionnaire.

With thanks in advance, we are,

Gratefully yours, . . .

The letter is clear and to the point; it *does* communicate readily. But there's a major flaw. It points out benefits the company will receive instead of suggesting how the program will help the recipient. The letter is writer- rather than reader-oriented.

Psychologists say that each of us is basically interested in himself or herself. We want to know "what's in it for me?" Once you routinely approach letter writing from this point of view, you'll find yourself telling your readers in specific terms how the letter will benefit them.

The questionnaire letter was rewritten this way.

Dear Sir:

Enclosed is a questionnaire on our proposed retail sales program. Your advance opinion on how this new plan would help you and others will be very useful in our evaluation of the program.

If you will fill out and return this questionnaire as soon as possible, we can let you and other retail contacts in this area know promptly of changes in the present program. Thank you.

Very truly yours, . . .

The revised version asks for your advance opinion, suggests how quick action might help you and *others*, and promises to let *you* know promptly of changes. There's also another improvement. The tired and outdated "With thanks in advance" has been replaced by a modern "Thank you."

The best way to persuade your readers to your point of view is to show them that it will be worth their while to do so. This rule holds true for just about every successful letter, sermon, sales presentation, or advertisement. A good sales letter, for example, is much like a good ad in that it attempts to dramatize benefits to the reader.

What does it take to get—and hold—a reader's attention? The most powerful letters appeal to basic needs and emotions rather than to purely logical reasons. Mainly, management people want to know how to save time, money, and effort. Show them how your product or service can help them do one or more of these things, and you're likely to get their attention.

With effort, almost any letter can be oriented to the reader, even the usually hard-to-write collection letter. Here's such a specimen, written almost entirely from the writer's point of view:

Dear Sir:

Our records show that you are three months delinquent in payment of your bill for $37.50.

Perhaps this is an oversight on your part. Otherwise we cannot understand why you have not taken care of this obligation.

Very truly yours, . . .

Keeping the reader's self-esteem in mind, the letter could have been rewritten this way:

Dear Sir:

We know you'll want to take care of your small past-due account for $37.50. This will help you to maintain the fine credit you have built up with us over the years.

Sincerely, . . .

To help develop the "you" attitude, put yourself in your reader's shoes, then write from his or her point of view. Once you've developed this attitude, you'll automatically start telling your readers what's in it for them. Instead of saying, "I wish to thank you," you'll write, "Thank you." Instead of writing, "We'd like to have your business," you'll write, "You'll find our service can help your business in many ways."

Personalize Your Letters (There's Power in Pronouns)

Some years ago, many would have considered this letter to have been perfectly proper and very effective:

Gentlemen:

Enclosed herewith are the subject documents which were requested in yours of the 10th. The documents will be duly reviewed and an opinion rendered as to their relevancy in the involved litigation.

Very truly yours, . . .

The letter *was* all right—back in the horse-and-buggy days! Phrases like "enclosed herewith," "duly received," and "involved litigation" would have marked the writer as learned. But the executive who makes a habit of writing like that today is generally regarded as an anachronism.

Current usage calls for clear, to-the-point letters, written mostly in conversational language. Like good conversation, your letters should generally be friendly, filled with personal references, and almost always informal in tone and language. Here's how the horse-and-buggy letter might have been rewritten by the modern executive:

Dear Sam:

Here are the documents you asked for. I'll look them over and let you know if we can use them in our lawsuit.

Cordially, . . .

When experts write a letter, even a form letter, they generally try to make it sound as personal as possible. Almost always, it contains a sprinkling of personal pronouns. In orienting your letter to the reader, fill it with "you," "your," and "yours." Use "I" and "me" sparingly.

Here's a case in point, a letter sent out by a mortgage company (emphasis added by the author):

Dear Mr. Jones:

We want to thank you for your query about *our* new mortgage insurance plan.

We are enclosing a pamphlet which outlines benefits of *our* new policy and gives testimonials from some of *our* policyholders.

We would like very much to enroll you within the next 30 days, since *we* are offering a special low premium rate as *our* introductory offer.

Very truly yours, . . .

The repeated use of *we* and *our* clearly shows the letter is written with the mortgage company's interests at heart. But notice how substituting *you* and *yours* orients the letter to the reader's interest. (Emphasis has again been added by the author.)

Dear Mr. Jones:

Thank *you* for *your* recent inquiry about our new mortgage insurance plan.

You'll find that the enclosed pamphlet outlines benefits of the policy in detail. *You'll* also probably be interested in the testimonials furnished by some policyholders.

If *you* sign up within the next 30 days, *you'll* be able to take advantage of special premiums we're offering on an introductory basis. Thank you.

Cordially, . . .

The word is out now in enlightened business circles. Companies are telling their executives to regard every letter as a personal contact: to write your own way, to develop your own style (within bounds), to make your letter distinctively *you*.

Mastering Tone (Your Personality in Print)

Writing a "rejection letter" that leaves the recipient's self-esteem intact and preserves his or her goodwill is a difficult task. It requires tact, diplomacy, and empathy—all of which must be effected through appropriate *tone*. For example, here's the way one banker turned down a builder, a long-time customer:

Dear Mr. Jones:

We regret to inform you that your request for an additional loan in the amount of $250,000 must be rejected. It was the judgment of the loan committee that, with your present commitment, such a loan would present too much of a risk for us.

Naturally, we look forward to doing business with you on your existing commitment.

Sincerely, . . .

What's wrong: Tone, mainly—the *way* the rejection is phrased. It deflates the reader's ego and makes it virtually certain the builder will do his banking elsewhere in the future.

True, the rejection was "justified." But why not let the reader down more gently and leave the door open for future business? For example:

Dear Mr. Jones:

One of the most distasteful tasks we have is to turn down a loan application, particularly when it is from a regular and respected customer like you.

We know you'll be disappointed, and so are we. We share your excitement about your plans to expand the Roseland Project, and hope that circumstances will later warrant our working with you on this and other projects.

However, the current economic outlook, combined with your delinquent status on your existing loan, makes your new loan application a questionable venture for us at the present time.

We will be glad to work with you in any way we can to resolve your current financial problems, and we look forward to helping you meet your future financial commitments.

Sincerely, . . .

The two letters say the same thing, but in vastly different ways. Suffice it to say that tone is as important to a letter as good muscle tone is to an athlete. A negatively phrased letter can have the same effect as an abrasive personality. As one New York Life executive put it:

> By its very nature, the "no" letter is a turndown and leaves the reader unsatisfied. Yet there are ways to soften the blow, and one of the best is simple candor. So, if you must say "no," state the reason first: "Currently there are no vacancies in that department. Therefore, I cannot offer you a position with the company at this time."
>
> A "no" response often requires positive alternatives if they are appropriate (for example, "Although, for the reasons mentioned, I cannot do as you ask, may I suggest that . . ."). You have to be more diplomatic and more sensitive if you're to have any chance of salvaging your reader's goodwill or ego.
>
> And that really is your goal in an effective "no" letter—to tell your readers something they don't want to hear in a way that compels understanding and, ideally, acceptance.

Unfortunately, tone requirements vary not only from person to person, but from one situation to another. For example, you would ordinarily use fast-paced, persuasive prose for a sales-promotion letter. In writing to a highly regarded law firm, you might use a slightly more "dignified" approach. If you're writing for a service-type organization, you might use a middle-of-the-road approach, as the government does.

Government letter writers are told to strive for a tone of "simple dignity," to make letters brief and to the point, and to avoid gobbledygook. "Don't act as if you're the only game in town," they're told. "On the other hand, don't bow and scrape just because you're a service organization."

Poor letters start with poor thinking on the part of the writer. Negative thoughts lead to negative words—and before you know it, there goes the old ball game. Here's a letter from a manager of a department store to a customer who complained that an appliance she had recently bought didn't work. (Negative words have been italicized by the author.)

Dear Sir:

I am in receipt of your letter in which you *state* that the hair dryer you purchased from us recently *failed to meet* the warranty requirements.

You *claim* that the dryer *failed* to do the things *you say* our salesman promised it would do.

Possibly *you misunderstood* the salesman's presentation. Or perhaps *you failed to follow instructions* properly. We *positively* know of no other customer who has made a similar complaint about the dryer. The feeling is that it will do all that is stated *if properly used*.

However, we are willing to make some concessions for the *alleged* faulty part. We will allow you to return it; however, *we cannot* do so *until* you sign the enclosed card and return it to us.

Very truly yours, . . .

The tone is unmistakably negative. "State" and "failed to meet" in the opening paragraph imply there's some doubt that the claim is valid. In the second paragraph, "you say" suggests the salesman didn't make the statement at all.

Such phrases as "you misunderstood," "you failed to follow instructions," and "if properly used" tell you in so many words that you're not too bright. And to wrap it up, the writer uses the negative "we cannot . . . until" instead of the positive "we will . . . as soon as."

Most letters aren't this negative, of course. But it doesn't take much to offend. Any of these negative words or phrases, in themselves, could have spoiled the tone of an otherwise effective letter.

If you've been guilty of taking a negative approach, study the following examples. In each case, the negative thought (emphasis added by the author) has been converted into a positive one.

Negative	Since you *failed* to say what size you wanted, we cannot send you the shirts.
Positive	You'll receive the shirts within two or three days after you send us your size on the enclosed form.
Negative	We *cannot* pay this bill in one lump sum as you requested.
Positive	We can clear up the balance in six months by paying you in monthly installments of $20.
Negative	We're sorry we *cannot* offer you billboard space for $200.
Positive	We can offer you excellent billboard space for $300.
Negative	We are *not* open on Saturday.
Positive	We are open from 8 A.M. to 8 P.M. daily, except Saturday and Sunday.

Negative words aren't the only cause of poor letter tone. Many letters are made more or less "neutral" by mechanical, impersonal, or discouraging language. Here's an example of each fault with a preferred alternative:

Impersonal	Many new names are being added to our list of customers. It is always a pleasure to welcome our new friends.
Personal	It's a pleasure to welcome you as our customer, Mr. Jones. We'll make every effort to serve you well.
Mechanical	This will acknowledge yours of the 10th requesting a copy of our company's annual report. A copy is enclosed herewith.
Friendly	Thanks for requesting a copy of our annual report, which is enclosed. We hope you will find it helpful.
Discouraging	Since we have a shortage of personnel at this time, we won't be able to process your order until the end of the month.
Encouraging	We should have more help shortly, which will enable us to get to your order by the end of the month.

Ideally, the tone of your letter should reflect the same ease in conversation that you enjoy when talking about your favorite hobby, business, or pastime.

How to Write (More) the Way You Talk

This letter was sent out by a large department store. Imagine yourself as the recipient.

Dear Sir:

　　We are in receipt of yours of July 10 and contents have been duly noted.

　　As per your request, we are forwarding herewith copies of our new fall brochure. Thanking you in advance for any business you will be so gracious as to do with us,

Yours truly, . . .

Conversational? Of course not. Who uses such language as "We are in receipt of . . . ," "duly noted . . . ," and "as per your request"? Practically no one. People just don't talk that way. Most of these phrases went out with the Model-T— or should have.

Face to face, the writer probably would have said, "Here's the fall brochure you requested. Let me know if we can serve you." It says the same thing, in less space, and without all the fuss.

Some business and professional people still feel it isn't quite proper to write conversationally, mainly because they have seen so much stilted business writing. But many progressive companies are telling their people to communicate in plain English, using only those technical terms that are absolutely necessary. As one executive of a major company said, "The best letters are more than just stand-ins for personal contact. They bridge any distance by the friendly way they have of talking things over person to person." And this from a U.S. Navy bulletin: "At best, writing is a poor substitute for talking. But the closer our writing comes to conversation, the better our exchange of ideas will be."

The consensus clearly is that informal, natural business writing is *in*; stilted business writing is *out*.

One word of caution about writing (more) the way you talk. Since World War II, readability experts have urged business people to "write more the way they talk" or "write as they talk."

Detractors have soft-pedaled the idea, claiming that most conversation is rambling, often incoherent, and frequently a bit too earthy. These are valid objections, but they miss the point. You're not being asked to write *exactly* the way you talk. Rather, you're being asked to bridge the gap between the spoken and the written word—to narrow the difference in the way you would *give* an order verbally and the way you would *write* that same order in a memo. Naturally, writing requires more restraint than speech, and the writer must normally use fewer words. But you can do these things and still capture the tone and cadence of spoken English.

The first step in making your correspondence more conversational is to rid your vocabulary of worn-out business phrases. Here are some of the more flagrant offenders. They were stylish once, but they've done their duty and need to be honorably discharged.

OLD HAT	CONVERSATIONAL
At a later date	Later
If this should prove to be the case	If this is the case
This will acknowledge receipt of	Thank you for
Attached herewith please find	Here is; Enclosed is
We shall advise you accordingly	We'll let you know
Due to the fact that	Because
With regard to	About
Please notify the writer as to	Please let me know
Enclosed please find a stamped envelope	I've enclosed a stamped envelope
We are submitting herewith a duplicate copy	Here is a copy
In compliance with your request	Here is
We are submitting herewith our check in the amount of $75	Here is our check for $75
We beg to advise (acknowledge) that	[Begging is unnecessary]
The information will be duly recorded	We'll record the information
The subject typewriter	This typewriter
In compliance with your request	As you requested
We will ascertain the facts and advise accordingly	We'll let you know
The writer wishes to state	[Just say it]

This list is far from complete but you get the idea. Once you're mentally geared to writing more conversationally, you'll detect many other clichés. Try to eliminate them.

Contractions will also make your writing more conversational. They play a part—a very large part—in almost everyone's everyday conversation. Even your most learned associate doesn't say, "We shall endeavor to be there at eight o'clock"; he's more likely to say, "We'll try to be there at eight o'clock." Instead of saying, "I am going to the ball game," he'll probably say, "I'm going to the ball game." It takes less effort to say, "You needn't bother to call," than to say, "You need not bother to call." Contractions tend to make the spoken words flow more smoothly. That's why they make writing appear more natural.

Probably the most common contractions are here's, there's, where's, what's, let's, haven't, hasn't, hadn't, won't, wouldn't, can't, couldn't, mustn't, don't, doesn't, didn't, aren't, isn't, and weren't. Then there are the pronoun contractions: I'll, I'm, I'd, I've, he's, he'll, he'd, and so forth.

Using these and other contractions when they facilitate flow of words will do much to give your writing a quality of spontaneity and warmth. But they must be used with discretion. Using too many contractions can sometimes make your writing too informal. And used in the "wrong" place, they might not "sound right." Indeed, the key is whether the contraction sounds right when the sentence is read.

Take this section from the Gettysburg Address: "But in a larger sense, we cannot dedicate, we cannot consecrate, we cannot hallow this ground." The passage would undoubtedly have lost its historic tone if *can't* had been used instead of *cannot*.

On the other hand, the advertising slogan "We'd rather fight than switch" would lose some of its punch if phrased, "We would rather fight than switch." Appropriate usage depends on how the contraction makes the sentence sound when it's read aloud.

Next time you get ready to write a letter, ask yourself, "How would I say this if I were talking to the person?" Then go ahead and write in that vein.

Letters That Sell

THE ROYAL BANK OF CANADA

Everyone writes letters that sell, and every letter has as its purpose the selling of something: goods, services, ideas or thoughts.

Someone may say that a family letter has no such purpose, but consider this: a letter telling about the children seeks to promote a favourable impression of their welfare and happiness; a letter telling about illness is designed to gain sympathy; the letter that says nothing but "I hope you are well" is selling the idea "I am thinking of you".

Family letters are usually rambling letters. They would be improved both in their readability and their informativeness if they adopted some of the principles that are used to sell goods and services. Business building letters, on the other hand, could with advantage incorporate some of the friendly informality of family letters.

Salesmanship of any kind is basically a person moving goods by persuading another person that he needs them, or winning that person's support or approval of an idea or a plan.

Some non-commercial type sales letters are those that champion good causes, such as community welfare or health standards or national unity. They seek to influence the thinking of individuals or groups.

It is not a simple task to compose a letter designed to sell. Like any other product of value, it calls for craftsmanship. There are techniques to be learned, techniques of conveying ideas, propositions, conclusions or advice appealingly and purposefully.

In the Beginning

In creating a letter to sell something we need to begin by thinking about the person to whom we are writing. A lawyer studies his opponent's case just as sharply as his client's; the manager of a baseball or hockey team analyses the qualities, good and bad, of members of the opposing team.

The writer must anticipate and answer in his letter questions that will occur to the reader: What is this about? How does it concern me? How can you prove it? What do you want me to do? Should I do it?

LETTERS THAT SELL © The Royal Bank of Canada (Monthly Letter 1974). Reprinted with the permission of The Royal Bank of Canada.

People buy goods or services because these will give them a new benefit or will extend or protect a benefit they already have, so the writer needs to translate what he offers into owner benefits.

The proffered benefits must be accessible and adapted to the reader's position, environment and needs. No letter is likely to sell sun-bonnets to people who live beyond the Arctic Circle or baby carriages to bachelors. We may classify a potential customer as a man, woman, company or institution that will have use for a product or service, has sufficient money to pay for it, and in whom a desire for possession may be created.

The reader's interest: that is the guiding star in sales letter writing. See his interests, his angle, and accommodate your stance to them. A simple precaution against sending a letter to the wrong person is to ask yourself what use you would have for the commodity if you were in the reader's place.

It is a good rule to spend more time thinking about the reader than about what you have to say. Otherwise you may become wrapped up in the virtues of your product so that you forget that the decision to buy rests with your prospect.

The self-interest of the person to whom you write is a major factor to consider in successful sales communication. When you remember it you give the impression that you have singled out this reader as being an important individual, and that is an excellent introduction.

It is not to be expected that the writer of letters that sell will know every person to whom he writes, but he must know certain facts: approximate income and age, occupational level, his business, and things like that. Then he is able to slant his sales points accurately toward the reader's needs, interests and purchasing power.

Know Your Product

The reader's attention should be attracted to the product or service, not to the grand style or picturesque phraseology of your letter. When you catch a person's attention you are focusing his consciousness on something. Concentrate on your commodity. The best magnet to draw and hold attention is what you say about the product, showing it to be useful and the means of fulfilling a desire.

It is no small accomplishment to analyse and marshal into order the facts about a product so as to win the thoughtful consideration of a person who has plenty of other things on his mind.

In purchasing almost any sort of commodity the buyer has a choice between what you are offering and what others are selling. Your sales job is to show the superiority of your product. Tell why what you offer is necessary or desirable, what it will accomplish in your reader's business, and how it can be fitted into his present layout and his plans. Do not content yourself with telling about the article as it sits on display: picture it in use in the reader's home or factory.

Your letter needs to convey the assurance that you are telling the truth about your goods. It is not a sensational offer that makes a letter convincing, but the feeling that the reader can depend upon what is said. He should feel assured that he will be buying what he thinks he is buying. Customer dissatisfaction caused by misleading sales talk can cause shock waves that affect the whole selling organization.

Let Your Personality Show

Make your letter sound friendly and human: put your personality on paper. Your letter is you speaking. Some of the features in your personality that you can display are: friendliness, knowledge, keen-mindedness, trustworthiness and interest in the prospect's welfare.

What you have in your mind about the good quality, appearance and usefulness of your product has to be communicated to your reader so as to arouse his interest, create a desire to possess, and induce him to buy.

Communication is not the easiest thing in the world to attain in writing, in art, or in music. Dr. Rollo May wrote in *Man's Search for Himself*: "We find in modern art and modern music a language which does not communicate. If most people, even intelligent ones, look at modern art without knowing the esoteric key, they can understand practically nothing."

It is not enough to write something so that it can be read. The degree to which communication occurs depends upon the degree to which the words represent the same thing for the reader as they do for the writer.

The recipient of a letter that is not clear is likely to blame its opacity on the lack of intelligence of the writer.

The art of composing sales letters is not one to be mastered by minds in which there is only a meagre store of knowledge and memories.

The art consists in having many mental references and associating them with new thoughts. Consider a poem. Its theme will likely have arisen from a single event, but the images used in its construction will have been drawn from the total life experience of the poet.

Put some flavour into your letters so that they taste good. Your letter will not be like anyone else's. That is a virtue, just as being an individual is a virtue in conversation. Who wishes to be a carbon copy of a textbook letter or to parrot phrases that other people use?

Practise talking on paper as if you were on the telephone. First write down the imagined questions asked by the person on the other end of the line and then your answers, given in simple, direct and pleasing words. To humanize your letters in this way with the natural idiom of conversation does not mean that you use cheap slang or clever verbal stunting.

Show Some Style

The style in which you write is not a casual feature of your letter. It is vital to your reader's understanding of what you are saying to him. It is not your job to please the reader's sense of the aesthetic, but to tell and explain plainly what is necessary to introduce your goods or your idea to his favourable attention. This may be done in a way that has grace and comeliness.

Never "talk down" to a reader. Make him feel that he knows a great deal, but here is something he may have missed. There is a big difference, when trying to build business, between making a suggestion and preaching a sermon.

It is highly important in writing a letter to sell something that it should be appropriate. Whatever your writing style may be, it will fit the occasion if it gives this particular correspondent information that will be useful to him, conveys to him a feeling of your interest in him and his business, and assures him of your goodwill.

Besides being grammatically correct, language should be suitable. At one extreme of unsuitability is the language that is too pompous for its load, and at the other is the language of the street which belittles the receiver's intellectual level.

Your words should be the most expressive for their purpose that the language affords, unobstructed by specialty jargon, and your sentences should be shaken free of adjectives—the most tempting of forbidden fruit to a person describing something.

Properly chosen words will convey your appreciation of the addressee as a person, and such friendliness is contagious. Some people are afraid to be friendly in their letters. They fear they will be thought of as "phonies" who have disguised themselves as Santa Claus for the occasion. Being friendly and showing it should not raise this scarecrow. It would be a grave mistake, indeed, for any of us to indulge in flowery language foreign to our natural talk; but it is no mistake at all to incorporate in our letters the warm, personal language that comes naturally to us in person-to-person social contacts.

Letter writing invites us to use the same etiquette as we use in courteous conversation. We look at the person with whom we are talking, converse on his level of understanding, speak gently, and discuss matters he considers important or interesting.

What the reader of your letter will notice is not its normal courtesy, but the extra touch that demonstrates care and understanding, a genuine interest in the reader's wants, a wish to do what is best for him, and the knowledge you show of how it can be done.

Everyone who writes a letter has a moral as well as a business reason to be intelligible. He is placing his reader under an obligation to spend time reading the letter, and to waste that time is to intrude upon his life plan.

There is an eloquence of the written as well as of the spoken word. It consists in adapting a statement to the receptive system of the reader so that he will have maximum help against confusion, against mistaking what is incidental from what is fundamental. A familiar device to use in this effort is to relate the new commodity you are offering to something that is familiar.

Use Suitable Formulas

There are formulas you may wish to make use of. Your letter must conform in some respects to what letters are expected to be. This does not mean pouring all letters into the same mould. Within the accepted pattern you are free to develop your talent for expression.

Skill is needed in the use of formulas. A form letter reveals itself to the reader and gets short shrift. It is possible to make use of the form as a guide to what points to cover, and then speak your piece on paper in a natural way.

Here are three formulas for letters. The first may be called the sales formula, the second the logical formula, and the third the rhetorical formula.

1. Get attention, provoke interest, rouse desire, obtain decision. Attention is curiosity fixed on something; interest is understanding of the nature and extent of what is new and its relationship to what is old; desire is the wish to take advantage of the proffered benefits; decision is based on confidence in what the writer says about his goods.

2. This is summarized: general, specific, conclusion. You start with a statement so broad and authoritative that it will not be disputed; you show that the general idea includes a specific idea; the conclusion is that what has been said about the general idea is also true of the specific.

3. This is very simple: picture, promise, prove, push. You write an attractive description of what you are selling; you promise that it will serve the reader well in such-and-such a way; you give examples of the commodity in use, proving that it has utility and worth; you urge the reader to take advantage of the promised values.

Selling Needs Ideas

Selling is done with ideas, so never throw away an idea even if it is of no use at the moment. Put it into your idea file where it will rub against other ideas and perhaps produce something new. The file is like an incubator. Thoughts and fancies you put into it will hatch out projects and plans.

Imagination helps in this operation. A correspondent of ordinary ability may never write anything that is not absolutely accurate and yet fail to interest his readers. This is a real weakness: to be perfect as to form but lacking in imagination and ideas.

Imagination should be given priority over judgment in preparing your first draft of a letter designed to sell. Then put reason to work: delete what is unnecessary, marshal your sentences into logical form so that your ideas advance in an orderly way; revise your words so that your thought is conveyed exactly as you wish it to be.

When you tell the advantages of your product or service or idea, and show how it will fill a need in the reader's life or job, in clear, truthful words placed in easily understood sentences brightened by ideas and imagination, you have done a good job of writing a sales letter.

Desire of the reader to do what you want done is created, just as in conversation, by both rational and emotional means, by proof and by persuasion, by giving reasons. Some goods and some buyers need nothing more than facts. An office manager buying pencils or pens for his staff will respond to an informative, factual, statistical sales letter. He is already sold on the idea of using pencils and pens, so you do not have to coach him about their usefulness; in fact, you may lose a sale if you give the impression of "teaching grandmother to suck eggs". What is needed is to catch his attention, give pertinent information about your product, and show him why buying from you will be profitable to him.

Try to make the information you give really enlightening. Comparing something unknown with something already known makes it possible to talk about the unknown. The analogy (like that between the heart and a pump) can be used as an aid in reasoning and in explaining or demonstrating.

The Soft Sell

The tone of a letter designed to sell something should be persuasive rather than insistent. It should seek to create a feeling of wanting, or at least an urge to "let's see".

People do not want to be told how to run their affairs, but anyone who shows them how to do things more economically or faster or better will find keen listeners. Soft sell gives the prospect credit for knowing a good thing when it is shown him, and acknowledges his right to make up his own mind.

The soft sell is recognition of the Missouri mule in human nature. Try to push a mule and he lashes out with his heels. Try to pull him by the halter rope and he braces his legs and defies you to budge him. "In the old cavalry," says A. C. Kemble in *Building Horsepower into Sales Letters*, "they said all it took to get a mule working for you was to recognize that he was an individualist who hated nagging and needed a chance to make up his own mind about things."

One hears a lot in advertising circles about "appeal". It is, according to the dictionary, "the power to attract, interest, amuse, or stimulate the mind or emotions."

Obviously, when you wish to influence someone you must take into account the kind of person you are addressing and what you want him to do. Your appeal must touch his feelings, needs and emotions. It strengthens your position if you can relate your own experience to that of the person you are addressing and write your message around the overlap of that experience.

The sort of mistake to be avoided with great care is slanting your appeal in a way that runs counter to the feelings of those whom you wish to influence.

It has been found in recent years that the advertising messages addressed to older people *as* older people did not win the desired response. In travel, for example, only a very small minority who want or need a sheltered situation are attracted by the semicustodial "trips for the elderly".

The Swiss Society for Market Research decided that "to sell anything to the over-65 age group it is important to keep one concept in mind: most senior citizens are vigorous and independent. Don't try to reach them with a head-on approach to the senior market. It probably won't work."

Writing a letter that pleases the recipient is not enough: it must be designed to lead to action. Do not fear to be explicit about what you want. Coyness in a letter is not attractive, and it exasperates the reader. Answer the reader's questions:

"What has this to do with me?" and "Why should I do what this person is asking me to do?"

You may answer these questions and encourage a purchase by appealing to emotional motives like pride, innovation, emulation, or social prestige; or to rational motives like money gain, economy, security, time-saving or safety.

Read Your Letter Critically

Imagine your letter to be your garden upon your return from vacation. You have to get into it and prune, clean up, tie up, and trim the edges.

Read the letter as if you were the recipient. How does it strike you? What can be added to attract attention? Is there anything irrelevant in it? Read the letter aloud to capture the conversational rhythm.

If you are not satisfied, do not crumple up the paper on which your draft is written. Try rearranging the paragraphs, the sentences, the words. Give the letter a new twist. Change the shape of your appeal. Delete anything that is distracting.

Be careful when trying to shorten a letter that seems to be too long. While a letter should be as short as possible, consistent with clearness and completeness, it is not the length that counts, but the depth. Since clearness and brevity sometimes get in the way of each other, remember that the right of way belongs to clearness. It will make a good impression if you find occasion to write: "I can be quite brief because this letter deals with a topic already well known to you."

The end of your letter, like the end of your pencil, should have a point. It should answer the reader's natural question: "So what?"

Follow Through

Do not let your customer forget you. When you produce a piece of copy that hits the bull's-eye, that is not the time to sit back and take things easy. It is a time to imagine what you would do if you were in your competitor's chair . . . and then do it first.

Competition is a fact of life. Wherever there are two wild animals trying to live on the same piece of land or two persons depending upon the same source of sustenance, there is competition. The customer who was a prospect to you before he bought your goods is now a prospect to your competitor. With the proper follow-through attention he will turn to you when he needs up-dating of equipment or new goods.

Writing a letter that sells goods or ideas, and following through so as to retain the customer, requires just as much specialized talent and mental ability as any other kind of advertising, if not more.

When you run into difficulties, composition of the sales or follow-up letter may give you a feeling of confusion. You may feel like throwing up your hands in despair of finding the exactly right slant or the perfect array of words. That is not unnatural. Nietzsche, the German philosopher, said in *Thus Spake Zarathustra*: "I tell you, one must still have chaos in one, to give birth to a dancing star."

The effort is worthwhile. When you set yourself to snap out of the depressing pedestrian type of letter that is so commonplace, you are raising yourself and your firm to a place where people will sit up and pay attention. As a student of sales letter writing you will generate ideas, as a philosopher you will assess the letters as to their purpose and usefulness, and as a writer you will energize them.

To summarize: the backbone of the principles of writing letters that sell is made up of these vertebrae—know why you are writing and what about; believe in what you are writing; be tactful and friendly and truthful; base your appeal on the prospect's interests . . . and check your letter and revise it.

"I Have Some Bad News for You"

ALLAN A. GLATTHORN

A consultant in management communications and the author of more than thirty
books on writing, Allan A. Glatthorn recently retired from the position of Senior
Faculty Member in the Teaching of Writing
Program at the University of Pennsylvania.

One of the most difficult letters or memos to write is the one containing bad news. A subordinate requests a salary increase which you cannot grant. A community organization asks for a contribution which you do not wish to make. An unqualified applicant asks for an appointment to discuss a position with your company, and you do not wish to take the time. You decide to have to dismiss a good worker because declining business mandates cutbacks. In each case you have some unpleasant news to deliver—but you wish to deliver it in a way that does not offend or alienate. How do you accomplish this difficult task? Let me offer some general guidelines and then explain the specific techniques.

The first guideline is to remind you that the successful manager is people-sensitive, able to empathize with others. When you receive a request, you stand in the shoes of the petitioner. You realize, to begin with, that from the standpoint of the asker, there are no foolish requests. People ask for things that they need, that they believe they are entitled to, that they hope to receive. And you also realize that there is really no good way to break bad news. No matter how empathic and tactful you may be, your bad news will inevitably cause disappointment and will often cause distress.

The second guideline derives from the first: remember that bad news is best delivered face to face. People getting bad news have some strong needs. They want an opportunity to express their negative feelings. They want the chance to press the request or appeal the decision. They want to explore the reasons more fully to be sure that there is no hidden message. These needs can best be met in a face-to-face meeting. So if you have bad news to give to an employee or a valued client, the best method is to confer with the individual, deliver the bad news in person, and then, if desirable, follow up with a written statement for the record. Don't avoid the unpleasant confrontation by writing a memo, hoping that the petitioner will go away quietly.

Finally, remember that everyone values honesty and forthrightness, especially when being disappointed. Typically, the receiver of bad news is inclined to be cynical, often resenting your attempts to be tactful and politic. You therefore should be sure that your desire to soften the blow does not beguile you into distorting the truth. Explain as tactfully as possible the real reasons for the bad news, instead of offering lame excuses.

With these general guidelines in mind, you should be able to send two kinds of "bad news" messages: the indirect and the direct.

The Indirect Bad News Message

The indirect message of bad news uses the soft and gentle approach. It tries to cushion the blow by burying the bad news in the middle of the letter or memo, surrounded by positive expressions of appreciation. You send the indirect message under one or more of these circumstances:

- You want further contact with the petitioner.

- You want to project the image of a caring individual.

- You believe that the petitioner won't be able to handle a more direct statement.

The formula is a simple one: THANKS . . . BECAUSE . . . SORRY . . . THANKS.

Thanks.

You begin with a positive statement. You express appreciation for the idea offered, the interest expressed, the petition received. Here's how an indirect bad news letter from an insurance company begins:

> Thank you very much for your recent inquiry about our automobile insurance coverage. We are pleased that you have considered transferring your account to our company.

Because.

You then continue with the reasons for the bad news. The strategy here is that stating the reasons first cushions the shock, preparing the reader for the bad news to come. Remember to use reasons that will make sense to the petitioner and that will at least project an image of sincerity. If at all possible, state reasons that will depersonalize the rejection, as the next paragraph of that letter does:

> In order to keep our premiums as low as possible, we find it necessary to accept only a small number of new accounts. And in fairness to our present customers, we accept applications only from those whose claims records are comparable to those of drivers we presently insure.

Sorry.

You next present the bad news itself, but you state it in a positive fashion. If you can suggest an alternative, do so. If you can find a way to leave the door open, make that clear—but do not give false hopes. Notice how the insurance letter continues:

> Even though we would like to include you among our insured drivers, we will not be able to do so at the present time. It seems to us that your best choice at this time is to remain with your present company. If your claims record improves during the coming year, we would be happy to have you reapply for coverage with us.

Thanks.

The indirect message of bad news closes with another expression of appreciation—and ends on a positive note, as this example illustrates:

> We do appreciate your considering our company. And we hope you will be able to reapply under more positive circumstances.

Figure [1] (p. 140) shows another example of this formula at work.

The Direct Message of Bad News

The direct message is a tough no-nonsense statement. While courteous, it gets right to the point and does not try to bury the bad news. It would be used under one or more of these circumstances:

- You want to slam the door shut, discouraging any other request from that petitioner.
- You want to project an image of toughness and directness.
- You are addressing an individual who prefers forthrightness and equates indirectness with softness or dishonesty.

The formula for the direct message is THANKS . . . SORRY . . . BECAUSE . . . THANKS. It uses the same ingredients as the indirect message, but it changes the order. And the language is less subtle and more direct.

Thanks.

You begin with a courteous expression of appreciation, since courtesy is expected even in the most direct communication. So a firm and direct letter rejecting an applicant might begin like this:

> Thank you for your letter and resume. We appreciate your interest in joining Mutual Life.

To: Bill Harkins
From: Joanne Clemens
Subject: Flex-Time Proposal
Date: February 19, 1985   *File:* A-342

   Bill, thanks very much for forwarding your proposal for a flex-time schedule for your department. I appreciate the creative energy—I can always count on getting good ideas from you.
   Our data suggest that flex time would result in an uneven distribution of worker hours at a time when uniformity seems desirable. As you are aware, the recent increase in customer demand is presenting us with the right kind of problem: our people and equipment are working at maximum capacity. My experience with other companies using flex time indicates that our productivity would suffer if we instituted it now.
   And my concern for maintaining productivity makes me reluctant to implement your excellent suggestion now. However, I have asked our personnel department to review the data. Because of my respect for your leadership, I want to give all of your ideas the most careful consideration.
   Thanks again for taking the time to share your ideas with me. I appreciate your developing a very sound proposal at a time when I know you are quite busy.

Figure [1] The Indirect Bad News Message

Sorry.

The direct message moves quickly to the bad news, to be sure that the message is heard as intended. The bad news is stated forthrightly—but without offending. So the rejection letter continues:

> Unfortunately, we do not have a position available that would match your qualifications, and it seems unlikely that such a position will develop in the future.

Because.

Now the reasons come, after the bad news has been delivered. The reasons are stated directly but not offensively, as in this example:

> We have found that our most successful middle-level managers are those who have had the benefit of working with Mutual in a variety of nonmanagerial positions. We therefore tend to promote from within and do not encourage applications for managerial positions from those who have not previously worked with us.

Thanks.

The message ends courteously—but the door is firmly closed. There must be no mistake about it: the news is bad. So the rejection letter ends like this:

> We hope you will be able to find employment with a company that can make use of your excellent qualifications, and we do appreciate your interest in applying with us.

The successful manager projects both people-sensitivity and toughness. The indirect message emphasizes sensitivity; the direct message affirms the toughness. . . .

How to Write Better Memos

HAROLD K. MINTZ

Harold K. Mintz was Senior Technical Editor for the RCA Corporation when he wrote this article.

Memos—interoffice, intershop, interdepartmental—are the most important medium of in-house communication. This article suggests ways to help you sharpen your memos so that they will more effectively inform, instruct, and sometimes persuade your coworkers.

Memos are informal, versatile, free-wheeling. In-house they go up, down or sideways.* They can even go to customers, suppliers, and other interested outsiders. They can run to ten pages or more, but are mostly one to three pages. (Short memos are preferable. Typed single-space and with double-space between paragraphs, Lincoln's Gettysburg Address easily fits on one page, and the Declaration of Independence on two pages.) They can be issued on a one-shot basis or in a series, on a schedule or anytime at all. They can cover major or minor subjects.

Primary functions of memos encompass, but are not limited to:

- Informing people of a problem or situation.
- Nailing down responsibility for action, and a deadline for it.
- Establishing a file record of decisions, agreements and policies.

Secondary functions include:

- Serving as a basis for formal reports.
- Helping to bring new personnel up-to-date.
- Replacing personal contact with people you cannot get along with. For example, the Shubert brothers, tyrannical titans of the American theatre for 40 years, often refused to talk to each other. They communicated by memo.

---

*We will return to this sentence later.

HOW TO WRITE BETTER MEMOS   By Harold K. Mintz. Reprinted by special permission from *Chemical Engineering* (January 26, 1970). Copyright © 1970, by McGraw-Hill, Inc., New York, N.Y. 10020.

142

- Handling people who ignore your oral directions. Concerning the State Dept., historian Arthur Schlesinger quoted JFK as follows: "I have discovered finally that the best way to deal with State is to send over memos. They can forget phone conversations, but a memorandum is something which, by their system, has to be answered."

Memos can be used to squelch unjustified time-consuming requests. When someone makes what you consider to be an unwarranted demand or request, tell him to put it in a memo—just for the record. This tactic can save you much time.

Organization of the Memo

Memos and letters are almost identical twins. They differ in the following ways: Memos normally remain in-house, memos don't usually need to "hook" the reader's interest, and memos covering a current situation can skip a background treatment.

Overall organization of a memo should ensure that it answer three basic questions concerning its subject:

1. What are the facts?

2. What do they mean?

3. What do we do now?

To supply the answers, a memo needs some or all of the following elements: summary, conclusions and recommendations, introduction, statement of problem, proposed solution, and discussion. Incidentally, these elements make excellent headings to break up the text and guide the readers.

In my opinion, every memo longer than a page should open with a summary, preferably a short paragraph. Thus, recipients can decide in seconds whether they want to read the entire memo.

Two reasons dictate placing the summary at the very beginning. There, of all places, you have the reader's undivided attention. Second, readers want to know, quickly, the meaning or significance of the memo.

Obviously, a summary cannot provide all the facts (Question 1, above) but it should capsule their meaning, and highlight a course of action.

When conclusions and recommendations are not applicable, forget them. When they are, however, you can insert them either right after the abstract or at the end of the memo. Here's one way to decide: If you expect readers to be neutral or favorable toward your conclusions and recommendations, put them up front. If you expect a negative reaction, put them at the end. Then, conceivably, your statement of the problem and your discussion of it may swing readers around to your side by the time they reach the end.

The introduction should give just enough information for the readers to be able to understand the statement of the problem and its discussion.

Literary Qualities

A good memo need not be a Pulitzer Prize winner, but it does need to be clear, brief, relevant. LBJ got along poorly with his science adviser, Donald Hornig, because Hornig's memos, according to a White House staffer, "were terribly long and complicated. The President couldn't read through a page or two and understand what Don wanted him to do, so he'd send it out to us and ask us what it was all about. Then we'd put a short cover-memo on top of it and send it back in. The President got mad as hell at long memos that didn't make any sense."

Clarity is paramount. Returning to the asterisked sentence in the second paragraph of the introduction, I could have said: "Memoranda are endowed with the capability of internal perpendicular and lateral deployment." Sheer unadulterated claptrap.

To sum up, be understandable and brief, but not brusque, and get to the point.

Another vitally important trait is a personal, human approach. Remember that your memos reach members of your own organization; that's a common bond worth exploiting. Your memos should provide them with the pertinent information they need (no more and no less) and in the language they understand. Feel free to use people's names, and personal pronouns and adjectives: you-your, we-our, I-mine. Get people into the act; it's they who do the work.

Lastly, a well-written memo should reflect diplomacy or political savvy. More than once, Hornig's memos lighted the fuse of LBJ's temper. One memo, regarded as criticizing James E. Webb (then the head of NASA), LBJ's friend, infuriated the President.

Another example of a politically naive memo made headlines in England three years ago. A hospital superintendent wrote a memo to his staff, recommending that aged and chronically ill patients should not be resuscitated after heart failure. Public reaction exploded so overwhelmingly against the superintendent that shock waves even shook Prime Minister Wilson's cabinet. Result? The Health Ministry torpedoed the recommendation.

Two other courses of action would have been more tactful for the superintendent: make the recommendation orally to his staff or, if he insisted on a memo, stamp it "private" and distribute it accordingly.

Literary style is a nebulous subject, difficult to pin down. Yet if you develop a clear, taut way of writing, you may end up in the same happy predicament as Lawrence of Arabia. He wrote "a violent memorandum" on a British-Arab problem, a memo whose "acidity and force" so impressed the commanding general that he wired it to London. Lawrence noted in his "Seven Pillars of Wisdom" that, "My popularity with the military staff in Egypt, due to the sudden help I had lent . . . was novel and rather amusing. They began to be polite to me, and to say that I was observant, with a pungent style. . . ."

Format of the Memo

Except for minor variations, the format to be used is standard. The memo dispenses with the addresses, salutations, and complimentary closes used in letters. Although format is a minor matter, it does rate some remarks.

To and From Lines—Names and departments are enough.

Subject—Capture its essence in ten words or less. Any subject that drones on for three or four lines may confuse or irritate readers.

Distribution—Send the memo only to people involved or interested in the subject matter. If they number less than say, ten, list them alphabetically on page 1; if more than ten, put them at the end.

Text—Use applicable headings listed after the three questions under *"Organization."*

Paragraphs—If numbering or lettering them helps in any way, do it.

Line Spacing—Single space within paragraphs, and double space between.

Underlines and Capitals—Used sparingly, they emphasize important points.

Number of Pages—Some companies impose a one-page limit, but it's an impractical restriction because some subjects just won't fit on one page. As a result, the half-baked memo requires a second or third memo to beef it up.

Figures and Tables—Use them; they'll enhance the impact of your memos.

Conclusion

Two cautions are appropriate. First, avoid writing memos that baffle people, like the one that Henry Luce once sent to an editor of *Time*. "There are only 30,000,000 sheep in the U.S.A.—same as 100 years ago. What does this prove? Answer???"

Second, avoid "memo-itis," the tendency to dash off memos at the drop of a pen, especially to the boss. In his book, "With Kennedy," Pierre Salinger observed that "a constant stream of memoranda" from Professor Arthur Schlesinger caused JFK to be "impatient with their length and frequency."

Clear Writing Means Clear Thinking Means . . .

MARVIN H. SWIFT

When he wrote this article, Marvin H. Swift
was Associate Professor of Communication
at the General Motors Institute.

I f you are a manager, you constantly face the problem of putting words
on paper. If you are like most managers, this is not the sort of problem
you enjoy. It is hard to do, and time consuming; and the task is doubly
difficult when, as is usually the case, your words must be designed to change the
behavior of others in the organization.

But the chore is there and must be done. How? Let's take a specific case.

Let's suppose that everyone at X Corporation, from the janitor on up to the
chairman of the board, is using the office copiers for personal matters; income tax
forms, church programs, children's term papers, and God knows what else are
being duplicated by the gross. This minor piracy costs the company a pretty
penny, both directly and in employee time, and the general manager—let's call
him Sam Edwards—decides the time has come to lower the boom.

Sam lets fly by dictating the following memo to his secretary:

To: All Employees
From: Samuel Edwards, General Manager
Subject: Abuse of Copiers

It has recently been brought to my attention that many of the people who
are employed by this company have taken advantage of their positions by
availing themselves of the copiers. More specifically, these machines are
being used for other than company business.

Obviously, such practice is contrary to company policy and must cease
and desist immediately. I wish therefore to inform all concerned—those
who have abused policy or will be abusing it—that their behavior cannot
and will not be tolerated. Accordingly, anyone in the future who is unable
to control himself will have his employment terminated.

146

If there are any questions about company policy, please feel free to contact this office.

Now the memo is on his desk for his signature. He looks it over; and the more he looks, the worse it reads. In fact, it's lousy. So he revises it three times, until it finally is in the form that follows:

> To: All Employees
> From: Samuel Edwards, General Manager
> Subject: Use of Copiers
>
> We are revamping our policy on the use of copiers for personal matters. In the past we have not encouraged personnel to use them for such purposes because of the costs involved. But we also recognize, perhaps belatedly, that we can solve the problem if each of us pays for what he takes.
>
> We are therefore putting these copiers on a pay-as-you-go basis. The details are simple enough. . . .
>
> *Samuel Edwards*

This time Sam thinks the memo looks good, and it *is* good. Not only is the writing much improved, but the problem should now be solved. He therefore signs the memo, turns it over to his secretary for distribution, and goes back to other things.

From Verbiage to Intent

I can only speculate on what occurs in a writer's mind as he moves from a poor draft to a good revision, but it is clear that Sam went through several specific steps, mentally as well as physically, before he had created his end product:

- He eliminated wordiness.
- He modulated the tone of the memo.
- He revised the policy it stated.

Let's retrace his thinking through each of these processes.

Eliminating Wordiness

Sam's basic message is that employees are not to use the copiers for their own affairs at company expense. As he looks over his first draft, however, it seems so long that this simple message has become diffused. With the idea of trimming the memo down, he takes another look at his first paragraph:

It has recently been brought to my attention that many of the people who are employed by this company have taken advantage of their positions by availing themselves of the copiers. More specifically, these machines are being used for other than company business.

He edits it like this:

ITEM: "recently"
COMMENT TO HIMSELF: Of course; else why write about the problem? So delete the word.

ITEM: "It has been brought to my attention"
COMMENT: Naturally. Delete it.

ITEM: "the people who are employed by this company"
COMMENT: Assumed. Why not just "employees"?

ITEM: "by availing themselves" and "for other than company business"
COMMENT: Since the second sentence repeats the first, why not coalesce?

And he comes up with this:

Employees have been using the copiers for personal matters.

He proceeds to the second paragraph. More confident of himself, he moves in broader swoops, so that the deletion process looks like this:

Obviously, such practice is contrary to company policy and ~~must cease and desist immediately. I wish therefore to inform all concerned—those who have abused policy or will be abusing it that their behavior cannot and will not be tolerated. Accordingly anyone in the future who is unable to control himself will have his employment terminated.~~ will result in dismissal.

The final paragraph, apart from "company policy" and "feel free," looks all right, so the total memo now reads as follows:

To: All Employees
From: Samuel Edwards, General Manager
Subject: Abuse of Copiers

Employees have been using the copiers for personal matters. Obviously, such practice is contrary to company policy and will result in dismissal.

If there are any questions, please contact this office.

Sam now examines his efforts by putting these questions to himself:

QUESTION: Is the memo free of deadwood?
ANSWER: Very much so. In fact, it's good, tight prose.
QUESTION: Is the policy stated?
ANSWER: Yes—sharp and clear.
QUESTION: Will the memo achieve its intended purpose?
ANSWER: Yes. But it sounds foolish.
QUESTION: Why?
ANSWER: The wording is too harsh; I'm not going to fire anybody over this.
QUESTION: How should I tone the thing down?

To answer this last question, Sam takes another look at the memo.

Correcting the Tone

What strikes his eye as he looks it over? Perhaps these three words:

- Abuse . . .

- Obviously . . .

- . . . dismissal . . .

The first one is easy enough to correct: he substitutes "use" for "abuse." But "obviously" poses a problem and calls for reflection. If the policy is obvious, why are the copiers being used? Is it that people are outrightly dishonest? Probably not. But that implies the policy isn't obvious; and whose fault is this? Who neglected to clarify policy? And why "dismissal" for something never publicized?
These questions impel him to revise the memo once again:

To: All Employees
From: Samuel Edwards, General Manager
Subject: Use of Copiers

Copiers are not to be used for personal matters. If there are any questions, please contact this office.

Revising the Policy Itself

The memo now seems courteous enough—at least it is not discourteous—but it is just a blank, perhaps overly simple, statement of policy. Has he really thought through the policy itself?
Reflecting on this, Sam realizes that some people will continue to use the copiers for personal business anyhow. If he seriously intends to enforce the basic

policy (first sentence), he will have to police the equipment, and that raises the question of costs all over again.

Also, the memo states that he will maintain an open-door policy (second sentence)—and surely there will be some, probably a good many, who will stroll in and offer to pay for what they use. His secretary has enough to do without keeping track of affairs of that kind.

Finally, the first and second sentences are at odds with each other. The first says that personal copying is out, and the second implies that it can be arranged.

The facts of organizational life thus force Sam to clarify in his own mind exactly what his position on the use of copiers is going to be. As he sees the problem now, what he really wants to do is put the copiers on a pay-as-you-go basis. After making that decision, he begins anew:

To: All Employees
From: Samuel Edwards, General Manager
Subject: Use of Copiers

We are revamping our policy on the use of copiers. . . .

This is the draft that goes into distribution and now allows him to turn his attention to other problems.

The Chicken or the Egg?

What are we to make of all this? It seems a rather lengthy and tedious report of what, after all, is a routine writing task created by a problem of minor importance. In making this kind of analysis, have I simply labored the obvious?

To answer this question, let's drop back to the original draft. If you read it over, you will see that Sam began with this kind of thinking:

- "The employees are taking advantage of the company."

- "I'm a nice guy, but now I'm going to play Dutch uncle."
- ∴ "I'll write them a memo that tells them to shape up or ship out."

In his final version, however, his thinking is quite different:

- "Actually, the employees are pretty mature, responsible people. They're capable of understanding a problem."

- "Company policy itself has never been crystallized. In fact, this is the first memo on the subject."

- "I don't want to overdo this thing—any employee can make an error in judgment."
- ∴ "I'll set a reasonable policy and write a memo that explains how it ought to operate."

Sam obviously gained a lot of ground between the first draft and the final version, and this implies two things. First, if a manager is to write effectively, he needs to isolate and define, as fully as possible, all the critical variables in the writing process and scrutinize what he writes for its clarity, simplicity, tone, and the rest. Second, after he has clarified his thoughts on paper, he may find that what he has written is not what has to be said. In this sense, writing is feedback and a way for the manager to discover himself. What are his real attitudes toward that amorphous, undifferentiated gray mass of employees "out there"? Writing is a way of finding out. By objectifying his thoughts in the medium of language, he gets a chance to see what is going on in his mind.

In other words, *if the manager writes well, he will think well.* Equally, the more clearly he has thought out his message before he starts to dictate, the more likely he is to get it right on paper the first time round. In other words, *if he thinks well, he will write well.*

Hence we have a chicken-and-the-egg situation: writing and thinking go hand in hand; and when one is good, the other is likely to be good.

Revision Sharpens Thinking

More particularly, rewriting is the key to improved thinking. It demands a real openmindedness and objectivity. It demands a willingness to cull verbiage so that ideas stand out clearly. And it demands a willingness to meet logical contradictions head on and trace them to the premises that have created them. In short, it forces a writer to get up his courage and expose his thinking process to his own intelligence.

Obviously, revising is hard work. It demands that you put yourself through the wringer, intellectually and emotionally, to squeeze out the best you can offer. Is it worth the effort? Yes, it is—if you believe you have a responsibility to think and communicate effectively.

4

REPORTS AND OTHER DOCUMENTS

Nearly everyone in business and industry writes reports. The word *report* is really just a generic term for a variety of documents that vary in form and purpose. Some reports are purely informative; others are persuasive or argumentative. Reports can be simple check lists, or they can take the form of interoffice memos, letters to clients, or more full-blown documents that are the results of weeks, if not months, of effort.

Some companies distinguish further between formal and informal reports. Formal reports generally follow a multi-part format and are used primarily to present the results of a detailed project. Such a project often involves a considerable outlay of capital. The format for a formal report may mandate a cover letter or a memo of transmittal attached to a bound document consisting of an abstract, a table of contents, a glossary, an introduction, a detailed discussion of all aspects of the topic, a set of conclusions and recommendations, and pages and pages of attachments. Informal reports tend to be shorter documents. Their formats are less complex, consisting only of such essential items as an introduction, a discussion, a set of conclusions, and, where appropriate, a set of recommendations. My earlier variation on the golden rule—write unto others as you would have them write unto you—is then especially applicable to the writing of reports, persuasive documents, and instructional materials.

To ensure that your reports are useful, you should take the same kind of process approach that you would when writing any other business or technical document. You should plan your reports carefully from the start so that you clearly define and stick to your intended purpose. Begin by asking yourself if your purpose is:

- to provide information

- to analyze information and draw conclusions

- to make recommendations.

Because they are often action-oriented, reports require that you analyze your audience—or your audiences—carefully. By virtue of their length, some reports can intimidate readers who need to know the information they contain.

Thomas Pearsall's classification of the kinds of audiences business and technical writing addresses is especially relevant to the audience, or readers, of reports. These readers can include:

- the layperson

- the executive

- the expert

- the technician

- the operator.[1]

Each brings a different background and a different set of needs to his or her reading of a report that must be taken into account when writing an effective document. In general, using abstracts and visual aids to supplement the contents of your reports will make them more accessible to larger groups of readers with varying degrees of expertise. You can also provide your readers with as many of the textual cues that Linda Flower suggested all writers use to guide readers through their prose (p. 58).

A proposal can take the form of a report, letter, or memo. Its primary purpose is to persuade readers to do something. Sales letters and requests for adjustments are two fairly simple proposals. Internal proposals, which are aimed at changing policies within an organization, and external proposals, such as documents seeking grants or funding, are more complex persuasive documents. Because proposals aim at convincing an audience to act in a way you want, a process approach will lead you to a successful proposal.

Instructional materials that explain processes and procedures are closely associated with persuasive writing. Such documents routinely fail to meet their objectives when business and technical people forget that instructional materials are written by people who know what to do to help people who don't.

[1] *Audience Analysis for Technical Writing* (Beverly Hills, CA: Glencoe, 1969).

In their selection that follows, J. C. Mathes and Dwight W. Stevenson return to a familiar theme in this anthology: the importance of audience analysis. They offer a detailed examination of the problem of audience analysis and offer a solution designed to meet the needs of the several audiences that reports in particular, and other business and technical documents in general, address.

Seconding this need for attention to audience, Richard W. Dodge reports on the results of a survey done at Westinghouse to determine the reading habits of busy managers. Dodge concludes that, while the body of the report may have required the most time for the writer to produce, busy managers read this section of the report with considerably less frequency than they read the other sections, usually giving more attention to the abstract. The importance of the abstract in meeting audience needs is further underscored by Christian K. Arnold, who discusses the key elements of an effective abstract.

A picture, the old saying tells us, is worth a thousand words. In business and technical illustrations, you'll want to make sure that the thousand words are the ones you intended. The pictures of the world of work are visual aids, and Charles T. Brusaw, Gerald J. Alred, and Walter E. Oliu offer easy-to-follow instructions for the effective use of four of the most widely-used visual aids: drawings, graphs, illustrations, and tables. It is possible, however, to misuse visual aids, intentionally and unintentionally. In a now classic piece, Darrell Huff suggests ways writers can use visual aids and statistics to manipulate the truth.

David W. Ewing next discusses the general problems of persuasive writing, addressing the wider issue of the different strategies needed to persuade, rather than simply to inform, readers. Ewing's general comments on persuasive writing are balanced by Charles H. Sides' specific approaches to the writing of procedures.

Vincent Vinci concludes Part Four with what amounts to a checklist business and technical writers can use as a last step in an effective writing process.

Audience Analysis: the Problem and a Solution

J. C. MATHES and
DWIGHT W. STEVENSON

Both J. C. Mathes and Dwight W. Stevenson are professors of humanities in the College of Engineering at the University of Michigan.

E very communication situation involves three fundamental components: a writer, a message, and an audience. However, many report writers treat the communication situation as if there were only two components: a writer and his message. Writers often ignore their readers because writers are preoccupied with their own problems and with the subject matter of the communication. The consequence is a poorly designed, ineffective report.

As an example, a student related to the class her first communication experience on a design project during summer employment with an automobile company. After she had been working on her assignment for a few weeks, her supervisor asked her to jot him a memo explaining what she was doing. Not wanting to take much time away from her work and not thinking the report very important, she gave him a handwritten memo and continued her technical activities. Soon after, the department manager inquired on the progress of the project. The supervisor immediately responded that he had just had a progress report, and thereupon forwarded the engineer's brief memo. Needless to say, the engineer felt embarrassed when her undeveloped and inadequately explained memo became an official report to the organization. The engineer thought her memo was written just to her supervisor, who was quite familiar with her assignment. Due to her lack of experience with organizational behavior, she made several false assumptions about her report audience, and therefore about her report's purpose.

The inexperienced report writer often fails to design his report effectively because he makes several false assumptions about the report writing situation. If the writer would stop to analyze the audience component he would realize that:

1. It is false to assume that the person addressed is the audience.

2. It is false to assume that the audience is a group of specialists in the field.

3. It is false to assume that the report has a finite period of use.

4. It is false to assume that the author and the audience always will be available for reference.

5. It is false to assume that the audience is familiar with the assignment.

6. It is false to assume that the audience has been involved in daily discussions of the material.

7. It is false to assume that the audience awaits the report.

8. It is false to assume that the audience has time to read the report.

Assumptions one and two indicate a writer's lack of awareness of the nature of his report audience. Assumptions three, four, and five indicate his lack of appreciation of the dynamic nature of the system. Assumptions six, seven, and eight indicate a writer's lack of consideration of the demands of day-by-day job activity.

A report has value only to the extent that it is useful to the organization. It is often used primarily by someone other than the person who requested it. Furthermore, the report may be responding to a variety of needs within the organization. These needs suggest that the persons who will use the report are not specialists or perhaps not even technically knowledgeable about the report's subject. The specialist is the engineer. Unless he is engaged in basic research, he usually must communicate with persons representing many different areas of operation in the organization.

In addition, the report is often useful over an extended period of time. Each written communication is filed in several offices. Last year's report can be incomprehensible if the writer did not anticipate and explain his purpose adequately. In these situations, even within the office where a report originated, the author as well as his supervisor will probably not be available to explain the report. Although organizational charts remain unchanged for years, personnel, assignments, and professional roles change constantly. Because of this dynamic process, even the immediate audience of a report sometimes is not familiar with the writer's technical assignment. Thus, the report writer usually must design his report for a dynamic situation.

Finally, the report writer must also be alert to the communication traps in relatively static situations. Not all readers will have heard the coffee break chats that fill in the details necessary to make even a routine recommendation convincing. A report can arrive at a time when the reader's mind is churning with other concerns. Even if it is expected, the report usually meets a reader who needs to act immediately. The reader usually does not have time to read through the whole report; he wants the useful information clearly and succinctly. To the reader, time probably is the most important commodity. Beginning report writers seldom realize they must design their reports to be used efficiently rather than read closely.

The sources of the false assumptions we have been discussing are not difficult to identify. The original source is the artificial communication a student is required to perform in college. In writing only for professors, a student learns to write for audiences of one, audiences who know more than the writer knows, and audiences who have no instrumental interests in what the report contains. The subsequent source, on the job, is the writer's natural attempt to simplify his task. The report writer, relying upon daily contact and familiarity, simply finds it easier to write a report for his own supervisor than to write for a supervisor in a different department. The writer also finds it easier to concentrate upon his own concerns than to consider the needs of his readers. He finds it difficult to address complex audiences and face the design problems they pose.

Audience Components and Problems They Pose

To write a report you must first understand how your audience poses a problem. Then you must analyze your audience in order to be able to design a report structure that provides an optimum solution. To explain the components of the report audience you must do more than just identify names, titles, and roles. You must determine who your audiences are as related to the purpose and content of your report. "Who" involves the specific operational functions of the persons who will read the report, as well as their educational and business backgrounds. These persons can be widely distributed, as is evident if you consider the operational relationships within a typical organization.

Classifying audiences only according to directions of communication flow along the paths delineated by the conventional organizational chart, we can identify three types of report audiences: *horizontal, vertical,* and *external.* For example, in the organization chart in Figure 1, *Part of organization chart for naval ship engineering center,*[1] horizontal audiences exist on each level. The Ship Concept Design Division and the Command and Surveillance Division form horizontal audiences for each other. Vertical audiences exist between levels. The Ship Concept Design Division and the Surface Ship Design Branch form vertical audiences for each other. External audiences exist when any unit interacts with a separate organization, such as when the Surface Ship Design Branch communicates with the Newport News Shipbuilding Company.

What the report writer first must realize is the separation between him and any of these three types of audiences. Few reports are written for horizontal audiences within the same unit, such as from one person in the Surface Ship Design Branch to another person or project group within the Surface Ship Design Branch itself. Instead, a report at least addresses horizontal audiences within a

[1]A reference in H. B. Benford and J. C. Mathes, *Your Future in Naval Architecture*, Richards Rosen, New York, 1968.

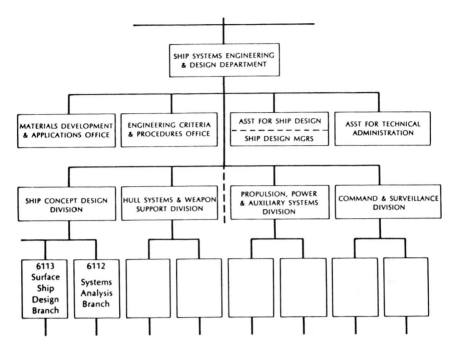

Figure 1 Part of organization chart for naval ship engineering center.

larger framework, such as from the Surface Ship Design Branch to the Systems Analysis Branch. Important reports usually have complex audiences, that is, vertical and horizontal, and sometimes external audiences as well.

An analysis of the problems generated by horizontal audiences—often assumed to pose few problems—illustrates the difficulties most writers face in all report writing situations. A systems engineer in the Systems Analysis Branch has little technical education in common with the naval architect in the Surface Ship Design Branch. In most colleges he takes only a few of the same mathematics and engineering science courses. The systems engineer would not know the wave resistance theory familiar to the naval architect, although he could use the results of his analysis. In turn, the naval architect would not know stochastics and probability theory, although he could understand systems models. But the differences between these audiences and writers go well beyond differences in training. In addition to having different educational backgrounds, the audiences will have different concerns, such as budget, production, or contract obligations. The audiences will also be separated from the writer by organizational politics and competition, as well as by personality differences among the people concerned.

When the writer addresses a horizontal audience in another organizational unit, he usually addresses a person in an organizational role. When addressed to the role rather than the person, the report is aimed at a department or a group. This means the report will have audiences in addition to the person addressed. It may be read primarily by staff personnel and subordinates. The addressee ultimately may act on the basis of the information reported, but at times he serves only to transfer the report to persons in his department who will use it. Furthermore, the report may have audiences in addition to those in the department addressed. It may be forwarded to other persons elsewhere, such as lawyers and comptrollers. The report travels routinely throughout organizational paths, and will have unknown or unanticipated audiences as well.

Consequently, even when on the same horizontal organizational level, the writer and his audience have little in common beyond the fact of working for the same organization, of having the same "rank," and perhaps of having the same educational level of attainment. Educational backgrounds can be entirely different; more important, needs, values, and uses are different. The report writer may recommend the choice of one switch over another on the basis of a cost-efficiency analysis; his audiences may be concerned for business relationships, distribution patterns, client preferences, and budgets. Therefore, the writer should not assume that his audience has technical competence in the field, familiarity with the technical assignment, knowledge of him or of personnel in his group, similar value perspectives, or even complementary motives. The differences between writer and audience are distinctive, and may even be irreconcilable.

The differences are magnified when the writer addresses vertical audiences. Reports directed at vertical audiences, that is, between levels of an organization chart, invariably have horizontal audience components also. These complex report writing situations pose significant communication problems for the writer. Differences between writer and audience are fundamental. The primary audiences for the reports, especially informal reports, must act or make decisions on the basis of the reports. The reports thus have only instrumental value, that is, value insofar as they can be used effectively. The writer must design his report primarily according to how it will be used.

In addition to horizontal audiences and to vertical audiences, many reports are also directed to external audiences. External audiences, whether they consist of a few or many persons, have the distinctive, dissimilar features of the complex vertical audience. With external audiences these features invariably are exaggerated, especially those involving need and value. An additional complication is that the external audience can judge an entire organization on the basis of the writer's report. And sometimes most important of all, concerns for tact and business relationships override technical concerns.

In actual practice the writer often finds audiences in different divisions of his own company to be "external" audiences. One engineer encountered this problem in his first position after graduation. He was sent to investigate the inconsistent test data being sent to his group from a different division of the company in another city. He found that the test procedures being used in that division were faulty. However, at his supervisor's direction he had to write a report that would not "step on any toes." He had to write the report in such a manner as to have the other division correct its test procedures while not implying that the division was in any way at fault. An engineer who assumes that the purpose of his report is just to explain a technical investigation is poorly prepared for professional practice.

Most of the important communication situations for an engineer during his first five years out of college occur when he reports to his supervisor, department head, and beyond. In these situations, his audiences are action-oriented line management who are uninterested in the technical details and may even be unfamiliar with the assignment. In addition, his audiences become acquainted with him professionally through his reports; therefore, it is more directly the report than the investigation that is important to the writer's career.

Audience components and the significant design problems they pose are well illustrated by the various audiences for a formal report written by an engineer on the development of a process to make a high purity chemical, as listed in Figure 2, *Complex audience components for a formal report by a chemical engineer on a process to make a high purity chemical* [p. 162]. The purpose of the report was to explain the process; others would make a feasibility study of the process and evaluate it in comparison to other processes.

The various audiences for this report, as you can determine just by reading their titles, would have had quite different roles, backgrounds, interests, values, needs, and uses for the report. The writer's brief analysis of the audiences yielded the following:

> He could not determine the nature of many of his audiences, who they were, or what the specifics of their roles were.

> His audiences had little familiarity with his assignment.

> His report would be used for information, for evaluation of the process, and for evaluation of the company's position in the field.

> Some of his audiences would have from a minute to a half hour to glance at the report, some would take the report home to study it, and some would use it over extended periods of time for process analysis and for economic and manufacturing feasibility studies.

> The useful lifetime of the report could be as long as twenty years.

> The report would be used to evaluate the achievements of the writer's department.

> The report would be used to evaluate the writing and technical proficiencies of the writer himself.

This report writer classified his audiences in terms of the conventional organization chart. Then to make them more than just names, titles, and roles he asked himself what they would know about his report and how they would use it. Even

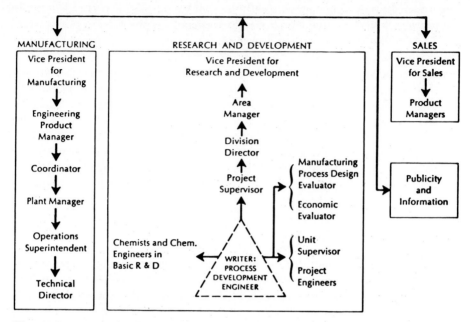

Figure 2 Complex audience components for a formal report by a chemical engineer on a process to make a high purity chemical.

then he had only partially solved his audience problem and had just begun to clarify the design problems he faced. To do so he needed to analyze his audiences systematically.

A Method for Systematic Audience Analysis

To introduce the audience problem that report writers must face, we have used the conventional concept of the organization chart to classify audiences as *horizontal, vertical,* and *external.* However, when the writer comes to the task of performing an instrumentally useful audience analysis for a particular report, this concept of the organization and this classification system for report audiences are not very helpful.

First, the writer does not view from outside the total communication system modeled by the company organization chart. He is within the system himself, so his view is always relative. Second, the conventional outsider's view does not yield sufficiently detailed information about the report audiences. A single bloc on the organization chart looks just like any other bloc, but in fact each bloc represents one or several human beings with distinctive roles, backgrounds, and personal characteristics. Third, and most importantly, the outsider's view does not help much to clarify the specific routes of communication, as determined by audience needs, which an individual report will follow. The organization chart may describe the organization, but it does not describe how the organization functions. Thus many of the routes a report follows—and consequently the needs it addresses—will not be signaled by the company organization chart.

In short, the conventional concept of report audiences derived from organization charts is necessarily abstract and unspecific. For that reason a more effective method for audience analysis is needed. In the remaining portion of this chapter we will present a three-step procedure. The procedure calls for preparing an egocentric organization chart to identify individual report readers, characterizing these readers, and classifying them to establish priorities. Based upon an egocentric view of the organization and concerned primarily with what report readers need, this system should yield the information the writer must have if he is to design an individual report effectively.

Prepare an Egocentric Organization Chart

An egocentric organization chart differs from the conventional chart in two senses. First, it identifies specific individuals rather than complex organizational units. A bloc on the conventional chart may often represent a number of people, but insofar as possible the egocentric chart identifies particular individuals who are potential readers of reports a writer produces. Second, the egocentric chart categorizes people in terms of their proximity to the report writer rather than in terms of their hierarchical relationship to the report writer. Readers are not identified as organizationally superior, inferior, or equal to the writer, but rather as near or distant from the writer. We find it effective to identify four different degrees of distance as is illustrated in Figure 3, *Egocentric organization chart* [p. 164]. In this figure, with the triangle representing the writer, each circle is an individual reader identified by his organizational title and by his primary operational concerns. The four degrees of distance are identified by the four concentric rings. The potential readers in the first ring are those people with whom the writer associates daily. They are typically those people in his same office or project group. The readers in the second ring are those people in other offices with whom the writer must normally interact in order to perform his job. Typically, these are persons in adjacent and management groups. The readers in the third ring are persons relatively more distant but still within the same organization. They are distant management, public relations, sales, legal department, production, purchasing, and so on. They are operationally dissimilar persons. The readers in the fourth ring are persons beyond the organization. They may work for the same company but in a division in another city. Or they may work for an entirely different organization.

Having prepared the egocentric organization chart, the report writer is able to see himself and his potential audiences from a useful perspective. Rather than seeing himself as an insignificantly small part of a complex structure—as he is apt to do with the conventional organizational chart—the writer sees himself as a center from which communication radiates throughout an organization. He sees

Figure 3 Egocentric organization chart.

his readers as individuals rather than as faceless blocs. And he sees that what he writes is addressed to people with varying and significant degrees of difference.

A good illustration of the perspective provided by the egocentric organization chart is the chart prepared by a chemical engineer working for a large corporation, Figure 4, *Actual egocentric organization chart of an engineer in a large corporation.* It is important to notice how the operational concerns of the persons even in close proximity vary considerably from those of the development engineer. What these people need from reports written by this engineer, then, has little to do with the processes by which he defined his technical problems.

The chemical engineer himself is concerned with the research and development of production processes and has little interest in, or knowledge of, budgetary matters. Some of the audiences in his group are chemists concerned with production—not with research and development. Because of this they have, as he said, "lost familiarity with the technical background, and instead depend mostly on experience." Other audiences in his group are technicians concerned only with operations. With only two years of college, they have had no more than introductory chemistry courses and have had no engineering courses.

Still another audience in his group is his group leader. Rather than being concerned with development, this reader is concerned with facilities and production operations. Consequently, he too is "losing familiarity with the technical material." Particularly significant for the report writer is that his group leader in his professional capacity does not use his B.S.Ch.E. degree. His role is that of manager, so his needs have become administrative rather than technical.

The concerns of the chemical engineer/report writer's audiences in close proximity to his group change again. Instead of being concerned with development or production operations, these audiences are primarily concerned with the budget. They have little technical contact, and are described as "business oriented." Both Manager I and Manager II are older, and neither has a degree in

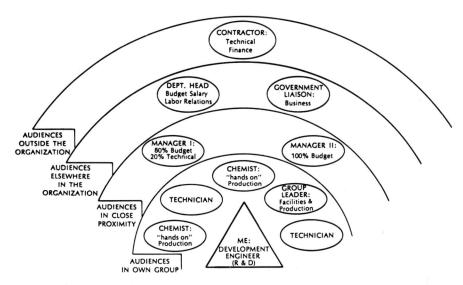

Figure 4 Actual egocentric organization chart of an engineer in a large corporation.

engineering. One has a Ph.D. degree in chemistry, the other an M.S. degree in technology. Both have had technical experience in the lab, but neither can readily follow technical explanations. As the chemical engineer said, both would find it "difficult to return to the lab."

The report writer's department head and the other persons through whom the group communicates with audiences elsewhere in the organization, and beyond it, have additional concerns as well as different backgrounds. The department head is concerned with budget, personnel, and labor relations. The person in contact with outside funding units—in this case, a government agency—has business administration degrees and is entirely business oriented. The person in contact with subcontractors has both technical and financial concerns.

Notice that when this writer examined his audiences even in his own group as well as those in close proximity to him, he saw that the natures, the backgrounds, and especially the operational concerns of his audiences vary and differ considerably. As he widened the scope of his egocentric organization chart, he knew less and less about his audiences. However, he could assume they will vary even more than those of the audiences in close proximity.

Thus, in the process of examining the audience situation with an egocentric organization chart, a report writer can uncover not only the fact that audiences have functionally different interests, but also the nature of those functional differences. He can proceed to classify the audiences for each particular report in terms of audience needs.

Preparation of the egocentric organization chart is the first step of your procedure of systematic audience analysis. Notice that this step can be performed once to describe your typical report audience situation but must be particularized for each report to define the audiences for that report. Having prepared the egocentric chart once, the writer revises his chart for subsequent reports by adding or subtracting individual audiences.

Characterize the Individual Report Readers

In the process of preparing the egocentric organization chart, you immediately begin to think of your individual report readers in particular terms. In preparing the egocentric chart discussed above, the report writer mentioned such items as a reader's age, academic degrees, and background in the organization as well as his operational concerns. All of these particulars will come to mind when you think of your audiences as individuals. However, a systematic rather than piecemeal audience analysis will yield more useful information. The second step of audience analysis is, therefore, a systematic characterization of each person identified in the egocentric organization chart. A systematic characterization is made in terms of *operational, objective,* and *personal* characteristics.

The *operational characteristics* of your audiences are particularly important. As you identify the operational characteristics for a person affected by your report, try to identify significant differences between his or her role and yours. What are his professional values? How does he spend his time? That is, will his daily concerns and attitudes enable him to react to your report easily, or will they make it difficult for him to grasp what you are talking about? What does he know about your role, and in particular, what does he know or remember about your technical assignment and the organizational problem that occasioned your report to come to him? You should also consider carefully what he will need from your report. As you think over your entire technical investigation, ask yourself if that person will involve staff personnel in action on your report, or if he will in turn activate other persons elsewhere in the organization when he receives the report. If he should, you must take their reactions into account when you write your report.

In addition, you should ask yourself, "How will my report affect his role?" A student engineer recently told us of an experience he had during summer employment when he was asked to evaluate the efficiency of the plant's waste treatment process. Armed with his fresh knowledge from advanced chemical engineering courses, to his surprise he found that, by making a simple change in the process, the company could save more than $200,000 a year. He fired off his report with great anticipation of glowing accolades—none came. How had his report affected the roles of some of his audiences? Although the writer had not considered the report's consequences when he wrote it, the supervisor, the manager, and related personnel now were faced with the problem of accounting for their waste of $200,000 a year. It should have been no surprise that they were less than elated over his discovery.

By *objective characteristics* we mean specific, relevant background data about the person. As you try to identify his or her educational background, you may note differences you might have otherwise neglected. Should his education seem to approximate yours, do not assume he knows what you know. Remember that the half-life of engineering education today is about five years. Thus, anyone five to ten years older than you, if you are recently out of college, probably will be only superficially familiar with the material and jargon of your advanced technical courses. If you can further identify his past professional experiences and roles, you might be able to anticipate his first-hand knowledge of your role and technical activities as well as to clarify any residual organizational commitments and value systems he might have. When you judge his knowledge of your technical area, ask yourself, "Could he participate in a professional conference in my field of specialization?"

For *personal characteristics*, when you identify a person by name, ask yourself how often the name changes in this organizational role. When you note his or her approximate age, remind yourself how differences in age can inhibit communication. Also note personal concerns that could influence his reactions to your report.

A convenient way to conduct the audience analysis we have been describing and to store the information it yields is to use an analysis form similar to the one in Figure 5, *Form for characterizing individual report readers* [p. 168]. It may be a little time-consuming to do this the first time around, but you can establish a file of audience characterizations. Then you can add to or subtract from this file as an individual communication situation requires.

One final point: This form is a means to an end rather than an end in itself. What is important for the report writer is that he think systematically about the questions this form raises. The novice usually has to force himself to analyze his audiences systematically. The experienced writer does this automatically.

Classify Audiences in Terms of How They Will Use Your Report

For each report you write, trace out the communication routes on your egocentric organization chart and add other routes not on the chart. Do not limit these routes to those specifically identified by the assignment and the addressees of the report. Rather, think through the total impacts of your report on the organization. That is, think in terms of the first, second, and even some third-order consequences of your report, and trace out the significant communication routes involved. All of these consequences define your actual communication.

When you think in terms of consequences, primarily you think in terms of the uses to which your report will be put. No longer are you concerned with your technical investigation itself. In fact, when you consider how readers will use your report, you realize that very few of your potential readers will have any real interest in the details of your technical investigation. Instead, they want to know the answers to such questions as "Why was this investigation made? What is the significance of the problem it addresses? What am I supposed to do with the

NAME: TITLE:

A. OPERATIONAL CHARACTERISTICS:
    1. His role within the organization and consequent value system:

    2. His daily concerns and attitudes:

    3. His knowledge of your technical responsibilities and assignment:

    4. What he will need from your report:

    5. What staff and other persons will be activated by your report
       through him:

    6. How your report could affect his role:

B. OBJECTIVE CHARACTERISTICS:
    1. His education—levels, fields, and years:

    2. His past professional experiences and roles:

    3. His knowledge of your technical area:

C. PERSONAL CHARACTERISTICS:
    Personal characteristics that could influence his reactions—age,
    attitudes, pet concerns, etc.

Figure 5 Form for characterizing individual report readers.

results of this investigation? What will it cost? What are the implications—for sales, for production, for the unions? What happens next? Who does it? Who is responsible?''

It is precisely this audience concern for nontechnical questions that causes so much trouble for young practicing engineers. Professionally, much of what the engineer spends his time doing is, at most, of only marginal concern to many of his audiences. His audiences ask questions about things which perhaps never entered his thoughts during his own technical activities when he received the assignment, defined the problem, and performed his investigation. These questions, however, must enter into his considerations when he writes his report.

Having defined the communication routes for a report you now know what audiences you will have and what questions they will want answered. The final step in our method of audience analysis is to assign priorities to your audiences. Classify them in terms of how they will use your report. In order of their importance to you (not in terms of their proximity to you), classify your audiences by these three categories:

- *Primary audiences*—who make decisions or act on the basis of the information a report contains.

- *Secondary audiences*—who are affected by the decisions and actions.

- *Immediate audiences*—who route the report or transmit the information it contains.

The *primary audience* for a report consists of those persons who will make decisions or act on the basis of the information provided by the report. The report overall should be designed to meet the needs of these users. The primary audience can consist of one person who will act in an official capacity, or it can consist of several persons representing several offices using the report. The important point here is that the primary audience for a report can consist of persons from any ring on the egocentric organization chart. They may be distant or in close proximity to the writer. They may be his organizational superiors, inferiors, or equals. They are simply those readers for whom the report is primarily intended. They are the top priority users.

In theory at least, primary audiences act in terms of their organizational roles rather than as individuals with distinctive idiosyncracies, predilections, and values. Your audience analysis should indicate when these personal concerns are likely to override organizational concerns. A typical primary audience is the decision maker, but his actual decisions are often determined by the evaluations and recommendations of staff personnel. Thus the report whose primary audience is a decision maker with line responsibility actually has an audience of staff personnel. Another type of primary audience is the production superintendent, but again his actions are often contingent upon the reactions of others.

In addition, because the report enters into a system, in time both the line and staff personnel will change; roles rather than individuals provide continuity. For this reason, it is helpful to remember the words of one engineer when he said, "A complete change of personnel could occur over the lifetime of my report." The report remains in the file. The report writer must not assume that his primary audience will be familiar with the technical assignment. He must design the report so that it contains adequate information concerning the reasons for the assignment, details of the procedures used, the results of the investigation, and conclusions and recommendations. This information is needed so that any future component of his primary audience will be able to use the report confidently.

The *secondary audiences* for a report consist of those persons other than primary decision makers or users who are affected by the information the report transmits into the system. These are the people whose activities are affected when a primary audience makes a decision, such as when production supervision has to adjust to management decisions. They must respond appropriately when a primary audience acts, such as when personnel and labor relations have to accommodate production line changes. The report writer must not neglect the needs of his secondary audiences. In tracing out his communication routes, he will identify several secondary audiences. Analysis of their needs will reveal what additional information the report should contain. This information is often omitted by writers who do not classify their audiences sufficiently.

The *immediate audience* for a report are those persons who route the report or transmit the information it contains. It is essential for the report writer to identify his immediate audiences and not to confuse them with his primary audiences. The immediate audience might be the report writer's supervisor or another middle management person. Yet usually his role will be to transmit information rather than to use the information directly. An information system has numerous persons who transmit reports but who may not act upon the information or who may not be affected by the information in ways of concern to the report writers. Often, a report is addressed to the writer's supervisor, but except for an incidental memo report, the supervisor serves only to transmit and expedite the information flow throughout the organizational system.

A word of caution: at times the immediate audience is also part of the primary audience; at other times the immediate audience is part of the secondary audience. For each report you write you must distinguish those among your readers who will function as conduits to the primary audience.

As an example of these distinctions between categories of report audiences, consider how audiences identified on the egocentric organization chart, Figure 4 [p. 165], can be categorized. Assume that the chemical engineer writes a report on a particular process improvement he has designed. The immediate audience might be his Group Leader. Another would be Manager I, transmitting the report to Manager II. The primary audiences might be Manager II and the Department Head; they would ask a barrage of nontechnical questions similar to those we mentioned a moment ago. They will decide whether or not the organization will implement the improvement recommended by the writer. The Department Head also could be part of the secondary audience by asking questions relating to labor relations and union contracts. Other secondary audiences, each asking different questions of the report, could be:

The person in contact with the funding agency, who will be concerned with budget and contract implications.

The person in contact with subcontractors, determining how they are affected.

The Group Leader, whose activities will be changed.

The "hands on" chemist, whose production responsibilities will be affected.

The technicians, whose job descriptions will change.

In addition to the secondary audiences on the egocentric organization chart, the report will have other secondary audiences throughout the organization—technical service and development, for example, or perhaps waste treatment.

At some length we have been discussing a fairly detailed method for systematic audience analysis. The method may have seemed more complicated than it actually is. Reduced to its basic ingredients, the method requires you, first, to identify all the individuals who will read the report, second, to characterize them, and third, to classify them. The *Matrix for audience analysis*, Figure 6, is a

Character-istics / Types of audiences	Operational	Objective	Personal
Primary	①	④	⑦
Secondary	②	⑤	⑧
Immediate	③	⑥	⑨

Figure 6 Matrix for audience analysis.

convenient device for characterizing and classifying your readers once you have identified them. At a glance, the matrix reveals what information you have and what information you still need to generate. Above all, the matrix forces you to think systematically. If you are able to fill in a good deal of specific information in each cell (particularly in the first six cells), you have gone a long way towards seeing how the needs of your audiences will determine the design of your report.

We have not introduced a systematic method for audience analysis with the expectation that it will make your communication task easy. We have introduced you to the problems you must account for when you design your reports—problems you otherwise might ignore. You should, at least, appreciate the complexity of a report audience. Thus, when you come to write a report, you are less likely to make false assumptions about your audience. To develop this attitude is perhaps as important as to acquire the specific information the analysis yields. On the basis of this attitude, you now are ready to determine the specific purpose of your report.

What to Report

RICHARD W. DODGE

At the time he wrote this article, Richard W. Dodge was the editor of *Westinghouse Engineer*.

Technical reports *can* be a useful tool for management—not only as a source of general information, but, more importantly, as a valuable aid to decision making. But to be effective for these purposes, a technical report must be geared to the needs of management.

Considerable effort is being spent today to upgrade the effectiveness of the technical report. Much of this is directed toward improving the writing abilities of engineers and scientists; or toward systems of organization, or format, for reports. This effort has had some rewarding effects in producing better written reports.

But one basic factor in achieving better reports seems to have received comparatively little attention. This is the question of audience needs. Or, expressed another way, *"What does management want in reports?"* This is an extremely basic question, and yet it seems to have had less attention than have the mechanics of putting words on paper.

A recent study conducted at Westinghouse sheds considerable light on this subject. While the results are for one company, probably most of them would apply equally to many other companies or organizations.

The study was made by an independent consultant with considerable experience in the field of technical report writing. It consisted of interviews with Westinghouse men at every level of management, carefully selected to present an accurate cross section. The list of questions asked is shown in Table 1. The results were compiled and analyzed and from the report several conclusions are apparent. In addition, some suggestions for report writers follow as a natural consequence.

What Management Looks for in Engineering Reports

When a manager reads a report, he looks for pertinent facts and competent opinions that will aid him in decision making. He wants to know right away whether he should read the report, route it, or skip it.

To determine this, he wants answers fast to some or all of the following questions:

WHAT TO REPORT   By Richard W. Dodge. Reprinted from *Westinghouse Engineer*, 22 (July–September, 1962), by permission of the Westinghouse Electric Corporation.

- What's the report about and who wrote it?

- What does it contribute?

- What are the conclusions and recommendations?

- What are their importance and significance?

- What's the implication to the Company?

- What actions are suggested? Short range? Long range?

- Why? By whom? When? How?

The manager wants this information in brief, concise, and meaningful terms. He wants it at the beginning of the report and all in one piece.

For example, if a summary is to convey information efficiently, it should contain three kinds of facts:

1. What the report is about;

2. The significance and implications of the work; and

3. The action called for.

To give an intelligent idea of what the report is about, first of all the problem must be defined, then the objectives of the project set forth. Next, the reasons for doing the work must be given. Following this should come the conclusions. And finally, the recommendations.

Such summaries are informative and useful, and should be placed at the beginning of the report.

The kind of information a manager wants in a report is determined by his management responsibilities, but how he wants this information presented is determined largely by his reading habits. This study indicates that management report reading habits are surprisingly similar. Every manager interviewed said he read the *summary* or abstract; a bare majority said they read the *introduction* and *background* sections as well as the *conclusions* and *recommendations*; only a few managers read the *body* of the report or the *appendix* material.

The managers who read the *background* section, or the conclusions and recommendations, said they did so ". . . to gain a better perspective of the material being reported and to find an answer to the all-important question: What do we do next?" Those who read the *body* of the report gave one of the following reasons:

1. Especially interested in subject;

2. Deeply involved in the project;

3. Urgency of problem requires it;

4. Skeptical of conclusions drawn.

Table 1 Questions Asked of Managers

---

1. What types of reports are submitted to you?
2. What do you look for *first* in the reports submitted to you?
3. What do you want from these reports?
4. To what depth do you want to follow any one particular idea?
5. At what level (how technical and how detailed) should the various reports be written?
6. What do you want emphasized in the reports submitted to you? (Facts, interpretations, recommendations, implications, etc.)
7. What types of decisions are you called upon to make or to participate in?
8. What type of information do you need in order to make these decisions?
9. What types of information do you receive that you don't want?
10. What types of information do you want but not receive?
11. How much of a typical or average report you receive is useful?
12. What types of reports do you write?
13. What do you think your boss wants in the reports you send him?
14. What percentage of the reports you receive do you think desirable or useful? (In kind or frequency.)
15. What percentage of the reports you write do you think desirable or useful? (In kind or frequency.)
16. What particular weaknesses have you found in reports?

And those few managers who read the *appendix* material did so to evaluate further the work being reported. To the report writer, this can mean but one thing: If a report is to convey useful information efficiently, the structure must fit the manager's reading habits.

The frequency of reading chart in Figure 1 [p. 176] suggests how a report should be structured if it is to be useful to management readers.

Subject Matter Interest

In addition to what facts a manager looks for in a report and how he reads reports, the study indicated that he is interested in five broad technological areas. These are:

1. Technical problems;

2. New projects and products;

3. Experiments and tests;

4. Materials and processes;

5. Field troubles.

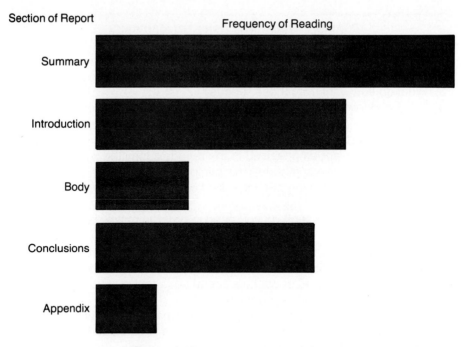

Figure 1 How managers read reports

Managers want to know a number of things about each of these areas. These are listed in Table 2. Each of the sets of questions can serve as an effective check list for report writers.

In addition to these subjects, a manager must also consider market factors and organization problems. Although these are not the primary concern of the engineer, he should furnish information to management whenever technical aspects provide special evidence or insight into the problem being considered. For example, here are some of the questions about marketing matters a manager will want answered:

- What are the chances for success?
- What are the possible rewards? Monetary? Technological?
- What are the possible risks? Monetary? Technological?
- Can we be competitive? Price? Delivery?
- Is there a market? Must one be developed?
- When will the product be available?

And, here are some of the questions about organization problems a manager must have answered before he can make a decision:

Table 2 What Managers Want to Know

Problems
What is it?
Why undertaken?
Magnitude and importance?
What is being done? By whom?
Approaches used?
Thorough and complete?
Suggested solution? Best? Consider others?
What now?
Who does it?
Time factors?
New Projects and Products
Potential?
Risks?
Scope of application?
Commercial implications?
Competition?
Importance to Company?
More work to be done? Any problems?
Required manpower, facilities and equipment?
Relative importance to other projects or products?
Life of project or product line?
Effect on Westinghouse technical position?
Priorities required?
Proposed schedule?
Target date?

Tests and Experiments
What tested or investigated?
Why? How?
What did it show?
Better ways?
Conclusions? Recommendations?
Implications to Company?
Materials and Processes
Properties, characteristics, capabilities? Limitations?
Use requirements and environment?
Areas and scope of application?
Cost factors?
Availability and sources?
What else will do it?
Problems in using?
Significance of application to Company?
Field Troubles and Special Design Problems
Specific equipment involved?
What trouble developed? Any trouble history?
How much involved?
Responsibility? Others? Westinghouse?
What is needed?
Special requirements and environment?
Who does it? Time factors?
Most practical solution? Recommended action?
Suggested product design changes?

- Is it the type of work Westinghouse should do?

- What changes will be required? Organization? Manpower? Facilities? Equipment?

- Is it an expanding or contracting program?

- What suffers if we concentrate on this?

These are the kinds of questions Westinghouse management wants answered about projects in these five broad technological areas. The report writer should answer them whenever possible.

Level of Presentation

Trite as it may sound, the technical and detail level at which a report should be written depends upon the reader and his use of the material. Most readers—certainly this is true for management readers—are interested in the significant material and in the general concepts that grow out of detail. Consequently, there is seldom real justification for a highly technical and detailed presentation.

Usually the management reader has an educational and experience background different from that of the writer. *Never* does the management reader have the same knowledge of and familiarity with the specific problem being reported that the writer has.

Therefore, the writer of a report for management should write at a technical level suitable for a reader whose educational and experience background is in a field different from his own. For example, if the report writer is an electrical engineer, he should write his reports for a person educated and trained in a field such as chemical engineering, or mechanical engineering, or metallurgical engineering.

All parts of the report *should preferably* be written on this basis. The highly technical, mathematical, and detailed material—if necessary at all—can and should be placed in the appendix.

Management Responsibilities

The information presented thus far is primarily of interest to the report writer. In addition, however, management itself has definite responsibilities in the reporting process. These can be summed up as follows:

1. Define the project and the required reports;

2. Provide proper perspective for the project and the required reporting;

3. See that effective reports are submitted on time; and

4. See that the reports are properly distributed.

An engineering report, like any engineered product, has to be designed to fill a particular need and to achieve a particular purpose within a specific situation. Making sure that the writer knows what his report is to do, how it is to be used, and who is going to use it—all these things are the responsibilities of management. Purpose, use, and reader are the design factors in communications, and unless the writer knows these things, he is in no position to design an effective instrument of communication—be it a report, a memorandum, or what have you.

Four conferences at selected times can help a manager control the writing of those he supervises and will help him get the kind of reports he wants, when he wants them.

Step 1—At the beginning of the project. The purpose of this conference is to define the project, make sure the engineer involved knows what it is he's supposed to do, and specify the required reporting that is going to be expected of him as the project continues. What kind of decisions, for example, hinge upon his report? What is the relation of his work to the decision making process of management? These are the kinds of questions to clear up at this conference.

If the project is an involved one that could easily be misunderstood, the manager may want to check the effectiveness of the conference by asking the engineer to write a memorandum stating in his own words his understanding of the project, how he plans to handle it, and the reporting requirements. This can assure a mutual understanding of the project from the very outset.

Step 2—At the completion of the investigation. When the engineer has finished the project assignment—but before he has reported on it—the manager should have him come in and talk over the results of his work. What did he find out? What conclusions has he reached? What is the main supporting evidence for these conclusions? What recommendations does he make? Should any future action be suggested? What is the value of the work to the Company?

The broader perspective of the manager, plus his extensive knowledge of the Company and its activities, puts him in the position of being able to give the engineer a much better picture of the value and implications of the project.

The mechanism for getting into the report the kind of information needed for decision making is a relatively simple one. As the manager goes over the material with the engineer, he picks out points that need to be emphasized, and those that can be left out. This is a formative process that aids the engineer in the selection of material and evidence to support his material.

Knowing in advance that he has a review session with his supervisor, the chances are the engineer will do some thinking beforehand about the project and the results. Consequently, he will have formed some opinions about the significance of the work, and will, therefore, make a more coherent and intelligent presentation of the project and the results of his investigation.

This review will do something for the manager, too. The material will give him an insight into the value of the work that will enable him to converse intelligently and convincingly about the project to others. Such a preview may, therefore, expedite decisions influencing the project in one way or another.

Step 3—After the report is outlined. The manager should schedule a third conference after the report is outlined. At this session, the manager and the author should review the report outline step-by-step. If the manager is satisfied with the outline, he should tell the author so and tell him to proceed with the report.

If, however, the manager is not satisfied with the outline and believes it will have to be reorganized before the kind of report wanted can be written, he must make this fact known to the author. One way he can do this is to have the author tell him why the outline is structured the way it is. This usually discloses the organizational weakness to the author and consequently he will be the one to suggest a change. This, of course, is the ideal situation. However, if the indirect approach doesn't work, the more direct approach must be used.

Regardless of the method used to develop a satisfactory outline, the thing the manager must keep in mind is this: It's much easier to win the author's consent to structural changes at the outline stage, i.e., *before* the report is written, than afterward. Writing is a personal thing; therefore, when changes are suggested in organization or approach, these are all too frequently considered personal attacks and strained relations result.

Step 4—After the report is written. The fourth interview calls for a review and approval by the manager of the finished report and the preparation of a distribution list. During this review, the manager may find some sections of the report that need changing. While this is to be expected, he should limit the extent of these changes. The true test of any piece of writing is the clarity of the statement. If it's clear and does the job, the manager should leave it alone.

This four-step conference mechanism will save the manager valuable time, and it will save the engineer valuable time. Also, it will insure meaningful and useful project reports—not an insignificant accomplishment itself. In addition, the process is an educative one. It places in the manager's hands another tool he can use to develop and broaden the viewpoint of the engineer. By eliminating misunderstanding and wasted effort, the review process creates a more helpful and effective working atmosphere. It acknowledges the professional status of the engineer and recognizes his importance as a member of the engineering department.

The Writing of Abstracts

CHRISTIAN K. ARNOLD

Christian K. Arnold was an instructor in English and a technical writer and editor before becoming Associate Executive Secretary of the Association of State Universities and Land-Grant Colleges.

T he most important section of your technical report or paper is the abstract. Some people will read your report from cover to cover; others will skim many parts, reading carefully only those parts that interest them for one reason or another; some will read only the introduction, results, and conclusions; but everyone who picks it up will read the abstract. In fact, the percentage of those who read beyond the abstract is probably related directly to the skill with which the abstract is written. The first significant impression of your report is formed in the reader's mind by the abstract; and the sympathy with which it is read, if it is read at all, is often determined by this first impression. Further, the people your organization wants most to impress with your report are the very people who will probably read no more than the abstract and certainly no more than the abstract, introduction, conclusions, and recommendations. And the people you should want most to read your paper are the ones for whose free time you have the most competition.

Despite its importance, you are apt to throw your abstract together as fast as possible. Its construction is the last step of an arduous job that you would rather have avoided in the first place. It's a real relief to be rid of the thing, and almost anything will satisfy you. But a little time spent in learning the "rules" that govern the construction of good abstracts and in practicing how to apply them will pay material dividends to both you and your organization.

The abstract—or summary, foreword, or whatever you call the initial thumbnail sketch of your report or paper—has two purposes: (1) it provides the specialist in the field with enough information about the report to permit him to decide whether he could read it with profit, and (2) it provides the administrator or executive with enough knowledge about what has been done in the study or project and with what results to satisfy most of his administrative needs.

It might seem that the design specifications would depend upon the purpose for which the abstract is written. To satisfy the first purpose, for instance, the abstract needs only to give an accurate indication of the subject matter and scope

THE WRITING OF ABSTRACTS   By Christian K. Arnold. © 1961 IRE. Reprinted, with permission, from *IRE Transactions on Engineering Writing & Speech*, Vol. EWS–4, pp. 80–82, December, 1961.

of the study; but, to satisfy the second, the abstract must summarize the results and conclusions and give enough background information to make the results understandable. The abstract designed for the purpose can tolerate any technical language or symbolic shortcuts understood at large by the subject-matter group; the abstract designed for the second purpose should contain no terms not generally understood in a semitechnical community. The abstract for the first purpose is called a *descriptive abstract*; that for the second, an *informative abstract*.

The following abstract, prepared by a professional technical abstracter in the Library of Congress, clearly gives the subject-matter specialist all the help he needs to decide whether he should read the article it describes:

> Results are presented of a series of cold-room tests on a Dodge diesel engine to determine the effects on starting time of (1) fuel quantity delivered at cranking speed and (2) type of fuel-injection pump used. The tests were made at a temperature of $-10°F$ with engine and accessories chilled at $-10°F$ at least 8 hours before starting.

Regardless of however useful this abstract might be on a library card or in an index or an annotated bibliography, it does not give an executive enough information. Nor does it encourage everyone to read the article. If fact, this abstract is useless to everyone except the specialist looking for sources of information. The descriptive abstract, in other words, cannot satisfy the requirements of the informative abstract.

But is the reverse also true? Let's have a look at an informative abstract written for the same article:

> A series of tests was made to determine the effect on diesel-engine starting characteristics at low temperatures of (1) the amount of fuel injected and (2) the type of injection pump used. All tests were conducted in a cold room maintained at $-10°F$ on a commercial Dodge engine. The engine and all accessories were "cold-soaked" in the test chamber for at least 8 hours before each test. Best starting was obtained with 116 cu mm of fuel, 85 per cent more than that required for maximum power. Very poor starting was obtained with the lean setting of 34.7 cu mm. Tests with two different pumps indicated that, for best starting characteristics, the pump must deliver fuel evenly to all cylinders even at low cranking speeds so that each cylinder contributes its maximum potential power.

This abstract is not perfect. With just a few more words, for instance, the abstracter could have clarified the data about the amount of fuel delivered; do the figures give flow rates (what is the unit of time?) or total amount of fuel injected (over how long a period?)? He could easily have defined "best" starting. He could have been more specific about at least the more satisfactory type of pump: what is the type that delivers the fuel more evenly? Clarification of these points would not have increased the length of the abstract significantly.

The important point, however, is not the deficiencies of the illustration. In fact, it is almost impossible to find a perfect, or even near perfect, abstract, quite possibly because the abstract is the most difficult part of the report to write. This difficulty stems from the severe limitations imposed on its length, its importance to the over-all acceptance of the report or paper, and, with informative abstracts, the requirement for simplicity and general understandability.

The important point, rather, is that the informative abstract gives everything that is included in the descriptive one. The informative abstract, that is, satisfies not only its own purpose but also that of the descriptive abstract. Since values are obtained from the informative abstract that are not obtained from the descriptive, it is almost always worth while to take the extra time and effort necessary to produce a good informative abstract for your report or memo. Viewed from the standpoint of either the total time and effort expended on the writing job as a whole or the extra benefits that accrue to you and your organization, the additional effort is inconsequential.

It is impossible to lay down guidelines that will lead always to the construction of an effective abstract, simply because each reporting job, and consequently each abstract, is unique. However, general "rules" can be established that, if practiced conscientiously and applied intelligently, will eliminate most of the bugs from your abstracts.

1. *Your abstract must include enough* specific *information about the project or study to satisfy most of the administrative needs of a busy executive.* This means that the more important results, conclusions, and recommendations, together with enough additional information to make them understandable, must be included. This additional information will most certainly include an accurate statement of the problem and the limitations placed on it. It will probably include an interpretation of the results and the principal facts upon which the analysis was made, along with an indication of how they were obtained. Again, *specific* information must be given. One of the most common faults of abstracts in technical reports is that the information given is too general to be useful.

2. *Your abstract must be a self-contained unit, a complete report-in-miniature.* Sooner or later, most abstracts are separated from the parent report, and the abstract that cannot stand on its own feet independently must then either be rewritten or will fail to perform its job. And the rewriting, if it is done, will be done by someone not nearly as sympathetic with your study as you are. Even if it is not separated from the report, the abstract must be written as a complete, independent unit if it is to be of the most help possible to the executive. This rule automatically eliminates the common deadwood phrases like "this report contains . . ." or "this is a report on . . ." that clutter up many abstracts. It also eliminates all references to sections, figures, tables, or anything else contained in the report proper.

3. *Your abstract must be short.* Length in an abstract defeats every purpose for which it is written. However, no one can tell you just how short it

must be. Some authorities have attempted to establish arbitrary lengths, usually in terms of a certain percentage of the report, the figure given normally falling between three and ten per cent. Such artificial guides are unrealistic. The abstract for a 30-page report must necessarily be longer, percentagewise, than the abstract for a 300-page report, since there is certain basic information that must be given regardless of the length of the report. In addition, the information given in some reports can be summarized much more briefly than can that given in other reports of the same over-all dimensions. Definite advantages, psychological as well as material, are obtained if the abstract is short enough to be printed entirely on one page so that the reader doesn't even have to turn a page to get the total picture that the abstract provides. Certainly, it should be no longer than the interest span of an only mildly interested and very busy executive. About the best practical advice that can be given in a vacuum is to make your abstract as short as possible without cutting out essential information or doing violence to its accuracy. With practice, you might be surprised to learn how much information you can crowd into a few words. It helps, too, to learn to blue-pencil unessential information. It is perhaps important to document that "a meeting was held at the Bureau of Ordnance on Tuesday, October 3, 1961, at 2:30 P.M." somewhere, but such information is just excess baggage in your abstract: it helps neither the research worker looking for source material nor the administrator looking for a status or information summary. Someone is supposed to have once said, "I would have written a shorter letter if I had had more time." Take the time to make your abstracts shorter; the results are worth it. But be careful not to distort the facts in the condensing.

4. *Your abstract must be written in fluent, easy-to-read prose.* The odds are heavily against your reader's being an expert in the subject covered by your report or paper. In fact, the odds that he is an expert in your field are probably no greater than the odds that he has only a smattering of training in any technical or scientific discipline. And even if he were perfectly capable of following the most obscure, tortured technical jargon, he will appreciate your sparing him the necessity for doing it. T. O. Richards, head of the Laboratory Control Department, and R. A. Richardson, head of the Technical Data Department, both of the General Motors Corporation, have written that their experience shows the abstract cannot be made too elementary: "We never had [an abstract] . . . in which the explanations and terms were too simple." This requirement immediately eliminates the "telegraphic" writing often found in abstracts. Save footage by sound practices of economy and not by cutting out the articles and the transitional devices needed for smoothness and fluency. It also eliminates those obscure terms that you defend on the basis of "that's the way it's always said."

5. *Your abstract must be consistent in tone and emphases with the report proper, but it does not need to follow the arrangement, wording, or proportion of the original.* Data, information, and ideas introduced into the

abstract must also appear in the report or paper. And they must appear with the same emphases. A conclusion or recommendation that is qualified in the report proper must not turn up without the qualification in the abstract. After all, someone might read both the abstract and the report. If this reader spots an inconsistency or is confused, you've lost a reader.

6. *Your abstract should make the widest possible use of abbreviations and numerals, but it must not contain any tables or illustrations.* Because of the space limitations imposed upon abstracts, the rules governing the use of abbreviations and numerals are relaxed for it. In fact, all figures except those standing at the beginning of sentences should be written as numerals, and all abbreviations generally accepted by such standard sources as the American Standards Association and "Webster's Dictionary" should be used.

By now you must surely see why the abstract is the toughest part of your report to write. A good abstract is well worth the time and effort necessary to write it and is one of the most important parts of your report. And abstract writing probably contributes more to the acquisition of sound expository skills than does any other prose discipline.

Drawings, Graphs, Illustrations, and Tables

CHARLES T. BRUSAW, GERALD J. ALRED, and WALTER E. OLIU

Charles T. Brusaw is a Senior Program Instructor for NCR Corporation. Gerald J. Alred is a member of the English Department at the University of Wisconsin-Milwaukee. Walter E. Oliu is a technical writer in the Division of Technical Writing and Document Control of the U.S. Nuclear Regulatory Commission. They are also the coauthors of *The Business Writer's Handbook* (3rd ed., St. Martin's, 1987).

Drawings

A drawing is useful when you wish to focus on details or relationships that a photograph cannot capture. A drawing can emphasize the significant part of a mechanism, or its function, and omit what is not significant. However, if the precise details of the actual appearance of an object are necessary to your report or document, a photograph is essential.

There are various types of drawings, each with unique advantages. The type of drawing used for an illustration should be determined by the specific purpose it is intended to serve. If your reader needs an impression of an object's general appearance or an overview of a series of steps or directions, a conventional drawing of the type illustrated by Figure 1 will suffice. Where it is necessary to show the internal parts of a piece of equipment in such a way that their relationship to the overall equipment is clear, a cutaway drawing is necessary, as in Figure 2 [p. 188]. To show the proper sequence in which parts fit together or when it is essential to show the details of each individual part, use an exploded-view drawing such as Figure 3 [page 189].

Tips for Creating and Using Drawings

Many organizations have their own format specifications. In the absence of such specifications, the following tips will be helpful:

EMERGENCY STOP. Arm extended, palm down, move hand rapidly right and left.

STOP. Arm extended, palm down, hold position rigidly.

RAISE BOOM. Arm extended, fingers closed, thumb pointing upward.

LOWER BOOM. Arm extended, fingers closed, thumb pointing downward.

SWING. Arm extended, point with finger in direction of swing of boom.

TRAVEL. Arm extended forward, hand open and slightly raised, make pushing motion in direction of travel.

Source: Harnischfeger Corporation

Hand Signals for Crane Operation

Figure 1 Drawing That Illustrates Instructions

Source: Harnischfeger Corporation

Detail View—Collector

Figure 2 Cutaway Drawing

1. Give the drawing a clear title and a figure number (if figure numbers are used), both of which should be centered below the drawing.

2. Place the source or courtesy line, if necessary, in the lower left corner.

3. Show the equipment from the point of view of the person who will use it.

4. When illustrating a subsystem, show its relationship to the larger system of which it is a part.

5. Draw the different parts of an object in proportion to one another, unless you indicate that certain parts are enlarged.

6. When a sequence of drawings is used to illustrate a process, arrange them from left to right or from top to bottom.

7. Label parts in the drawing so that text references to them are clear.

1. Wheel Nut	22. Spacer
2. Water Seal	23. Torsion Bar
3. Felt Seal	23A. Pin
4. Snap Ring	24. Valve Spool
5. Washer	24A. Housing Assembly
6. Brass Washer	25. 5/16″ Steel Ball
7. Teflon Washer	26. Ball Retaining Spring
8. Seal	27. 13/16″ Steel Ball
9. Upper Cover	28. Seal (2)
9A. Upper Cover Screw	29. Spacer
10. Seal Ring	30. Drive Link
11. Needle Bearing	31. Metering Element
12. Shims	31A. Stator
13. Snap Ring	31B. Rotor
14. Thrust Washer	32. Manifold
15. Thrust Bearing	33. Commutator Ring
16. Thrust Washer	33A. Commutator
17. Wave Spring Washer	34. Seal Retainer
18. Spacer	35. Washer
19. Input Shaft	36. End Cover Assembly
20. Pin	36A. End Cover Screw (7)
21. Drive Ring	

Source: Harnischfeger Corporation

Power Steering Valve

Figure 3 Exploded-View Drawing

8. Depending on the complexity of what is shown, labels may be placed on the parts themselves, or the parts may be given letter or number symbols, with an accompanying key (see Figure 3). . . .

Graphs

A graph presents numerical data in visual form. This method has several advantages over presenting data in tables or within the text. Trends, movements, distributions, and cycles are more readily apparent in graphs than they are in tables. By providing a means for ready comparisons, a graph often shows a significance in the data not otherwise immediately apparent. Be aware, however, that although graphs present statistics in a more interesting and comprehensible form than tables do, they are less accurate. For this reason, they are often accompanied by tables giving the exact figures. The main types of graphs are line graphs, bar graphs, pie graphs, and picture graphs. This entry also includes a compact discussion of computer graphics and provides guidelines for integrating graphs into the text.

Line Graphs

The line graph shows the relationship between two sets of numbers by means of points plotted in relation to two axes drawn at right angles. The points, once plotted, are connected to one another to form a continuous line. In this way, what was merely a set of dots having abstract mathematical significance becomes graphic, and the relationship between the two sets of figures can easily be seen.

The line graph's vertical axis usually represents amounts, and its horizontal axis usually represents increments of time, as shown in Figure 4.

Line graphs with more than one line are common because they allow for comparisons between two sets of statistics for the same period of time. In creating such graphs, be certain to identify each line with a label or a legend, as shown in Figure 5 [p. 192]. The difference between the two lines can be emphasized by shading the space between them.

Tips on Preparing Line Graphs

1. Give the graph a title that describes the data clearly and concisely. Either center the title below the graph or align it with the left margin. If the title is too long to fit within the margins of the graph on one line, break the title into two or more lines of roughly equal length. In this case, the figure number should precede the first line of the title, and the other lines should begin directly beneath the first word of the title. See Figure 12 [p. 196].

2. Assign a figure number if your report includes five or more illustrations. The figure number precedes the title, as in the examples throughout this entry.

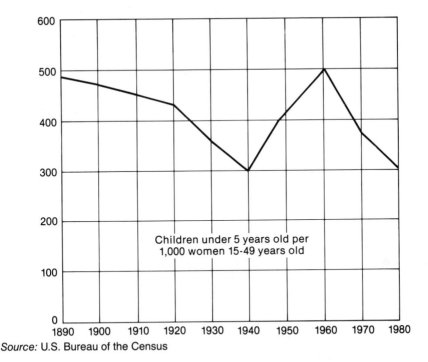

Source: U.S. Bureau of the Census

Fertility Ratio: 1890–1970

Figure 4 Single-Line Graph

3. Indicate the zero point of the graph (the point where the two axes meet). If the range of data shown makes it inconvenient to begin at zero, insert a break in the scale, as in Figure 6 [p. 193].

4. Graduate the vertical axis in equal portions from the least amount at the bottom to the greatest amount at the top. Ordinarily the caption for this scale is placed at the upper left.

5. Graduate the horizontal axis in equal units from left to right. If a caption is necessary, center it directly beneath the scale.

6. Graduate the vertical and horizontal scales so that they give an accurate visual impression of the data, since the angle at which the curved line rises and falls is determined by the scales of the two axes. The curve can be kept free of distortion if the scales maintain a constant ratio with each other. See Figures 7 and 8 [p. 193].

7. Hold grid lines to a minimum so that curved lines stand out. Since precise values are usually shown in a table of data accompanying a graph, detailed grid lines are unnecessary. Note the increasing clarity of the three graphs in Figures 9, 10, and 11 [pp. 194–95].

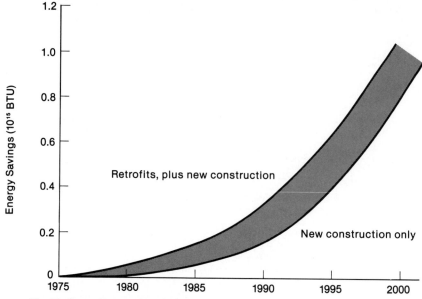

Source: Electric Power Research Institute

Projected energy savings for residences heating by solar power

Figure 5 Double-Line Graph with Difference Shaded

8. Include a key (which lists and explains symbols) when necessary, as in Figure 10. At times a label will do just as well, as in Figure 11.

9. If the information comes from another source, include a source line below and on the same left margin as the caption, as in Figure 1 in this entry.

10. Place explanatory footnotes below the graph, to the lower left.

11. Place all lettering horizontally if possible.

Bar Graphs

Bar graphs consist of horizontal or vertical bars of equal width but scaled in length to represent some quantity. They are commonly used to show (1) quantities of the same item at different times, (2) quantities of different items for the same time period, or (3) quantities of the different parts of an item that make up the whole.

Figure 12 [p. 196] is an example of a bar graph showing varying quantities of the same item at the same time. Here each bar, which represents a different quantity of the same item, begins at the left scale. The left scale also provides additional information in the form of the percentage of the whole population each bar (and therefore each state) represents.

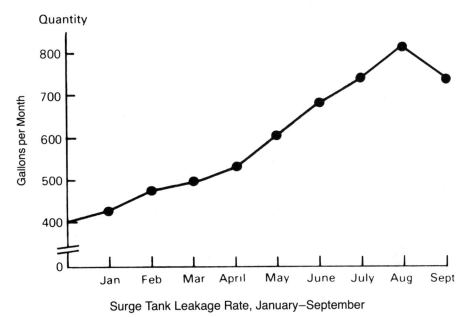

Surge Tank Leakage Rate, January–September

Figure 6 Line Graph with Vertical Axis Broken

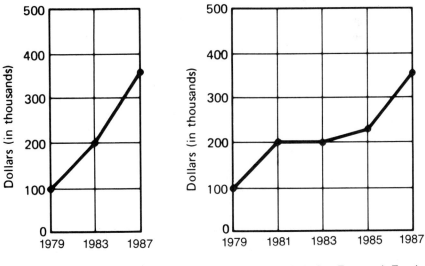

Growth in Engineering Research Funds

Figure 7 Distorted Curve

Growth in Engineering Research Funds

Figure 8 Distortion-Free Curve

Figure 9 Line Graph that Is Difficult to Read

Figure 10 A More Legible Version of Figure 9

Auto Production, 1977–1987

Figure 11 A Clear Version of Figure 9

Some bar graphs show the quantities of different items for the same period of time. See Figure 13 [on p. 197]. (A bar graph with vertical bars is also called a column graph.)

Bar graphs can also show the different portions of an item that make up the whole. Here the bar is equivalent to 100 percent. It is then divided according to the appropriate proportions of the item sampled. This type of graph can be constructed vertically or horizontally and can indicate more than one whole when comparisons are necessary. See Figures 14 and 15 [pp. 197–98].

If the bar is not labeled, each portion must be marked clearly by shading or crosshatching. Include a key that identifies the subdivisions.

Pie Graphs

A pie graph presents data as wedge-shaped sections of a circle. The circle must equal 100 percent, or the whole, of some quantity (a tax dollar, a bus fare, the hours of a working day), with the wedges representing the various ways in which the whole is divided. In Figure 16 [p. 198], for example, the circle stands for a city tax dollar, and it is divided into units equivalent to the percentage of the tax dollar spent on various city services.

Pie graphs provide a quicker way of presenting the same information that can be presented in a table; in fact, a table often accompanies a pie graph with a more detailed breakdown of the same information.

Supercity*	1960 Population	Land Area (Square Miles)	Population Density (People per Square Mile)
New York City/ Northeastern New Jersey/ Southern Connecticut	17,606,680	3,656	4,616
Los Angeles/Long Beach/ San Bernardino/Riverside	10,184,611	2,187	4,657
Chicago/Northwest Indiana Aurora/Elgin/Joliet	7,212,778	1,675	4,306
Philadelphia/ Wilmington/Trenton	4,779,796	1,270	3,764
San Francisco/San Jose	4,434,650	1,122	3,952
Detroit	3,809,327	1,044	3,649
Boston/Brockton/Lowell/ Lawrence/Haverhill	3,225,386	1,064	2,975
Miami/Fort Lauderdale/ Hollywood/West Palm Beach	3,103,729	816	3,804
Washington, D.C.	2,763,105	807	3,424
Houston/ Texas City/Lamarque	2,521,856	1,169	2,157
Cleveland/Akron/ Lorain/Elyria	2,493,475	989	2,521
Dallas/Fort Worth	2,451,390	1,280	1,915
St. Louis	1,848,590	597	3,096
Pittsburgh	1,810,038	713	2,539
Seattle/ Everett/Tacoma	1,793,612	672	2,669
Minneapolis/St. Paul	1,787,564	980	1,824
Baltimore	1,755,477	523	3,357
San Diego	1,704,352	611	2,789
Atlanta	1,613,357	905	1,783
Phoenix	1,409,279	641	2,199
Tampa/St. Petersburg	1,354,249	527	2,570
Denver	1,352,070	439	3,080
Cincinnati/Hamilton	1,228,438	465	2,642
Milwaukee	1,207,008	496	2,433
Newport News/Hampton/ Norfolk/Portsmouth	1,099,360	614	1,790
Kansas City	1,097,793	589	1,864
New Orleans	1,078,299	230	4,688
Portland	1,026,144	349	2,940
Buffalo	1,002,285	266	3,768

*Cities in bold type lost population in the 1970s.

Source: "The Slowing of Urbanization in the U.S.," Larry Long, Diana DeArc. © 1983 Scientific American, Inc.

Urban areas of 1 million or more population, with land area and population density.

Figure 12 Bar Graph of Varying Quantities of the Saqme Item at the Same Time

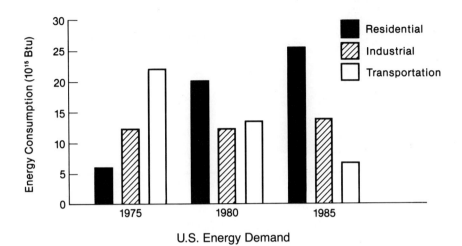

U.S. Energy Demand

Figure 13 Bar Graph of Quantities of Different Items for the Same Period
(shown for three separate years)

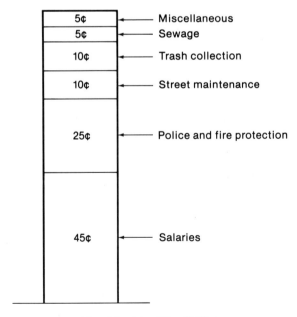

Your Municipal Tax Dollar

Figure 14 Bar Graph of Quantities of Different Parts Making Up a Whole

Figure 15 Bar Graph Showing Variables in Three Samples

Tips on Preparing Pie Graphs

1. The complete 360° circle is equivalent to 100 percent; therefore, each percentage point is equivalent to 3.6°

2. To make the relative percentages clear, begin at the 12 o'clock position and sequence the wedges clockwise, from largest to smallest.

3. If you shade the wedges, do so clockwise and from light to dark.

4. Keep all labels horizontal, and most important, give the percentage value of each wedge.

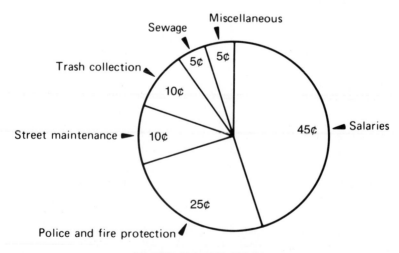

Your Municipal Tax Dollar

Figure 16 Pie Graph

5. Finally, check to see that all wedges, as well as the percentage values given for them, add up to 100 percent.

Although pie graphs have strong visual impact, they also have drawbacks. If more than five or six items are presented, the graph looks cluttered. Also, since they usually present percentages of something, they must often be accompanied by a table listing precise statistics. Further, unless percentages are shown on the sections, the reader cannot compare the values of the sections as accurately as with a bar graph. (The terms that identify each segment of the graph are referred to as *callouts*.)

Picture Graphs

Picture graphs are modified bar graphs that use picture symbols of the item presented. Each symbol corresponds to a specified quantity of the item. See Figure 17 [p. 200]. Note that precise figures are included, since the graph can present only approximate figures.

Tips on Preparing Picture Graphs

1. Make the symbol self-explanatory.

2. Have each symbol represent a single unit.

3. Show larger quantities by increasing the number of symbols rather than by creating a larger symbol. (It is difficult to judge relative sizes accurately.)

4. Consult a good graphics manual for details about preparing graphs. . . .

Computer Graphics

Many computer systems, including microcomputers, have sophisticated graphics programs that allow you to create, in seconds, complex six-color graphs, such as multiple bar graphs and pie graphs. Computer graphics help you display and interpret data at a glance, resulting in faster decision making. By integrating computer graphics and word-processing programs, you can rapidly insert your visual aids anywhere in the text of a report, delete them, or store them for later use. With the right software, you can create all of the illustrations shown in this entry. Some other features of computer graphics are the capability of:

- using an electronic stylus (a pen with an electronic signal) for drawing pictures displayed on a monitor.

- mapping densities and concentrations in different colors.

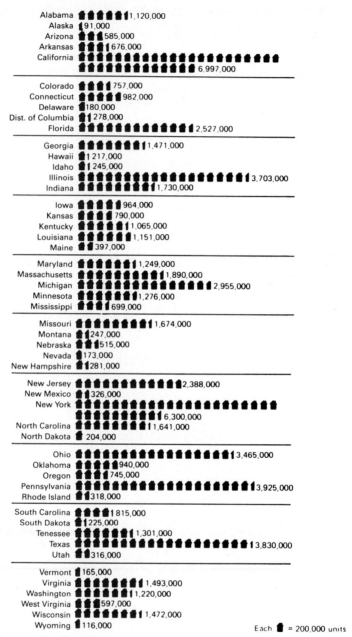

Alabama ▮▮▮▮▮▮1,120,000
Alaska ▮91,000
Arizona ▮▮▮585,000
Arkansas ▮▮▮▮676,000
California ▮▮▮▮▮▮▮▮▮▮▮▮▮▮▮▮▮▮▮▮▮▮▮▮▮▮▮▮▮▮▮▮▮6,997,000

Colorado ▮▮▮▮757,000
Connecticut ▮▮▮▮▮982,000
Delaware ▮180,000
Dist. of Columbia ▮▮278,000
Florida ▮▮▮▮▮▮▮▮▮▮▮▮▮2,527,000

Georgia ▮▮▮▮▮▮▮1,471,000
Hawaii ▮▮217,000
Idaho ▮▮245,000
Illinois ▮▮▮▮▮▮▮▮▮▮▮▮▮▮▮▮▮▮3,703,000
Indiana ▮▮▮▮▮▮▮▮▮1,730,000

Iowa ▮▮▮▮▮964,000
Kansas ▮▮▮▮790,000
Kentucky ▮▮▮▮▮▮1,065,000
Louisiana ▮▮▮▮▮▮1,151,000
Maine ▮▮397,000

Maryland ▮▮▮▮▮▮▮1,249,000
Massachusetts ▮▮▮▮▮▮▮▮▮1,890,000
Michigan ▮▮▮▮▮▮▮▮▮▮▮▮▮▮▮2,955,000
Minnesota ▮▮▮▮▮▮▮1,276,000
Mississippi ▮▮▮▮699,000

Missouri ▮▮▮▮▮▮▮▮▮1,674,000
Montana ▮▮247,000
Nebraska ▮▮▮515,000
Nevada ▮173,000
New Hampshire ▮▮281,000

New Jersey ▮▮▮▮▮▮▮▮▮▮▮▮2,388,000
New Mexico ▮▮326,000
New York ▮▮▮▮▮▮▮▮▮▮▮▮▮▮▮▮▮▮▮▮▮▮▮▮▮▮▮▮▮▮▮▮▮6,300,000
North Carolina ▮▮▮▮▮▮▮▮1,641,000
North Dakota ▮204,000

Ohio ▮▮▮▮▮▮▮▮▮▮▮▮▮▮▮▮▮▮3,465,000
Oklahoma ▮▮▮▮▮940,000
Oregon ▮▮▮▮745,000
Pennsylvania ▮▮▮▮▮▮▮▮▮▮▮▮▮▮▮▮▮▮▮▮▮3,925,000
Rhode Island ▮▮318,000

South Carolina ▮▮▮▮815,000
South Dakota ▮▮225,000
Tenessee ▮▮▮▮▮▮▮1,301,000
Texas ▮▮▮▮▮▮▮▮▮▮▮▮▮▮▮▮▮▮▮▮3,830,000
Utah ▮▮316,000

Vermont ▮165,000
Virginia ▮▮▮▮▮▮▮1,493,000
Washington ▮▮▮▮▮▮1,220,000
West Virginia ▮▮▮597,000
Wisconsin ▮▮▮▮▮▮▮1,472,000
Wyoming ▮116,000

Each ▮ = 200,000 units

Source: Bureau of the Census

Number of Housing Units, by States: 1970

Figure 17 Picture Graph

- using shading and shadows to create three-dimensional effects.

- creating and revising mathematical models, animations, or simulated events.

- using computer-assisted design (CAD) to direct and automate computer-assisted manufacturing (CAM).

Identifying Graphs and Integrating Them into the Text

Observe the following guidelines when you plan to integrate graphs into your text:

1. Give each graph a title that describes the data clearly and concisely. Either center the title below the graph or align it with the left margin. If the title is too long to fit within the margins of the graph on one line, break the title into two or more lines of roughly equal length. The figure number should precede the first line of the title; the other lines should begin directly below the first word of the title.

2. Assign a figure number if your report contains five or more graphs. The figure number precedes the title, as in the examples throughout this entry.

3. Relate the graph to the text around it by referring to it by figure number and title.

4. Locate the graph as close as possible to its first mention in the text. However, the graph should never precede its first text mention; its appearance without an introduction will confuse readers.

5. If the graph is central to the discussion, illuminating or strongly reinforcing it, include the graph in the text. But if the graph is lengthy, detailed, and peripheral to the discussion, place it in an appendix. However, even material in an appendix should be mentioned or referred to in the text; otherwise, the information in the appendix is superfluous. . . .

6. The amount of text discussion each graph requires will vary with its importance to the discussion. A graph showing an important trend over time may be the central focus of an entire discussion. The level of complexity of the graph will also affect the discussion, as will how knowledgeable your readers are. Nonexperts require lengthier explanations than experts do, as a rule. . . .

Illustrations

The objective of using an illustration is to help your reader absorb the facts and ideas you are presenting. When used well, an illustration can convey an idea that words alone could never really make clear. Notice how the description in Figure 18 depends on its illustration:

EXAMPLE   The 682-100 Card Reader, a serial Reader that uses photo-electric sensing for data detection, can read a maximum of 300 cards per minute, with the actual rate dependent upon the processor's demand for input. Each time the processor requests that a card be input, the Reader completes one cycle of the following concurrent steps: (1) the card in the read station moves past the photoelectric cells to the output hopper (the photoelectric cells sense the data in the card for transmission to the processor's main memory), (2) the card in the ready station moves to the read station, and (3) a card feeds from the input hopper to the ready station.

Output hopper

Input hopper

Photoelectric
cells

Read
Station

Card ready
Station

Figure 18 Drawing Illustrating a Process

Illustrations should never be used as ornaments, however; they should always be functional working parts of your writing. Be careful not to overillustrate; use an illustration only when you are sure that it makes a direct contribution to your reader's understanding of your subject. When creating illustrations, you must always consider your objective and your reader. You would use a different illustration of an x-ray machine, for example, for a high school science class than you would for a group of medical doctors. Many of the attributes of good writing—simplicity, clarity, conciseness, directness—are equally important in creating and using illustrations.

The most common types of illustrations are photographs, graphs, tables, drawings, flowcharts, organizational charts, schematic diagrams, and maps. Your material will normally suggest one of these types when an illustration is needed.

Tips for Creating and Using Illustrations

Each type of illustration has its unique strengths and weaknesses. . . . The guidelines presented here apply to most visual material you use to supplement the information in your text. Following these tips should help you create and present your visual material to good effect.

1. Keep the information as brief and simple as possible.

2. Try to present only one type of information in each illustration.

3. Label or caption each illustration carefully.

4. Include a key that identifies all symbols, when necessary.

5. Specify the proportions used or include a scale of relative distances, when appropriate.

6. If possible, make the lettering horizontal for easy reading.

7. Keep terminology consistent. Do not refer to something as a "proportion" in the text and as a "percentage" in the illustration.

8. Allow enough white space around and within the illustration.

9. Position the illustration as close as possible to the text that refers to it; however, an illustration should normally not appear ahead of the first text reference to it.

10. Be sure the significance of an illustration is clear in the text.

11. If figure numbers or table numbers are used, as they should be if five or more illustrations or tables are used, number the illustrations or tables consecutively.

12. If more than five illustrations or tables appear in a report, list them by title, together with figure and page numbers, under a separate heading ("List of Figures" or "List of Tables") following the table of contents.

Identifying Illustrations and Integrating Them into the Text

Presented with clarity and consistency, illustrations can help your reader focus on key portions of your report. Be aware, though, that even the best illustration can only supplement the text. Your writing must carry the major burden of providing the context for the illustration and pointing out its significance. To do so effectively, adhere to the following guidelines:

1. Give each illustration a concise title that clearly describes the information. Either center the title below the illustration or align it with the left

margin. If the title is too long to fit within the margins of the illustration on one line, break the title into two or more lines of roughly equal length. The figure number should precede the first line of the title; the other lines should begin directly below the first word of the title.

2. Assign a figure number if your report contains five or more illustrations. The figure number precedes the title. If figure numbers are used, number the illustrations consecutively as Figure 1, Figure 2, and so on.

3. If more than five illustrations appear in a formal report, list them by title, together with figure and page numbers, under a separate heading ("List of Figures") following the report's table of contents.

4. Relate the illustration to the text around it by referring to it by figure number and title.

5. Locate the illustration as close as possible to its first mention in the text. However, the illustration should never precede its first text mention; its appearance without an introduction will confuse readers.

6. If the illustration is central to the discussion, illuminating or strongly reinforcing it, place the illustration in the text. But, if the illustration is lengthy, detailed, and peripheral to the discussion, place it in an appendix. However, even material in an appendix should be mentioned or referred to in text; otherwise, the information in the appendix is superfluous. . . .

7. The amount of discussion that each illustration requires will vary with its importance to the text. An illustration showing an important feature or system may be the central focus of an entire discussion. The complexity of the illustration will also affect the discussion, as will how knowledgeable your readers are. Nonexperts require lengthier explanations than experts do, as a rule. . . .

Tables

A table is useful for showing large numbers of specific, related facts or statistics in a small space. A table can present data more concisely than the text can, and it is more accurate than graphic presentations are because it provides numerous facts that a graph cannot convey. A table facilitates comparisons among figures because of the arrangement of the figures into rows and columns. Overall trends about the information, however, are more easily seen in charts and graphs. But do not rely on a table (or any illustration) as the only method of conveying significant information. (See Figure 19.)

Guidelines for Creating Tables

Table Number. If you are using several tables, assign each a number, and then center the number and title above the table. The numbers are usually arabic, and

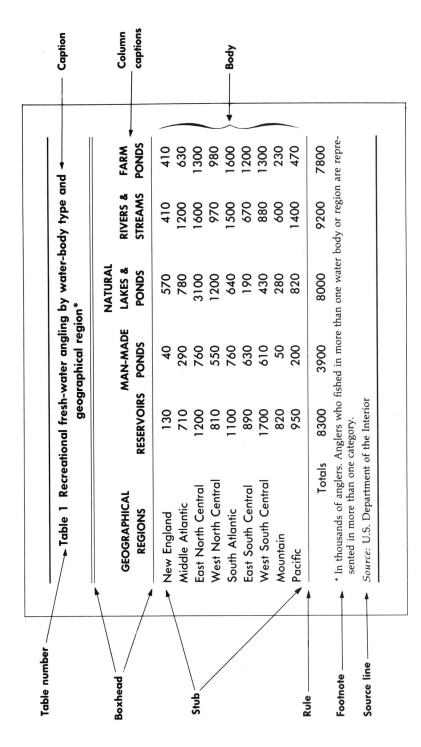

Table number

Caption

Column captions

Body

Boxhead

Stub

Rule

Footnote

Source line

Table 1   Recreational fresh-water angling by water-body type and geographical region*

GEOGRAPHICAL REGIONS	RESERVOIRS	MAN-MADE PONDS	NATURAL LAKES & PONDS	RIVERS & STREAMS	FARM PONDS
New England	130	40	570	410	410
Middle Atlantic	710	290	780	1200	630
East North Central	1200	760	3100	1600	1300
West North Central	810	550	1200	970	980
South Atlantic	1100	760	640	1500	1600
East South Central	890	630	190	670	1200
West South Central	1700	610	430	880	1300
Mountain	820	50	280	600	230
Pacific	950	200	820	1400	470
Totals	8300	3900	8000	9200	7800

* In thousands of anglers. Anglers who fished in more than one water body or region are represented in more than one category.

Source: U.S. Department of the Interior

Figure 19   Table of Data

they should be assigned sequentially to the tables throughout the text. Tables should be referred to in the text by table number rather than by direction ("Table 4" rather than "the above table"). If there are more than five tables in your report or paper, give them a separate heading ("List of Tables"), and list them by title and page number, together with any figure numbers, on a separate page immediately after the table of contents. The first text reference to the table should *precede* the table. If a document contains several chapters or sections, tables can be numbered by chapter or section (Table 1-1, 1-2, . . . 3-1, 3-2).

Title. The title, which is placed just above the table, should describe concisely what the table represents.

Boxhead. The boxhead carries the column headings. These should be kept concise but descriptive. Units of measurement, where necessary, should be specified either as part of the heading or enclosed in parentheses beneath the heading. Avoid vertical lettering if possible.

Stub. The left-hand vertical column of a table is the stub. It lists the items about which information is given in the body of the table.

Body. The body comprises the data below the boxhead and to the right of the stub. Within the body, columns should be arranged so that the terms to be compared appear in adjacent rows and columns. Leaders are sometimes used between figures to aid the eye in following data from column to column. Where no information exists for a specific item, leave an empty space to acknowledge the gap.

Rules. These are the lines that separate the table into its various parts. Horizontal lines are placed below the title, below the body of the table, and between the column headings and the body of the table. They should not be closed at the sides. The columns within the table may be separated by vertical lines if they aid clarity.

Footnotes. Footnotes are used for explanations of individual items in the table. Symbols (*, #) or lowercase letters, rather than numbers, are ordinarily used to key table footnotes, because numbers might be mistaken for the data in a numerical table.

Source Line. The source line, which identifies where the data were obtained, appears below any footnotes (when a source line is appropriate).

Continued Lines. When a table must be divided so that it can be continued on another page, repeat the boxhead and give the table number at the head of each new page with a "continued" label ("Table 3, continued").

How to Lie with Statistics

DARRELL HUFF

Darrell Huff, a free-lance writer, expanded
this article into a book with the same title
(Norton, 1954).

T he average Yaleman, Class of '24," *Time* magazine reported last year
after reading something in the New York *Sun*, a newspaper published
in those days, "makes $25,111 a year."

Well, good for him!

But, come to think of it, what does this improbably precise and salubrious
figure mean? Is it, as it appears to be, evidence that if you send your boy to Yale
you won't have to work in your old age and neither will he? Is this average a mean
or is it a median? What kind of sample is it based on? You could lump one Texas
oilman with two hundred hungry free-lance writers and report *their* average
income as $25,000-odd a year. The arithmetic is impeccable, the figure is
convincingly precise, and the amount of meaning there is in it you could put in
your eye.

In just such ways is the secret language of statistics, so appealing in a fact-
minded culture, being used to sensationalize, inflate, confuse, and oversimplify.
Statistical terms are necessary in reporting the mass data of social and economic
trends, business conditions, "opinion" polls, this year's census. But without
writers who use the words with honesty and understanding and readers who
know what they mean, the result can only be semantic nonsense.

In popular writing on scientific research, the abused statistic is almost crowd-
ing out the picture of the white-jacketed hero laboring overtime without time-and-
a-half in an ill-lit laboratory. Like the "little dash of powder, little pot of paint,"
statistics are making many an important fact "look like what she ain't." Here are
some of the ways it is done.

The sample with the built-in bias. Our Yale men—or Yalemen, as they say in
the Time-Life building—belong to this flourishing group. The exaggerated esti-
mate of their income is not based on all members of the class nor on a random or
representative sample of them. At least two interesting categories of 1924-model
Yale men have been excluded.

First there are those whose present addresses are unknown to their class-mates. Wouldn't you bet that these lost sheep are earning less than the boys from prominent families and the others who can be handily reached from a Wall Street office?

There are those who chucked the questionnaire into the nearest wastebasket. Maybe they didn't answer because they were not making enough money to brag about. Like the fellow who found a note clipped to his first pay check suggesting that he consider the amount of his salary confidential: "Don't worry," he told the boss. "I'm just as ashamed of it as you are."

Omitted from our sample then are just the two groups most likely to depress the average. The $25,111 figure is beginning to account for itself. It may indeed be a true figure for those of the Class of '24 whose addresses are known and who are willing to stand up and tell how much they earn. But even that requires a possibly dangerous assumption that the gentlemen are telling the truth.

To be dependable to any useful degree at all, a sampling study must use a representative sample (which can lead to trouble too) or a truly random one. If *all* the Class of '24 is included, that's all right. If every tenth name on a complete list is used, that is all right too, and so is drawing an adequate number of names out of a hat. The test is this: Does *every* name in the group have an equal chance to be in the sample?

You'll recall that ignoring this requirement was what produced the *Literary Digest's* famed fiasco.* When names for polling were taken only from telephone books and subscription lists, people who did not have telephones or *Literary Digest* subscriptions had no chance to be in the sample. They possibly did not mind this underprivilege a bit, but their absence was in the end very hard on the magazine that relied on the figures.

This leads to a moral: You can prove about anything you want to by letting your sample bias itself. As a consumer of statistical data—a reader, for example, of a news magazine—remember that no statistical conclusion can rise above the quality of the sample it is based upon. In the absence of information about the procedures behind it, you are not warranted in giving any credence at all to the result.

The truncated, or gee-whiz, graph. If you want to show some statistical information quickly and clearly, draw a picture of it. Graphic presentation is the thing today. If you don't mind misleading the hasty looker, or if you quite clearly *want* to deceive him, you can save some space by chopping the bottom off many kinds of graph.

Suppose you are showing the upward trend of national income month by month for a year. The total rise, as in one recent year, is 7 per cent. It looks like this:

Editor's note: The Literary Digest predicted that Alfred Landon would defeat Franklin Roosevelt in the 1936 presidential election. Landon carried only two states.

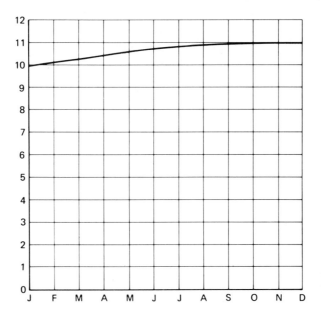

That is clear enough. Anybody can see that the trend is slightly upward. You are showing a 7 per cent increase and that is exactly what it looks like.

But it lacks schmaltz. So you chop off the bottom, this way:

The figures are the same. It is the same graph and nothing has been falsified—except the impression that it gives. Anyone looking at it can just feel prosperity throbbing in the arteries of the country. It is a subtler equivalent of editing "National income rose 7 per cent" into " . . . climbed a whopping 7 per cent."

It is vastly more effective, however, because of that illusion of objectivity.

The souped-up graph. Sometimes truncating is not enough. The trifling rise in something or other still looks almost as insignificant as it is. You can make that 7 per cent look livelier than 100 per cent ordinarily does. Simply change the proportion between the ordinate and the abscissa. There's no rule against it, and it does give your graph a prettier shape.

But it *exaggerates,* to say the least, something awful:

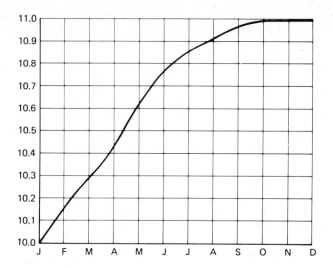

The well-chosen average. I live near a country neighborhood for which I can report an average income of $15,000. I could also report it as $3,500.

If I should want to sell real estate hereabouts to people having a high snobbery content, the first figure would be handy. The second figure, however, is the one to use in an argument against raising taxes, or the local bus fare.

Both are legitimate averages, legally arrived at. Yet it is obvious that at least one of them must be as misleading as an out-and-out lie. The $15,000-figure is a mean, the arithmetic average of the incomes of all the families in the community. The smaller figure is a median; it might be called the income of the average family in the group. It indicates that half the families have less than $3,500 a year and half have more.

Here is where some of the confusion about averages comes from. Many human characteristics have the grace to fall into what is called the "normal" distribution. If you draw a picture of it, you get a curve that is shaped like a bell. Mean and median fall at about the same point, so it doesn't make very much difference which you use.

But some things refuse to follow this neat curve. Income is one of them. Incomes for most large areas will range from under $1,000 a year to upward of $50,000. Almost everybody will be under $10,000, way over on the left-hand side of that curve.

One of the things that made the income figure for the "average Yaleman" meaningless is that we are not told whether it is a mean or a median. It is not that one type of average is invariably better than the other; it depends upon what you are talking about. But neither gives you any real information—and either may be highly misleading—unless you know which of those two kinds of average it is.

In the country neighborhood I mentioned, almost everyone has less than the average—the mean, that is—of $10,500. These people are all small farmers, except for a trio of millionaire week-enders who bring up the mean enormously.

You can be pretty sure that when an income average is given in the form of a mean nearly everybody has less than that.

The insignificant difference or the elusive error. Your two children Peter and Linda (we might as well give them modish names while we're about it) take intelligence tests. Peter's IQ, you learn, is 98 and Linda's is 101. Aha! Linda is your brighter child.

Is she? An intelligence test is, or purports to be, a sampling of intellect. An IQ, like other products of sampling, is a figure with a statistical error, which expresses the precision or reliability of the figure. The size of this probable error can be calculated. For their test the makers of the much-used Revised Stanford-Binet have found it to be about 3 per cent. So Peter's indicated IQ of 98 really means only that there is an even chance that it falls between 95 and 101. There is an equal probability that it falls somewhere else—below 95 or above 101. Similarly, Linda's has no better than a fifty-fifty chance of being within the fairly sizeable range of 98 to 104.

You can work out some comparisons from that. One is that there is rather better than one chance in four that Peter, with his lower IQ rating, is really at least three points smarter than Linda. A statistician doesn't like to consider a difference significant unless you can hand him odds a lot longer than that.

Ignoring the error in a sampling study leads to all kinds of silly conclusions. There are magazine editors to whom readership surveys are gospel; with a 40 per cent readership reported for one article and a 35 per cent for another, they demand more like the first. I've seen even smaller differences given tremendous weight, because statistics are a mystery and numbers are impressive. The same thing goes for market surveys and so-called public-opinion polls. The rule is that you cannot make a valid comparison between two such figures unless you know the deviations. And unless the difference between the figures is many times greater than the probable error of each, you have only a guess that the one appearing greater really is.

Otherwise you are like the man choosing a camp site from a report of mean temperature alone. One place in California with a mean annual temperature of 61 is San Nicolas Island on the south coast, where it always stays in the comfortable range between 47 and 87. Another with a mean of 61 is in the inland desert, where the thermometer hops around from 15 to 104. The deviation from the mean marks the difference, and you can freeze or roast if you ignore it.

The one-dimensional picture. Suppose you have just two or three figures to compare—say the average weekly wage of carpenters in the United States and another country. The sums might be $60 and $30. An ordinary bar chart makes the difference graphic.

That is an honest picture. It looks good for American carpenters, but perhaps it does not have quite the oomph you are after. Can't you make that difference appear overwhelming and at the same time give it what I am afraid is known as eye-appeal? Of course you can. Following tradition, you represent these sums by pictures of money bags. If the $30 bag is one inch high, you draw the $60 bag two inches high. That's in proportion, isn't it?

The catch is, of course, that the American's money bag, being twice as tall as that of the $30 man, covers an area on your page four times as great. And since your two-dimensional picture represents an object that would in fact have three dimensions, the money bags actually would differ much more than that. The volumes of any two similar solids vary as the cubes of their heights. If the unfortunate foreigner's bag holds $30 worth of dimes, the American's would hold not $60 but a neat $240.

You didn't say that, though, did you? And you can't be blamed, you're only doing it the way practically everybody else does.

The ever-impressive decimal. For a spurious air of precision that will lend all kinds of weight to the most disreputable statistics, consider the decimal.

Ask a hundred citizens how many hours they slept last night. Come out with a total of, say, 781.3. Your data are far from precise to begin with. Most people will miss their guess by fifteen minutes or more and some will recall five sleepless minutes as half a night of tossing insomnia.

But go ahead, do your arithmetic, announce that people sleep an average of 7.813 hours a night. You will sound as if you knew precisely what you are talking about. If you were foolish enough to say 7.8 (or "almost 8") hours it would sound like what it was—an approximation.

The semi-attached figure. If you can't prove what you want to prove, demonstrate something else and pretend that they are the same thing. In the daze that follows the collision of statistics with the human mind, hardly anybody will notice the difference. The semi-attached figure is a durable device guaranteed to stand you in good stead. It always has.

If you can't prove that your nostrum cures colds, publish a sworn laboratory report that the stuff killed 31,108 germs in a test tube in eleven seconds. There may be no connection at all between assorted germs in a test tube and the whatever-it-is that produces colds, but people aren't going to reason that sharply, especially while sniffling.

Maybe that one is too obvious and people are beginning to catch on. Here is a trickier version.

Let us say that in a period when race prejudice is growing it is to your advantage to "prove" otherwise. You will not find it a difficult assignment.

Ask that usual cross section of the population if they think Negroes have as good a chance as white people to get jobs. Ask again a few months later. As Princeton's Office of Public Opinion Research has found out, people who are most unsympathetic to Negroes are the ones most likely to answer yes to this question.

As prejudice increases in a country, the percentage of affirmative answers you will get to this question will become larger. What looks on the face of it like growing opportunity for Negroes actually is mounting prejudice and nothing else. You have achieved something rather remarkable: the worse things get, the better your survey makes them look.

The unwarranted assumption, or post hoc *rides again.* The interrelation of cause and effect, so often obscure anyway, can be most neatly hidden in statistical data.

Somebody once went to a good deal of trouble to find out if cigarette smokers make lower college grades than non-smokers. They did. This naturally pleased many people, and they made much of it.

The unwarranted assumption, of course, was that smoking had produced dull minds. It seemed vaguely reasonable on the face of it, so it was quite widely accepted. But it really proved nothing of the sort, any more than it proved that poor grades drive students to the solace of tobacco. Maybe the relationship worked in one direction, maybe in the other. And maybe all this is only an indication that the sociable sort of fellow who is likely to take his books less than seriously is also likely to sit around and smoke many cigarettes.

Permitting statistical treatment to befog casual relationships is little better than superstition. It is like the conviction among the people of the Hebrides that body lice produce good health. Observation over the centuries had taught them that people in good health had lice and sick people often did not. *Ergo*, lice made a man healthy. Everybody should have them.

Scantier evidence, treated statistically at the expense of common sense, has made many a medical fortune and many a medical article in magazines, including professional ones. More sophisticated observers finally got things straightened out in the Hebrides. As it turned out, almost everybody in those circles had lice most of the time. But when a man took a fever (quite possibly carried to him by those same lice) and his body became hot, the lice left.

Here you have cause and effect not only reversed, but intermingled.

There you have a primer in some ways to use statistics to deceive. A well-wrapped statistic is better than Hitler's "big lie": it misleads, yet it can't be pinned onto you.

Is this little list altogether too much like a manual for swindlers? Perhaps I can justify it in the manner of the retired burglar whose published reminiscences amounted to a graduate course in how to pick a lock and muffle a footfall: The crooks already know these tricks. Honest men must learn them in self-defense.

Strategies of Persuasion

DAVID W. EWING

David W. Ewing is Executive Editor-Planning of the *Harvard Business Review* and a member of the faculty of the Harvard Business School.

When we review reports, letters, and memoranda that get the intended results, we find a fascinating diversity of approaches. Some are gentle in approach, taking readers by the hand and leading them to a certain finding or recommendation. Others are brisk and abrupt. Some are objective in approach, carefully examining both sides of an idea, like a judge writing a difficult decision—at least until the end. Others burst with impatience to explain one side, and only one side, of a proposal or argument. Some flow swimmingly, others erupt like Mount Vesuvius.

How is it possible that communications taking such different approaches can all be effective? It is not sufficient to answer glibly, "It depends on the situation," or "Communications should mirror the personal style of the communicator." How does a written communication depend on the situation? Which style of the communicator should be reflected in a given communication? Examine the writing of most business executives, professionals, and public leaders, and you will find not one but *many* styles of exposition.

Rules Every Persuader Should Know

The explanation lies in a set of relationships among the communicator, the reader, the message, and the time-space environment. These relationships work in predictable ways and are an important part of the knowledge of every good business and professional writer. They come into play in the planning stages of writing, when the writer is considering how he or she will proceed, and in the main body of the presentation, to accomplish what he or she has promised in the opening paragraphs. The relationships affect some of the most important decisions a writer makes—the choice of ideas to use, the comparative emphasis to be given various arguments pro and con, the types of reasons and supporting material used, the establishment of credibility, and other matters.

It is convenient but self-defeating to follow fixed prescriptions for persuasion, such as to put your strongest arguments first or last or to identify with the readers.

STRATEGIES OF PERSUASION   By David W. Ewing. From *Writing for Results*, 2nd ed., by David W. Ewing, copyright © 1979 by John Wiley & Sons, Inc. Reprinted by permission of John Wiley & Sons, Inc.

Such nostrums were fine for the age of patent medicines and snake-oil peddlers, but not for the age of diagnostic medicine. What is more, they are belittling. They assume that writers are witless. Good writers vary their approaches in response to their readings of different situations. Just as a good golfer plays an approach to a green differently depending on the wind, so a good writer uses different strategies depending on the crosscurrents of mood and feeling.

How should you choose your approach to a group of readers? What elements of the approach should be tailored to the situation? These are the topics of this chapter. Let us assume that the substance of the intended message is clear in your mind. . . .

1. Consider Whether Your Views Will Make Problems for Readers.

J. C. Mathes and Dwight W. Stevenson tell of the student engineer who was asked to evaluate the efficiency of the employer plant's waste-treatment process.[1] He found that by making a simple change, the company could save more than $200,000 a year. Anticipating an enthusiastic response, he wrote up and delivered his report. Although he waited with great expectations, no accolades came. Why? What he hadn't counted on was that now his supervisors would have to explain to their bosses why they had allowed a waste of $200,000 a year. They were far from elated to read his report.

"If you want to make a man your enemy," Henry C. Link once said, "tell him simply, 'You are wrong.' This method works every time." Under the illusion that their sciences are "hard," physicists, biologists, and others may assume that it is necessary only to worry about setting the facts forth accurately. From posterity's standpoint, perhaps yes—but not from the standpoint of writing for current results. As Kenneth Boulding, head of the American Association for the Advancement of Science, has pointed out, the so-called "hard" sciences are in many ways "soft," and vice versa. "You can knock forever on a deaf man's door," said Zorba the Greek, and the deaf man can be a physicist as well as a marketing manager or public official.

If your views are bad news for readers, you proceed to report them, but with empathy and tact and an effort to put yourself in the reader's shoes. You work as carefully as if you were licking honey off a thorn.

2. Don't Offer New Ideas, Directives, or Recommendations for Change until Your Readers Are Prepared for Them.

"Should I state my surprising findings at the very beginning of my memorandum?" a writer asks. "Should I go slow with my heretical proposal and hold the reader's hand?" asks another.

Generally speaking, the answer to all such questions depends on the extent of your audience's resistance to change, the amount of change you are asking for,

[1] J. C. Mathes and Dwight W. Stevenson, *Designing Technical Reports* (Indianapolis: Bobbs-Merrill, 1976), pp. 18–19.

the uncertainty in readers' minds as to your understanding of their situation, and what psychologists call the "perceived threat" of your communication, that is, how much it seems (to readers) to upset their values and interests. The more change, uncertainty, and/or threat, the slower you should proceed, the more carefully you should prepare your readers.

For instance, if your boss is enthusiastic about a new promotion scheme that he (or she) has paid a consultant $25,000 to devise, naturally you will want to go slow in shooting it down (at least if you want to stay in his good graces). In fact, any written criticism of the scheme is probably out of order until you have had a chance to talk with him and get a feel for the proper timing of any forthcoming criticism. When you do commit yourself to writing, you should probably review the arguments for the new scheme as fairly as possible, making it crystal clear to him that you understand them. Only then does it become timely to turn to the facts or conditions that, in your opinion, raise serious questions about the plan.

On the other hand, suppose the faulty promotion scheme is of little personal interest to your boss—it is not his (or her) "baby." Now the situation is different. You can launch right into the shortcomings, throwing your heaviest objections first. The fact is that the boss may not even want to know about the lesser objections, much less the supporting arguments once advanced for the plan; the main things he should know are that (a) the plan is in trouble and (b) the major, most compelling reasons why.

Clearly, this strategy is plain, everyday common sense—what you would normally do in communicating orally instead of in writing. Only in writing you must be more explicit and thorough, because a document lacks the expressiveness and visual advantages of a spoken dialogue.

Now consider another type of situation. Suppose it is your unhappy task to write a department manager that the extra appropriations he (or she) was promised have been cancelled. First of all, how would you handle it if you saw him often and could talk with him personally? . . . You would not (we hope) pussyfoot around trying to withhold the bad news from him. Also, once you had indicated the main message, you would probably backtrack a little and make it clear that the step is being taken with reluctance.

"Joe, it looks as if we're not going to be able to give you the extra budget we promised," you might say, getting down to business. That is the message in a nutshell—now for the review of common ground. "We know how much you have counted on getting those people and funds. There's no doubt you could manage them well and put them to good use. And we know that the morale of your people is involved in this, too. But the fact is that the sales we counted on are not coming in. We've got to cut somewhere, and, frankly, we feel it's got to be your department because . . ."

If you are communicating by letter or memorandum, the strategy is exactly the same (only "Joe" may now be "Mr. Wyncoop"). After your lead, you review the main needs as he and you understand them, perhaps spelling them out more than you would have in a face-to-face meeting but choosing the same ones. Only then do you turn to the new conditions that make it necessary to do an about-face.

3. Your Credibility with Readers Affects Your Strategy.

In general, communication research indicates that the chances of opinion change vary with the communicator's authority with his or her readers. In their succinct summary of the field, *Persuasion*, social scientists Marvin Karlins and Herbert I. Abelson point out that credibility itself is a variable; that is, it can be influenced by the words of the communicator.[2] Above all, as psychologists repeatedly emphasize, credibility lies in the eye of the beholder.[3] . . .

In written communications there are two types of credibility. It may be given or it may be acquired. Between the two lies a world of practical difference.

Given credibility may result from your position in an organization. If, let us say, you are the boss writing directions to a subordinate, your credibility is likely to be high. Given credibility also may result from reputation—a well-known chemist has more credibility in communications about polymers than a good industrial engineer has, but the latter would possess more credibility in communications about time-and-motion studies. It may result from the individuals and groups the writer is associated with—if he or she is a member of the same trade union the reader belongs to, a union held in high esteem by both, he or she has more credibility in a memorandum on grievance procedures than a member of the board of directors would have.

Though you may be high in given credibility, you may yet need to remind some readers of the fact. In the case of an obvious credential, such as a position in an important organization, a letterhead may be enough to do the trick. Another device is to insert a few lines of biographical data at the head of a report or brochure. If you have had experience or associations that carry weight with the reader, perhaps you can interject them early in the message. "During a visit I had last week with Zach Jarvis," you might say, knowing that Dr. Zachary P. Jarvis is a magic name with your reader, or, "The Executive Committee of the Aberjona Basin Association asked me to join their meeting on Monday . . ." knowing that group carries a triple-A rating in the mind of the reader.

Of course, you do not want to overplay your hand at such name dropping. A report to a fairly diverse audience by a famous black organization began simply:

> The National Association for the Advancement of Colored People has for many years been dedicated to the task of defending the economic, social and political rights and interests of black Americans. The growing national debate about energy has led us to examine the question to ascertain the implications for black Americans.[4]

Again, an attorney of the American Civil Liberties Union, in a letter to members of the organization soliciting donations, began:

[2]Marvin Karlins and Herbert I. Abelson. *Persuasion* (New York, Springer, 1970); see pp. 107–132.

[3]See, for example, Ralph L. Rosnow and Edward J. Robinson, Eds. *Experiments in Persuasion* (New York, Academic, 1967).

[4]*The Wall Street Journal*, January 12, 1978.

My dear friend:

I am the ACLU lawyer who went into court last April to defend freedom of speech in Skokie, Illinois, for a handful of people calling themselves "nazis."

The case has had an enormous impact on my life.

It has also gravely injured the ACLU financially. . . . [5]

Acquired credibility, on the other hand, is earned by thoughts and facts in the written message. I may not know you from Adam. Yet if you send me a letter or report that carefully, helpfully describes something I am interested in, you gain credibility in my estimation.

Some studies suggest that if you are low in given credibility and seek to acquire it with an audience, a useful technique is to cite ideas or evidence that support the reader's existing views.[6] As Disraeli once said, "My idea of an agreeable person is a person who agrees with me." The very fact that you feel confident and knowledgeable enough to articulate these views is likely to lift you several notches in the reader's estimation.

Still another approach is that old standby of persuaders—identifying yourself, in an early section, with the goals and interests of the audience. Possibly the most famous example of this strategy is the opening of Marc Antony's funeral oration in Shakespeare's *Julius Caesar:* "I come to bury Caesar, not to praise him. . . ."

Finally, you can acquire credibility by citing authorities who rate highly with your intended audience, or by exhibiting documentary evidence that, because of its source, lends prestige and authority to your proposals or ideas.

"For success in negotiation," says C. Northcote Parkinson and Nigel Rowe, "it is vitally important that people will believe what you say and assume that any promise you make will be kept. But it is no good saying: 'Trust me. Rely on my word.' Only politicians say that."[7]

Even if you have prestigious credentials, you cannot take too much for granted. In an age of television sets, radios, cassettes, and record players in every home, credibility—at least with the public—may come quicker for the singer or comedian than for the judge, business executive, or medical researcher. In fact, because of an association with an organization or profession, you may be stereotyped as a member of "them" or "the establishment." It may behoove you to establish that you are a person with a name, a personality, certain interests, certain experiences—not just a nameless representative.

[5]David Goldberger, letter dated March 20, 1978.

[6]Karlins and Abelson, *op. cit.*, pp. 115–119.

[7]C. Northcote Parkinson and Nigel Rowe, "Better Communication: Business's Best Defense," *The McKinsey Quarterly*, Winter 1978, p. 26.

4. If Your Audience Disagrees with Your Ideas or is Uncertain about Them, Present Both Sides of the Argument.

Behavioral scientists generally find that if an audience is friendly to a persuader, or has no contrary views on the topic and will get none in the near future, a one-sided presentation of a controversial question is most effective.[8] For instance, if your point is that sales of product X in the St. Louis territory could be doubled and you are writing to enthusiastic salespeople of product X, your best course is to concentrate on facts and examples showing the enormous potential of product X. There is no shortage of evidence showing that people generally prefer reading material that confirms their beliefs, and that they develop resistance to material that repudiates their beliefs. (As we shall see presently, however, this does not mean you cannot change their minds.)

But suppose your audience has not made up its mind, so far as you know? In this case you would do well to deal with *both* sides of the argument (or all sides, if there are more than two). Follow the same approach if the reader disagrees with you at the outset. For one thing, a two-sided presentation suggests to an uncertain or hostile audience that you possess objectivity. For another, it helps the reader remember your view by putting the pros and cons in relationship to one another. Also, it meets the reader's need to be treated as a mature, informed individual. As Karlins and Abelson point out:

> Conspicuously underlying your presentation is the assumption that the audience would be on your side if they only knew the truth. The other points of view should be presented with the attitude "it would be natural for you to have this idea if you don't know all the facts, but when you know all the facts, you will be convinced."[9]

Karlins and Abelson tested the reactions of audiences in post-war Germany to Voice of America broadcasts. They found that the most persuasive programs were those that included admissions of shortcomings in United States living conditions.[10]

Again, observation of businessmen's reactions to scores of *Harvard Business Review* articles advocating controversial measures convinces me that the most influential articles have been those that have acknowledged the shortcomings, weaknesses, and limitations of their arguments. When an author wants to sell a new idea to a sophisticated audience, he or she should be candid about the soft spots in his argument.

[8]Experiments supporting this conclusion are reported by Carl I. Hovland, Arthur A. Lumsdaine, and F. Sheffield in *Experiments on Mass Communication* (Princeton, Princeton University Press, 1949). Cited by Karlins and Abelson, *op. cit.*, p. 22.

[9]Karlins and Abelson, *op. cit.*, p. 26.

[10]See *Factors Affecting Credibility in Psychological Warfare Communications* (Washington, D.C., Human Resources Research Office, George Washington University, 1956).

5. Win Respect by Making Your Opinion or Recommendation Clear.

Although strategy may call for a two-sided argument, this does not mean you should be timid in setting forth your conclusions or proposals at the end. We assume here that you have definite views and seek to persuade your audience to adopt them. The two-sided approach is a *means* to that end; it does not imply compromising or obfuscating your conclusions. An official at Armour & Company once criticized many reports from subordinates to bosses on the ground that, after presenting much data, they concluded, in effect, "Here is what I found out and maybe we should do this or maybe we should do that." The typical response of a boss to such a memorandum, he noted, was to do nothing. Hence, the time taken both in writing and reading was wasted.[11]

6. Put Your Strongest Points Last if the Audience Is Very Interested in the Argument, First If It Is Not So Interested.

This question is referred to by social scientists as the "primacy-recency" issue in persuasion. The argument presented first is said to have primacy; the argument presented last, recency. Although studies of the question have produced inconsistent findings and no firm rules can be drawn, it appears that if your audience is deeply concerned with your subject you can afford to lead it along from the weakest points to the strongest. The audience's great interest will keep it reading, and putting the weaker points at the start tends to create rising reader expectations about what is coming. When you end with your strongest punch, therefore, you do not let readers down.

If your audience is not so concerned with the topic, on the other hand, it may be best to use the opposite approach. Now you cannot risk leading readers along a winding path. They may drop out before you reach the end. So grab their attention right at the beginning with your strongest argument or idea.

In any case, put the recommendation, facts, or arguments you most want the reader to *remember* first or last. Although experiments by social scientists on the primacy-recency issue are inconclusive, there is a firm pattern on the question of recall. The ideas you state first or last have a better chance of being remembered than the ideas stated in the middle of your appeal or case.

7. Don't Count on Changing Attitudes by Offering Information Alone.

"People are hostile to big business because they don't know enough facts about it," businesspeople are heard to say. Or, "If customers knew the truth about our costs, they would not object to our prices." Companies have poured large sums into advertising and public relations campaigns on this assumption; civic organizations have often based their hopes on it.

[11]John Ball and Cecil B. Williams, *Report Writing* (New York, Ronald, 1955).

"The trouble with the assumption," states Karlins and Abelson, "is that it is almost never valid. There is a substantial body of research findings indicating that cognition—knowing something new—increasing information—is effective as an attitude change agent only under very specialized conditions."[12]

Social scientists do concede, however, that presentations of facts alone may strengthen the opinions of people who already agree with the persuader. The information reassures them and helps them defend themselves in discussions with others.

8. "Testimonials" Are Most Likely to be Persuasive if Drawn from People with Whom Readers Associate.

It is well known that a person's attitudes and opinions are strongly influenced by the groups to which he or she belongs or wants to belong—work units in a company, labor unions, bowling teams, social clubs, church associations, ethnic associations, and so on. To muster third-party support for your proposal or idea, therefore, you would do well to cite the behavior, findings, or beliefs of groups to which your readers belong. In so doing, you allay any feelings of isolation readers might have if tempted to follow your ideas. You suggest that they are not alone with you, that there is group support for the points being made.

As every school child learns, the predominant attitudes of a group toward individuals or regarding standards of behavior, performance, or status influence an individual member's perceptions. For instance, a study of boys at a camp demonstrated that their ratings of various individuals' performances at shooting and canoeing were biased by their knowledge of the status of the rated individuals in the camp society. Thus a boy generally regarded as a leader was seen as performing better with the rifle or canoe than was a boy generally regarded as a follower, even though the first boy's performance was not actually superior.[13]

In addition, it seems fair to say that as modern television, radio, records, and cassettes have brought national celebrities into the home and automobile, these people, too, have been stamped with approval or disapproval by millions of groups across the country.

Accordingly, if your readers are young, dissident, or "long hairs," refer to a Richard Dreyfus or a Joan Baez for supporting statements, not to a Gerald Ford or an Arnold Palmer. If your readers are electrical engineers, quote well-regarded scientific sources as your authority, not star salespeople or public relations people. Take into account also that the more deeply attached your readers are to a group, the greater the influence of the group norms on them. For instance, one experiment by social scientists showed that the opinions of Catholic students who took

[12]Karlins and Abelson, *op. cit.*, p. 33.

[13]*Ibid.*, p. 50.

their religion seriously were less influenced by the answers of nonserious Catholics than were the opinions of Catholic students who placed little value on their church membership.[14]

9. Be Wary of Using Extreme or "Sensational" Claims and Facts.

Both research in behavioral science and common sense confirm this rule.[15] Do not be misled by the fact that flashy journalists make successful use of extreme and bizarre cases to dramatize a story. The situation in business and professional writing is different from that in journalism.

When you seek the confidence and cooperation of your readers—and typically you do in the kinds of communications we deal with in this book—it is best to write in terms of the real world as you and they perceive it. Observable, believable, realistic statements carry more weight than any other kind. Although you want reader attention, you do not want to shock your audience with outlandish examples or arguments. These may help you to succeed in making the reader sit up—but they will also provoke distrust and suspicion.

Examples are common in the letters sections of newspapers. A writer who identified himself as a former vice-president of a well-known bank opposed a large power company's plan to build a new plant in a rural area near his town. His letter began as follows: "A great many of us . . . are profoundly disturbed by the proposal now being considered to disrupt and destroy the marvelous little valley southwest of [name of town], in order to build bigger and better power plants. This would be a devastating blow to the last unspoiled bit of country left in Connecticut. . . ."[16]

Like a batter who hits the first two pitches foul and quickly gets two strikes against him, this writer managed to distort the first two sentences he wrote. The proposed plant, though a very large one, would not "disrupt and destroy" the valley—only a small section of the valley area would be affected. Moreover, the valley was not "the last unspoiled bit of country" in the state—it was only a small parcel of the state's beautiful countryside. These exaggerations might have drawn cheers from rabid foes of the project, but the writer wasn't interested in appealing to them; he wanted to win uncommitted readers. At the very beginning, however, he antagonized them with hyperbole.

[14]See H. Kelley, "Salience of Membership and Resistance to Change of Group-Anchored Attitudes," *Human Relations*, August 1955, pp. 255–289. Cited in Karlins and Abelson, *op. cit.*, p. 58.

[15]See, for example, *Building Opposition to the Excess Profits Tax* (Princeton, Opinion Research Corporation, August 1952), and R. Weiss, "Conscious Technique for the Variation of Source Credibility," *Psychological Reports*, Vol. 20, 1969, p. 1159. Both cited in Karlins and Abelson, *op. cit.*, pp. 36–37.

[16]*Lakeville Journal*, April 2, 1970. p. 11.

10. Tailor Your Presentation to the Reasons for Readers' Attitudes, if You Know Them.

Your chances of persuading readers are better if you can plan your appeal or argument to meet the main feelings, prejudices, or reasons for their beliefs. For instance, if reader beliefs are the result of their wanting to go along with certain groups they like or associate with, your best bet (as indicated earlier) is to show the acceptability of your point to these groups. If their attitudes reflect personal biases, such as an old grudge against someone in power, it is best to tailor your presentation to that prejudice. And so on.

Summarizing the implications of several behavioral studies, Karlins and Abelson present the example of three people who say they are against private ownership of industry. How should their reasons for this position influence one's choice of a strategy of persuasion? The authors explain:

> One of them feels that way because he has only been exposed to one side of the story and has nothing else on which to base his opinion. The way to change this man's opinion may be to expose him to facts, take him to visit some factories, meet some workers and supervisors. A second person is against private owner-ship because that is the prevailing norm or social climate in the circles in which he finds himself. His attitudes are caused by his being a part of a group and conforming to its standards. You cannot change this fellow just by showing him facts. The facts must be presented in an atmosphere which suggests a social reward for changing his opinion. Some kind of status appeal might be a start in that direction. A third person may have negative attitudes toward private industry because by making business the scapegoat for all his troubles, he can unload his pent-up feelings of bitterness and disappointment at the world for not giving him a better break. . . . Trying to change this third person with facts may actually do more harm than good. The more the evidence shows how wrong he is, the more he looks for reasons to support his beliefs. This kind of person can sometimes be influenced by helping him to understand why he has a particular attitude.[17]

11. Never Mention Other People without Considering Their Possible Effect on the Reader.

Other people may, as we saw earlier, be introduced for the sake of "testimonials." More commonly, however, other people's names are mentioned in the course of explaining a situation, narrating an event, or completing the format of a message. This use of names, too, may affect the power of your message.

A reference to the actions of another person—however simple and unobtru-sive it may seem to you the writer—may alter your relationship with readers. If readers consider that person a friend or enemy, their natural reaction is to begin thinking of the possible bearing of your communication on their friendship or antagonism. This reaction can have significant implications for your approach.

To illustrate, a doctoral student who had failed to meet his school's program

[17]Karlins and Abelson, *op. cit.*, p. 92.

requirements tried to muster faculty opinion in support of his petition for readmission by appearing daily at the entrance to the dining hall and handing out leaflets to faculty members. One such leaflet contained these words: "I am very unhappy about the strain my case has created for Professor [name of the program director]. I am distressed if last Friday's handout . . . created the impression that I was harping on his mistakes. I have told him and I tell you that I could understand his actions and decisions. . . ." The leaflet went on at some length to explain the doctoral student's feelings about the problem.

What this writer did not realize was the impact of the professor's name on his communication strategy. Almost everyone who received the leaflet was a colleague of the professor in question. Therefore the leaflet made it necessary for them to think of their relationship with the professor when they made up their minds about the petition. And their relationship with the professor was more important to them than their relationship with the doctoral student.

If the doctoral student considered it essential to mention the professor, he could have elected to: (1) try to win readers over while convincing them that their relations with the professor would not be affected, or (2) show that the professor was so far off base that readers were morally bound to risk their relationship with him. In the latter case, the leaflet should have contained ready-to-use arguments that readers could draw on in explaining to the professor why they sympathized with the doctoral student. Since the leaflet did neither of these things, it was a failure in persuasion.

Don't overlook the possible effect of distribution. Letters often go to third parties, with "cc" typed at the bottom followed by the names of those people. A memorandum often contains the names of several addressees in the "To" line at the top. Covering letters with reports may indicate several groups of readers. All this may affect your strategy. The background information that you could omit if writing only to Jones may be quite necessary if Brown, too, is an important reader; and the rather offhand treatment you give to a certain test or episode if writing to Jones and Brown might not be fitting at all if Larabee also is an intended reader. Many times the wise manager or professional rewrites part of a letter or memo after deciding to send a copy of it to an additional person who was not considered when the first draft was made.

Many people have strong feelings about "blind copies," that is, copies sent to persons other than those indicated after "cc" at the end of a letter or in the "To" line of a memorandum. Some people feel that blind copies never should be sent. Others feel that since a letter or memo is the property of the writer, he or she can distribute it at will. Although the latter view is legally correct, only an obtuse writer will distribute copies thoughtlessly if the content is in any way confidential, personal, or politically sensitive.

Sizing up Your Readers

We have a tendency to abstract written communications from real life, to act as if the customary ground rules of influence and persuasion don't apply to a message that is in writing. We act with a naiveté almost unheard of in our face-to-face relationships. Not seeing readers, we act as if they weren't real people. "If we write the information clearly, accurately, and correctly," we think wishfully to ourselves, "surely that satisfies the requirements of a piece of paper." But Josh Billings' puckish maxim, "As scarce as truth is, the supply has always been in excess of the demand," applies to truth on paper as well as truth in conversation.

Think of your intended readers as the real people they will be when they take your letter or report out of the "in-box." Only then can you decide intelligently what information and ideas to emphasize and in what order to present them. To help you think of readers as three-dimensional people, ask yourself some questions about their situation and relationships with you. Are they:

- Deeply or only mildly interested in the subject of your communication?

- Familiar or unfamiliar with your views, competence, and feelings about them?

- Knowledgeable or ignorant of your authority in the area discussed, your status, and your associations of possible importance to them?

- Committed or uncommitted to a viewpoint, opinion, or course of action other than the one you favor in your letter, report, or other document?

- Likely or unlikely to find your proposal, idea, finding, or conclusion threatening or requiring considerable change in their thought or behavior?

- Inclined or uninclined to think and feel the way they do about the subject because of identifiable reasons, prejudices, or experiences?

- Associated formally or informally with groups or organizations involved in some way with the idea or proposal you deal with?

With answers to questions like these in mind, you will not see your readers as shadows on the wall. They will sit across from you. You can write as if talking *with* them, not talking to them.

How to Write Procedures

CHARLES H. SIDES

Charles H. Sides is Lecturer in the Writing Program and Coordinator of the Cooperative Writing Program with the School of Engineering at MIT.

About five years ago, suffering from the delusion that I was "good with my hands," I bought my wife a bureau in a box. Like most people when they start work on a kit, the first thing I did was open one end of the box and dump all the contents out onto the living room floor. The last thing that fluttered out was the instructions. The first thing it said was, "Remove contents from box in an orderly fashion." The wisdom of this was immediately apparent. There was no parts list, no handy little plastic bags containing the hardware, just a lot of wood and metal scattered on my floor. The next thing I noticed was that the instructions had only three steps. There were at least forty "things" on my floor, and even though the project was supposedly simple, looking at this mess, I had my doubts. So, I did what most people do when they find themselves in this predicament. I threw the instructions away. Little by little, the bureau got built, and it even looked like a bureau, capable of doing bureau things. But there was one little problem. The last piece of wood, a restraining piece which looked as if it should fit across the back between the two legs, was four inches longer than the top of the bureau. Nothing suggested that it should fit diagonally, and anyway, I thought, that would look odd. So again I allied myself with the majority of kit builders, sawed the excess four inches off, and nailed the piece in place.

This story serves an important purpose. It identifies the single most common problem of poor procedure writing: procedure writers who have no idea who they are writing for and under what conditions the procedures will be used. Consequently, the worst technical writing tends to be "how to" writing. Based on the procedures with which most of us have had experience, some people have even suggested that the persons who write procedures are those deemed least valuable to the organization. While I would not go that far, such an attitude does suggest a personal relations problem for those of us who write procedures. Our product often does not inspire confidence that even *we* know what we are doing. That is reason enough for considering how to write procedures. This [selection], then, will examine a system for writing procedures—planning, writing, and testing.

HOW TO WRITE PROCEDURES By Charles H. Sides. From *How to Write Papers and Reports about Computer Technology* published by ISI Press. © 1984 ISI Press and written by Charles H. Sides.

Planning for Procedures

Before readers can be told how to do something, they must be told what that something is, what its purpose is. In other words, give the readers a rationale for following the procedure. Doing so suggests to readers that you have considered them and what they are up against in their day-to-day activities, that it is in your best interest that readers do not waste time trying to figure out what it is you are wanting them to do. This consideration has an obvious positive effect: readers are more likely to follow procedures accurately.

Procedures, regardless of the format in which they are written, may do any or all of the following:

- give steps for operating something

- give steps for assembling something

- give steps for troubleshooting, repairing, adjusting, or maintaining something

- give steps for unpacking or shipping

- give steps for ordering parts, optional attachments, tools, etc.

- furnish a parts list

- teach skills, as in a training manual.

The important thing to remember when writing procedures is that you must become a *teacher*. You are the expert, and it is your responsibility to impart your knowledge to readers who know less about the subject than you do. If it is true of any type of writing within the computer industry, it is especially true of writing procedures: the written product has value only insofar as it can be used.

One of the ways you can ensure the usability of your procedures and a way you can instill confidence in your readers that *you* know what you are talking about is through the language you use. Use the *command* voice, not the descriptive voice.

Example:

COMMAND VOICE   Use the command voice.
DESCRIPTIVE VOICE   You should use the command voice.

Notice that the descriptive voice suggests that there might be alternatives to what you want done, that the reader only "should" use it, not that he absolutely has to use it, no questions asked. As long as you don't fail your readers with inaccuracies, the command voice is convincing.

Vocabulary is also important in procedures. The procedures must be written in the language of the readers. Impressing them with your erudition is worthless. If readers are to follow a procedure accurately, they at least have to understand the individual steps. This is just another indication of the necessity of audience analysis and adaptation. As a writer of procedures, you have to know who your readers are intended to be, what level of expertise they have attained in the area covered by the procedures. Depending on what you know about the readers, you may have to define terms and explain unfamiliar concepts. Clarity is your goal, and that means explicitness. Make a mistake on the side of too much information rather than too little. Too much information may aggravate readers who find they know much of what you have included, but that is a small price to pay. Too little information means that the procedure cannot be followed.

All of this calls to mind what a former professor of mine once said about the process of writing procedures. He was convinced that the people who were assigned the task of writing procedures and instructions were those whom management thought to be expendable, the flunkies. I'm not sure that I would agree with that assessment, but often that's the impression our procedures leave readers with. Consequently, well-planned and well-written procedures are public relations documents for our companies.

The planning for procedures begins before you start to write. First, you have to know your subject. This means doing a number of things. You should find out how the subject came into being. If it is something which has been designed, new software, for example, why was it designed? What needs will it fill? Who will it be marketed to? You should examine the subject itself. If it is something that must be assembled, assemble it. If it is a programming procedure that must be followed, do it. See if it works. Find out what the purposes of the subject are, who will use it, and under what conditions it will be used. What are its good and bad features? Even though you may not be able to say anything about its weak points, every subject has them. Learn how they may be avoided, and you can impart that to your readers with advisory comments.

If your subject is complex, divide it into parts. These parts will later form the basis for sections in short procedures or chapters in manuals. You may even have to subdivide the divisions. These divisions, with plenty of headings, enable readers to see the important parts of the procedure and how they interrelate.

If your subject lends itself to things which might go wrong should the procedures not be followed accurately, make a list of precautions. These have widely accepted meanings.

- DANGER

  Reserved for steps which might lead to serious injury or loss of life if readers do not know what they are doing (poking around inside the CPU with a screwdriver, for instance)

- WARNING

  Used for steps which could result in damage to the subject if the procedures are not followed carefully

- CAUTION

  Applied to steps where faulty results might occur if the reader does not follow the procedures accurately

- NOTE

  Used to alert readers to potential problems

- ADVICE

  Reserved for making suggestions which would make the readers' tasks easier

Once you have analyzed the subject, considered the projected audience, made an outline, and listed the precautions which will apply, you are ready to write the procedure.

Writing Procedures

Writing procedures begins with determining the purpose of the procedures for the intended audience. This includes choosing an explicit title that includes the date and all appropriate models and operations to which the procedures apply. It also often includes writing a short purpose statement introduction. This is the aspect of procedure writing most often overlooked. Many writers assume that, since they will be telling readers what to do, nothing is served by telling them why to do it. This is a dangerous fallacy because it assumes that readers will automatically see the wisdom of doing it your way. Not so! Once these concerns have been met, you will have to choose a format which suits your purpose and communicates the information efficiently to your readers. There are a variety of choices. The following examples are the same LOGON procedure written in a variety of formats.

Example: Paragraph procedure

> To logon using the IBM 3278 display terminal, type L, skip one space, and type your assigned user ID number. Then press ENTER. At this point you will be prompted on the screen for your password. Type it in and press ENTER again. Now a message will appear on the screen. When it is complete, press ENTER. More messages will appear. At the end of these, you will see either MORE or HOLDING. At this point, hold down the ALT key and press the CURSOR SELECT key. Another message will appear followed by R. You are now logged on and ready to use the system.

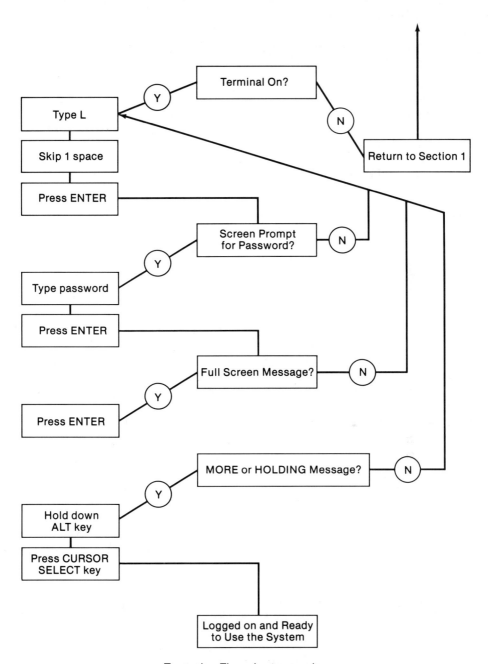

Example: Flow chart procedure

Example: Listed procedure

To LOGON to the IBM 3278 display terminal, proceed as follows:

1. Type L.
2. Skip 1 space.
3. Type your user ID number.
4. Press ENTER.
5. After the screen prompt for your password, type in your password.
6. Press ENTER.
7. Following a long displayed message, press ENTER again.
8. MORE or HOLDING will appear on the screen; hold down the ALT key and press the CURSOR SELECT key.

You are now logged on and ready to use the system.

Example: Map layout procedure

1. Is terminal turned on?   YES—Proceed to Step 2.
                            NO—Return to Section 1.
2. Type L.
   Skip 1 space.
   Type user ID number.
   Press ENTER.
3. Does screen prompt you for your password?
                    YES—Type password.
                         Press ENTER.
                         Proceed to Step 4.
                    NO—Return to Step 2.
4. Does a full screen message appear?   YES—Press ENTER.
                                             Proceed to Step 5.
                                        NO—Return to Step 2.
5. Does MORE or HOLDING appear on the screen?
             YES—Hold down ALT key.
                  Press CURSOR SELECT key.
             NO—Return to Step 2.

You are now logged on and ready to use the system.

Testing Procedures

The final task procedure writers have to concern themselves with could be called quality control. Usually we think of quality control as something which applies to production items, something which industrial engineers do. But quality control also applies to written documents, particularly to procedures.

To check the quality of your procedures, make sure that two different types of people read and evaluate the procedures before they are made public: an expert who can check the steps for technical accuracy and a person representing the intended user who can check the procedure for whether it can be understood and used.

Then beta test the procedure in the environment in which it is intended to be used with persons intended to use it. This is a common procedure for evaluating the functions of newly developed hardware and software. It should extend to procedures.

Procedure	Step	Condition	Y/N	Action
LOGON				
	1.	Terminal On?	Y	Type L Skip 1 space Press ENTER
			N	Return to Section 1
	2.	Password Screen Prompt?	Y	Type Password Press ENTER
			N	Return to Step 2
	3.	Screen Message?	Y	Press ENTER
			N	Return to Step 2
	4.	MORE or HOLDING	Y	Hold down ALT key Press CURSOR SELECT key
			N	Return to Step 2
		Logged on and ready to use system		

Example: Structure style procedure

Ten Report Writing Pitfalls: How to Avoid Them

VINCENT VINCI

Vincent Vinci was Director of Public Relations for Lockheed Electronics when he wrote this article.

T he advancement of science moves on a pavement of communications. Chemists, electrical engineers, botanists, geologists, atomic physicists, and other scientists are not only practitioners but interpreters of science. As such, the justification, the recognition and the rewards within their fields result from their published materials.

Included in the vast field of communications is the report, a frequently used medium for paving the way to understanding and action. The engineering manager whose function is the direction of people and programs receives and writes many reports in his career. And therefore the need for technical reports that communicate effectively has been internationally recognized.

Since scientific writing is complicated by specialized terminology, a need for precision and the field's leaping advancement, the author of an engineering report can be overwhelmed by its contents. The proper handling of contents and communication of a report's purpose can be enhanced if the writer can avoid the following 10 pitfalls.

Pitfall 1: Ignoring Your Audience

In all the forms of communications, ignoring your audience in the preparation of a report is perhaps the greatest transgression. Why? All other forms of communication such as instruction manuals, speeches, books and brochures, are directed to an indefinable or only partially definable audience. The report, on the other hand, is usually directed to a specific person or group and had a specific purpose. So, it would certainly seem that if one knows both the "who" and the "why," then a report writer should not be trapped by this pitfall.

But it is not enough to know the who and why, you need to know "how." To get to the how, let's assume that the reader is your boss and has asked you to write a trip report. You are to visit several plants and report on capital equipment requirements. Before you write the first word you will have to find out what your boss already knows about these requirements. It is obvious that he wants a new assessment of the facilities' needs. But, was he unsatisfied with a recent assessment and wants another point of view, or is a new analysis required because the previous report is outdated—or does he feel that now is the time to make the investment in facilities so that production can be increased over the next five years? That's a lot of questions, but they define both the who and why of your trip and, more importantly, your report.

By this time you may get the feeling that I suggest you give him exactly what he wants to read. The answer is yes and no. No, I don't mean play up to your boss's likes and dislikes. I do mean, however, that you give him all the information he needs to make a decision—the pros and the cons.

I mean also that the information be presented in a way that he is acclimated to in making judgments. For example, usually, a production-oriented manager or executive (even the chief executive) will think in terms of his specialty. The president of a company who climbed the marketing ladder selling solvents will think better in marketing terms. Therefore, perhaps the marketing aspects of additional equipment and facilities should be stressed. You should also be aware that if you happen to be the finance director, your boss will expect to see cost/investment factors too.

A simple method for remembering, rather than ignoring, your audience is to place a sheet of paper in front of you when you start to write your report. On the paper have written in bold letters WHO, WHY and HOW, with the answers clearly and cogently defined. Keep it in front of you throughout the preparation of your report.

Pitfall 2: Writing to Impress

Nothing turns a reader off faster than writing to impress. Very often reports written to leave a lasting scholarly impression on top management actually hinder communication.

Generally, when a word is used to impress, the report writer assumes that the reader either knows its meaning or will take the trouble to look it up. Don't assume that a word familiar to you is easily recognized by your reader. I recall a few years ago, there was a word "serendipity" which became a fashionable word to impress your reader with. And there was "fulsome," and "pejorative," and more. All are good words, but they're often misused or misapplied. They were shoved into reports to impress, completely disregarding the reader. Your objective is that your reader comprehend your thoughts, and there should be a minimum of impediments to understanding—understanding with first reading, and no deciphering.

Unfortunately, writing to impress is not merely restricted to use of obscure words but also includes unnecessary detail and technical trivia. Perhaps the scientist, chemist, chemical engineer and others become so intrigued with technical fine points that the meaningful (to your audience) elements of a report are buried. And quite often the fault is not so much a lack of removing the chaff from the grain but an attempt to technically impress the reader. Of course there exist reports that are full of technical detail because the nature of the communication is to impart a new chemical process, compound or technique. Even when writing this kind of report, you should eliminate any esoteric technical facts that do not contribute to communication, even though you may be tempted to include them to exhibit your degree of knowledge in the field.

Pitfall 3: Having More than One Aim

A report is a missile targeted to hit a point or achieve a mission. It is not a barrage of shotgun pellets that scatter across a target indiscriminately.

Have you ever, while reading a report, wondered where or what it was leading to—and even when you finished you weren't quite sure? The writer probably had more than one aim, thereby preventing you from knowing where the report was heading.

Having more than one aim is usually the sign of a novice writer, but the pitfall can also trip up an experienced engineer if he does not organize the report toward one objective.

It is too easy to say that your report is being written to communicate, to a specific audience, information about your research, tests, visit, meeting, conference, field trip, progress or any other one of a range of activities that may be the subject. If you look at the first part of the sentence, you will see that "specific audience" and "information" are the key words that have to be modified to arrive at the goal of your report. For instance, you must define the specific audience such as the "members of the research council," "the finance committee" or "the chief process engineer and his staff."

Secondly, you need to characterize the information, such as "analysis of a new catalytic process," "new methods of atomic absorption testing" or "progress on waste treatment programs." You should be able to state the specific purpose of your report in one sentence: e.g., "The use of fibrous material improves scrubber efficiency and life—a report to the product improvement committee."

When you have arrived at such a definition of your purpose and audience, you can then focus both the test results and analysis toward that purpose, tempered with your readers in mind.

The usual error made in writing reports is to follow the chronology of the research in the body of the report with a summary of a set of conclusions and recommendations attached. The proper procedure to follow is to write (while focusing on your report goal) the analysis first (supported by test essentials or any other details), then your introduction or summary—sort of reverse chronology. But be sure that your goal and audience are clearly known, because they become the basis of organizing your report.

Pitfall 4: Being Inconsistent

If you work for an international chemical firm, you may be well aware of problems in communicating with plant managers and engineers of foreign installations or branches. And I'm not referring to language barriers, because for the most part these hurdles are immediately recognized and taken care of. What is more significant is units of measure. This problem is becoming more apparent as the United States slowly decides whether or not to adopt the metric system. Until it is adopted, your best bet is to stick to one measurement system throughout the report. Preferably, the system chosen should be that familiar to your audience. If the audience is mixed you should use both systems with one (always the same one) in parentheses. Obviously, don't mix units of measure because you will confuse or annoy your readers.

Consistency is not limited to measurements but encompasses terms, equations, derivations, numbers, symbols, abbreviations, acronyms, hyphenation, capitalization and punctuation. In other words, consistency in the mechanics of style will avoid work for your reader and smooth his path toward understanding and appreciating the contents of the report.

If your company neither has a style guide nor follows the general trends of good editorial practice, perhaps you could suggest instituting a guide. In addition to the U.S. Government Printing Office Style Manual, many scientific and engineering societies have set up guides which could be used.

Pitfall 5: Overqualifying

Chemical engineers, astronomers, geologists, electrical engineers, and scientists of any other discipline have been educated and trained to be precise. As a result, they strive for precision, accuracy, and detail. That tends to work against the scientist when it comes to writing. Add to that the limited training received in the arts, and you realize why written expression does not come easily.

Most reports, therefore, have too many modifiers—adjectives, clauses, phrases, adverbs and other qualifiers. Consider some examples: the single-stage, isolated double-cooled refractory process breakdown, or, the angle of the single-rotor dc hysteresis motor rotor winding. To avoid such difficult-to-comprehend phrases, you could in the first example write "the breakdown of the process in single-stage, isolated double-cooled refractories," and in the second, "the angle of the rotor winding in single-rotor dc hysteresis motors can cause . . . ," and so on. This eliminates the string of modifiers and makes the phrase easier to understand.

Better still, if your report allows you to say at the beginning that the following descriptions are only related to "single-stage, isolated double-cooled refractories" or "single-rotor dc hysteresis motors," you can remove the cumbersome nomenclature entirely.

In short, to avoid obscuring facts and ideas, eliminate excessive modifiers. Try to state your idea or main point first and follow with your qualifying phrases.

Pitfall 6: Not Defining

Dwell, lake, and barn, all are common words. Right? Right and wrong. Yes, they are common to the non-scientist. To the mechanical engineer, dwell is the period a cam follower stays at maximum lift; to a chemical engineer, lake is a dye compound; and to an atomic physicist, a barn is an atomic cross-sectional area (10^{-24} cm^2).

These three words indicate two points: first, common words are used in science with other than their common meaning; and second, terms need to be defined.

In defining terms you use in a report, you must consider what to define and how to define. Of the two, I consider what to define a more difficult task and suggest that you review carefully just which terms you need defined. If you analyze the purpose, the scope, the direction and your audience (reader/user), you will probably get a good handle on such terms.

"How to define" ranges from the simple substitution of a common term for an uncommon one, to an extended or amplified explanation. But whatever the term, or method of definition, you need to slant it both to the reader and to the report purpose.

Pitfall 7: Misintroducing

Introductions, summaries, abstracts and forewords—whatever you use to lead your reader into your report, it should not read like an exposition of a table of contents. If it does, you might as well let your audience read the table of contents.

The introduction, which should be written after the body of the report, should state the subject, purpose, scope, and the plan of the report. In many cases, an introduction will include a summary of the findings or conclusions. If a report is a progress report, the introduction should relate the current report to previous reports. Introductions, then, not only tell the sequence or plan of the report, but tell the what, how and why of the subject as well.

Pitfall 8: Dazzling with Data

Someone once said that a good painter not only knows what to put in a painting, but more importantly he knows what to leave out. It's much the same with report writing. If you dazzle your reader with tons of data, he may be moved by the weight of the report but may get no more out of it than that.

The usual error occurs in supportive material that many engineers and scientists feel is necessary to give a report scientific importance. The truth is that successful scientific writing (which includes reports) is heavily grounded in reality, simplicity, and understanding—not quantity.

The simplest way to evaluate the relevancy of information is to ask yourself after writing a paragraph, "What can I remove from this paragraph without destroying its meaning and its relationship to what precedes and what will follow?'' Then, ask another question, ''Does my reader require all that data to comprehend, evaluate or make a decision with?'' If you find you can do without excess words, excess description and excess supportive data, you will end up with a tighter, better and more informative report.

These principles should also be used to evaluate graphs, photographs, diagrams and other illustrations. Remember, illustrations should support or aid comprehension rather than being a crutch on which your report leans. The same should be kept in mind when determining just how much you should append to your report. There is no need to copy all your lab notes to show that detailed experimentation was performed to substantiate the results. A statement that the notes exist and are available will suffice.

Pitfall 9: Not Highlighting

Again, I believe the analogy of the painter applies. A good painter also knows what to highlight and what to subdue in a portrait or scene.

If you don't accent the significant elements, findings, illustrations, data, tests, facts, trends, procedures, precedents, or experiments pertinent to the subject and object of your report, you place the burden of doing so on your reader. As a result, he may consider the report a failure, draw his own conclusions, or hit upon the significant elements by chance. In any event, don't leave it up to your reader to search out the major points of your report.

Highlighting is one step past knowing what goes into your report and what to leave out (see Pitfall 8 above). All the key points of your report should define and focus on the purpose of your report. They must be included in your summary or conclusions, but these sections are not the only places to highlight. Attention should be called to key elements needed for the understanding of your material throughout the body of the report. Several methods may be used: you can underline an important statement or conclusion, you can simply point out that a particular illustration is the proof of the results of an experiment, or, as most professional writers do, you can make the key sentence the first or last sentence of a paragraph.

Pitfall 10: Not Rewriting

Did you ever hear of an actor who hadn't rehearsed his lines before stepping before an audience? An actor wouldn't chance it—his reputation and his next role depend on his performance. The engineer shouldn't chance it either. Don't expect the draft of your report to be ready for final typing and reproduction without rewriting.

Once you have judged what your report will contain and how it will be organized, just charge ahead and write the first draft. Don't worry about choosing the precise word, turning that meaningful phrase, or covering all the facts in one paragraph or section. Once you have written your first draft (and the quicker you accomplish this the more time you will have to perfect the text), you are in a better position to analyze, tailor, and refine the report as a whole. Now you are also able to focus all the elements toward your purpose and your audience.

As you begin the rewriting process simply pick up each page of your draft, scan it, and ask yourself what role the material on that page plays in the fulfillment of the report's objective and understanding. You will find that this will enable you to delete, add, change and rearrange your material very quickly.

After you have completed this process, then rewrite paragraph by paragraph, sentence by sentence, and word by word. Your final step is to repeat the procedure of examining each page's contents. When you are satisfied with its flow and cohesion, then you will have a good report, one you know will be well received and acted upon.

5

RESUMES AND OTHER WRITTEN MATERIALS FOR A JOB SEARCH

The written materials that are part of your application for a job face one of the most difficult audiences imaginable: an experienced recruiting manager. Because the selections that follow offer extensive advice on how to prepare and write resumes, cover letters, and writing samples, I will limit my remarks to some general comments.

First, there is no *one* way to write a resume or a cover letter. Slavishly following some format that you think represents the ideal can defeat your purpose in writing: to get an interview. The shelves of bookstores across the country are filled with guides offering advice on how to write resumes and cover letters. These guides offer advice, not commandments. Read as many of them as you want, read the essays that follow, but in the end let common sense be your guide when you write what is essentially an advertisement for yourself.

When you are unsure, or when common sense doesn't seem to be forthcoming, remember what recruiting managers look for when they read resumes and cover letters. Two years ago, my own university's placement bureau sponsored a panel featuring the recruiting managers from the four companies that had hired the greatest number of our graduates in previous years. All four managers stressed that they looked at cover letters and resumes to determine as quickly as possible what preparation and experience candidates had in the following skills and areas:

- oral and written communication skills

- interpersonal relations, as demonstrated by the ability to work as a member of a team

- a sense of what the world of work demands

- specific skills in one technical area, supplemented by secondary skills in a variety of related areas

- basic computer literacy

- a sense of business ethics

- an ability to manage time, set priorities, and work under stress.

While you won't be expected to excel in all these areas or possess all these skills, this list does provide you with some general guidelines for communicating with recruiting managers by cover letters and resumes—or, for that matter, in person during an interview.

Part V begins with John L. Munschauer's detailed discussion of how to write a resume and cover letter. Based on his many years of work with the Cornell University Career Center, Munschauer places the writing of resumes and cover letters within the context of how they are read by busy recruiting managers. Yana Parker takes Munschauer's advice a step further by providing a handy checklist designed to answer ten tough questions you may have to answer on paper or in person during a job search. Marcia R. Fox then offers some practical suggestions about the mechanics of a good cover letter.

Because of the increasing importance of writing skills in nearly all areas of the world of work, Part 5 concludes with a discussion by Warren S. Feld of how to submit an appropriate writing sample when you are asked to do so by a potential employer to supplement your cover letter and resume.

Communicating Your Message through Letters and Resumes

JOHN L. MUNSCHAUER

John L. Munschauer is Director Emeritus of
the Cornell University Career Center.

Why Use a Resume?

he purpose of a resume is to convey a message, a purpose easily
forgotten in the ritual of preparing it. At every turn, you will get
conflicting advice about how to conduct the ritual:

You must have a resume to get a job.
The purpose of a resume is to get an interview.
Every resume must have a job objective.
A resume should never, ever be longer than one page.
On a resume, list experience chronologically.

On the other hand, others advise:

Don't use a resume if you are looking for an executive position or
merely seeking information.
Resumes typecast you and narrow your options.
Interview for information first, determine what an employer wants,
and then decide whether offering a resume will suit your purposes.
Two or more pages present no problem if your resume follows a
logical, easy-to-read outline.
List your experience by function, not chronologically.

The more opinions you get, the more confused you become, but you finally
work up something. You send it out. You get little or no response. You change
your resume from one page to two pages—or from two pages to one. The results
are no better. Somebody says to try pink paper, *that* will get attention. You decide
you should have used blue. You fiddle and fiddle with your resume, trying to find

COMMUNICATING YOUR MESSAGE THROUGH LETTERS AND RESUMES   By John L. Munschauer. Reprinted
with permission from Peterson's Guides, Inc., from the publication entitled *Jobs for English Majors
and Other Smart People* (Revised Edition, 1986), Stock No. 3916, available from Peterson's Guides,
Inc., 166 Bunn Drive, Princeton, N.J. 08540. Price $7.95.

the magic formula that will get you what you want. You are caught up in the ritual, forgetting that the purpose of a resume is to send a message.

It is hard not to be distracted from the message. You concentrate on developing a format, forgetting the message, instead of concentrating on the message and *then* working on a format that will convey it best. But what is your message? To find the answer, use your imagination to step out of yourself and become an employer. Think about what the employer is trying to accomplish and the talent required to get it done. Now, from your imaginary employer's chair, look back at yourself and ponder the answer. If you can't come up with one, you will have difficulty writing a resume that will say to the employer, "I have something to offer you."

Resumes are not tickets to a job. They are just one of several ways to court employers. And, as in any courtship, sometimes it's just as well not to put everything in print when the other party might draw the wrong conclusion. Take the case of Cheryl Fender, an alto who learned that the Springfield Opera Company was auditioning for an alto to sing *Carmen*. Cheryl was well qualified, and her voice teacher was well known as a coach of only the most gifted singers. On the other hand, her resume, which was incomplete, with gaps in her history, showed extensive experience as a secretary. Wisely, she did not send the resume, because it might have established her as a secretary who wanted to sing, rather than as a singer who had supported herself by being a secretary. Instead, she asked herself, What is important to a director? Voice, of course, so she outlined her training in a letter. But dramatic ability also mattered, so she included pictures of herself on stage in roles that beautifully illustrated her dramatic ability. She got an audition. Cheryl followed a good marketing rule: Don't confuse customers by flaunting things that don't speak to their needs.

Giving Your Message

While the language of employment for you is "I want" and for employers it is "I need," you can create resumes and letters in your language that will be read by employers in theirs. I don't mean statements such as, "I have analyzed my qualifications and feel confident that they fit your needs." If you were one of the thousands of employers who read this kind of thing, wouldn't you ask, what qualifications and what needs? If the answer isn't clear—and it rarely is—there won't be a message.

It isn't all that difficult to create one that is effective. Think of letters as offering the most creative method to communicate with employers. Even if you are going to be approaching them in person, go through the exercise of writing letters. Otherwise, like most people, you can get caught up in the resume ritual and neglect to develop the prose that can be more effective in telling your story. People sweat over resumes, then dash off letters without much thought. Perfect resumes arriving in the mail won't even be read if the cover letters don't impress and engage employers.

I recall being asked to review an applicant's proposed application letter for a job on the staff of a yachting magazine. The letter was beautifully written, but it left the impression of being all "I": "I want to write so very much, and I am sure I can learn if you give me a chance . . . I got straight A's in English . . . I love boats . . . I am a sailor . . . I was captain of the sailing team in college. . . . "

What do you say to a person who has written a letter like that? He had obviously spent hours composing it. In its appearance and use of language, it met the highest standards. I could not squelch the young man's hopes, so I had him read *Book Publishing*,[1] a pamphlet Daniel Melcher wrote when he was president of R. R. Bowker Company. Although the pamphlet is concerned only with book publishing, I thought its message would be useful for someone interested in magazines as well.

Let me paraphrase a portion of Melcher's pamphlet:

> I like publishing and you might like it too. It is only fair to warn you, however, that publishing attracts a great many more people than the industry can possibly absorb. Sometimes it seems as though half of the English majors in the country besiege publishing offices for jobs each year. While we hope that you will have something to offer us, you might as well face it. Publishers are experts in the art of the gentle brush-off.
>
> The interviewer hopes that you have what he needs, but it turns out that you have never looked into any of the industry's trade journals nor read any books about the industry. You haven't even acquainted yourself with the work of your university press. You tell the interviewer that you are willing to start anywhere, but it develops that a file clerk's job would not interest you, you do not want to type, you don't think you can sell, and you know nothing about printing.
>
> The fact is, all you have thought about is what you want, but it is his needs that create jobs, and you must address yourself to needs.
>
> Your problem, therefore, is to learn as much as possible about the industry before you go looking for a job. Only in this way will you be able to put yourself in the publisher's place and talk to him about his needs rather than about your wants.

After reading Melcher's advice, the fellow said he got the point, thanked me, and left, returning about three weeks later to show me his revised letter. It began in much the same way as his earlier effort—with "I's": "I majored in English . . . I have done considerable sailing . . . "; but after a few short sentences, he suddenly changed his tack. A new three-sentence paragraph began like this: "With my interests, naturally I want to work for you. But more to the point is not what I need but what you need." He followed this with . . . : "I can type." Right away, he showed that he knew he must be useful.

So much for the easy part of the letter. Next came the difficult part. Although he had had no experience, and had never submitted an article to a magazine or even written for a student newspaper, he still had to come up with something that would interest the editor. He found the solution. The letter continued in this manner:

> . . . In looking into the field of journalism, I visited the editor of our alumni magazine, and I talked to magazine space salesmen and to executives responsible for placing ads in magazines. I also visited a printer who has contracts with magazines. In addition, I have been reading trade journals and several books on the industry. As I looked into publishing, it occurred to me that of all the things I have done, the one I could most closely relate to the field was, strangely enough, an experience I had as a baby-sitter.

Immediately, he had the editor's full attention. How could babysitting fit in with publishing? During the summer of his junior year in college he had taken a job as a sailing instructor, tutor, and companion for the children of a wealthy family that summered on the coast of Maine. The parents often went away for a week or more at a time, leaving a governess in charge, with a cook, chauffeur, maid, and gardener to do the chores and the student to keep the children busy. While the parents were on a cruise, the governess suffered a stroke, sending the cook into a tizzy, the maid into tears, and the chauffeur and gardener to the local bar. Only the student could cope, and he took charge and managed the estate for the rest of the summer.

In his letter of application he described the crisis, and subsequent problems he had faced, and told how he had met them. Then he related those experiences to the problems that he had learned editors, advertisers, printers, and others encounter in the publishing industry. Reading his letter, you could picture the student working for a publisher. There would be no slipups with the printers. Advertisers and authors would be handled with tact, yet he would get them to turn in their copy on time. He came through as someone with ingenuity, energy, and reliability; and the letter itself testified to his writing ability.

Did he get the job? Yes, and no. He got an offer, but because of the publisher's urgent needs the job had to be filled immediately, and he could not accept it. He was teaching school at the time and felt that in fairness to his pupils he should finish the school year. However, a while later, the letter surfaced again when a group of editors at a meeting chatted during lunch. The subject of good editorial help came up. It followed the usual theme, "They don't make 'em like they used to." The editor of another sailing magazine complained that he had been looking for an assistant, but despite hundreds of applicants had found none suitable. At this point, the editor of the yachting magazine described the young man's letter and agreed to share it. The upshot was, again, a job offer. This time the timing was right, and the young man took the job. There is nothing quite like the staying power of a well-written letter. It is remembered.

Later, I complimented the young man, telling him I had never read a better letter. "It was easy," he said. "The first letter was the tough one. I didn't have anything to say other than 'I have a good record. Please give me a chance,' but I knew everyone else was saying the same thing, so I would have to say it better. I struggled with every word, trying to make an ordinary message extraordinary, but even elegant words can't make something out of fluff. I didn't know anything about publishing, so I didn't have anything to say to publishers; nor could I be really convincing without knowing enough about the work to decide whether I wanted that kind of job or not. But publishing sounded exciting, so I thought I would give it a fling."

The Importance of Knowing What the Job Is All About

"When I looked into the field in depth," the young man continued, "I became confident that I had something to offer. Thanks to a few good high school teachers and college professors, I knew where to place a comma and a colon, so I had a technical skill to offer publishers. And I knew sailing. But the big need I saw was one I discovered when I was teaching school and again when I was an assistant manager at a McDonald's—a need for people who can get things done. Such a quality is hard to describe without an analogy. I could have alluded to any number of jobs I had held, but I chose the baby-sitting job because I thought it would be different and would introduce an element of surprise. Apparently, the analogy worked. I got a job. More important, I wanted it. If I had received a job offer after sending the first letter, before I had really investigated publishing, I would have taken the job with an attitude of 'teach me.' That's a passive role, one of an observer, and observers tend to be critical. The chances are fifty-fifty that I would not have known how or where to contribute and would have quit after a while. Instead of offering my employer solutions to his problems, I would have become one of his problems."

I asked the young man if he had used any other supporting documents, such as a resume, to help him get the job. "I had a resume," he replied, "but I held it back, because my task was to transfer the qualities I had demonstrated as a baby-sitter to the needs of a publisher, and I couldn't seem to do that in a resume. A resume is a good way to outline facts, but I had to use prose to develop the analogy.

"I did think about including a writing sample, but when I studied the magazine I realized that most of the articles were written by contributors rather than the staff. Their job was to select and edit articles. If I presented myself as a writer, I wouldn't have received an offer; the magazine didn't hire authors. When a friend of mine saw an advertisement for an editing job, he made a list of the required qualifications, then presented his case point by point, right on target. Then the dope attached his resume that said loud and clear, 'I want to be a writer.' He should have either skipped the resume or prepared a new one."

Are these examples intended to be good arguments for not using resumes? No. They simply emphasize that it is important to determine the best way to get a message across. There are times when there is no substitute for a resume. When employers advertise and list the qualifications they seek, there is no better way to respond than to send a resume outlining qualifications.

Letters of Application

Sometimes, however, it is hard to figure out how to make the letter of application you send with your resume more effective than those of the hundreds of people who are responding to the ad. Imagine being on the receiving end of applications at General Motors or Exxon, organizations that list jobs in Peterson's annual *Engineering, Science, and Computer Jobs*[2] and *Business and Management Jobs*[3] and in the *CPC Annual*.[4]

To find out about the effectiveness of letters and resumes, I visited corporations and asked employment managers for their comments. "Here," said one employment manager, as he picked up an eighteen-inch stack of letters and handed it to me. "This is my morning's mail. Read these letters and you'll have your answer."

"I can't," I protested. "I have only two hours, and there's a day's reading here."

"Yes, you can," he replied. "Unfortunately, you'll get through the pack in a half hour, because a glance will tell you that most are not worth reading."

It was hard to believe that the letters could be that bad, but he was right. The typical letter was an insult. Among the letters that I did not finish reading was one on onionskin paper, in very light type—it must have been the fifth carbon in the typewriter. It began:

Dear Sir:

I am writing to the top companies in each industry and yours is certainly that. I want to turn my outstanding qualities of leadership and my can-do abilities to . . .

Enough of that. Also, the applicant hadn't even bothered to type in the employment manager's name, which he could easily have found in the *CPC Annual* or in Peterson's Job Guides.

The next letter was written in pencil on notepaper. There may have been an Einstein behind that one, but I can't imagine anyone taking the time to find it out. Many other letters were smudged and messy. Some applicants tried to attract attention with stunts, such as putting cute cartoons on their letters. One piece of mail contained a walnut and a note that read, "Every business has a tough nut to crack. If you have a tough nut to crack and need someone to do it, crack this nut." Inside the nut, all wadded up, was a resume. Cute tricks and cleverness don't work at the General Mammoth Corporation.

At the same time, the good letters stood out like gold. Five letters, only five letters in that pile of hundreds, were worth reading. They had this in common:

They looked like business letters. Their paragraphing, their neatness, and their crisp white 8½" x 11" stationery attracted attention like good-looking clothing and good grooming.

They were succinct.

There were no misspellings or grammatical errors.

As I read them, I heard a voice—the voice of a fusty old high school English teacher—commanding out of the past:

If you can't spell a word, look it up in a dictionary.

Use a typewriter. Pen and ink are for love letters.

Clean your typewriter. Avoid fuzzy type. You wouldn't interview in a dirty shirt, so don't send a dirty resume or letter.

For format, use a secretarial manual. If you don't have one, get one from the library. What do you think libraries are for?

How that English teacher would have loved the following advice from Malcolm Forbes. the editor-in-chief of *Forbes* magazine:

> Edit ruthlessly. Somebody ~~has~~ said that words are ~~a lot~~ like inflated money—the more ~~of them that~~ you use, the less each one ~~of them~~ is worth. ~~Right on.~~ Go through your entire letter ~~just~~ as many times as it takes. ~~Search out and~~ Annihilate all unnecessary words ~~and~~ sentences—even ~~entire~~ paragraphs.[5]

The following letter is typical of those I saw that day. Give it the Forbes treatment, and see what you can do with it. You may need a scissors as well as a pencil.

Dear Mr. Employer,

I am writing to you because I am going to be looking for employment after I graduate which will be from Michigan where I studied Chemical Engineering and I will be getting a Bachelor of Science degree in June. The field in which I am interested and hope to pursue is process design and that is why I am writing your company to see if you have openings like that. I think I have excellent qualifications and you will find them described in the resume which I have attached to this letter.

The five letters that stood out favorably were characterized by their simplicity. Here [on page 250] is a letter, fictitious of course, but enough like the letter I remember to give you an idea of the ones that created a favorable impression.

Thompson's effective letter, and three of the four others, followed a similar pattern:

(1) The first paragraph stated who the writer was and what he wanted;

(2) The second paragraph, sometimes the third, and in one case a fourth paragraph, indicated why the writer wrote to the employer and mentioned areas of mutual interest, special talents that might be of interest to employers, or other

February 1, 1986

Mr. Paul Boynton
Manager of Employment
The United States Oil Company
1 Chicago Plaza
Chicago, Illinois 60607

Dear Mr. Boynton:

This June I will receive a Bachelor of Science in Chemical Engineering from the University of Michigan, and I hope to work in process design or instrumentation. I was glad to see your description in Peterson's Engineering, Science, and Computer Jobs 1986,[2] soliciting applicants with my interests. I am enclosing a resume to help you evaluate my qualifications.

While I find all aspects of refining interesting, my special interest in process design and instrumentation developed while working as a laboratory assistant for Professor Juliard Smith, who teaches process design. I wrote my senior thesis under him on the subject of instrumentation, and part of what I wrote will be used in a textbook he is writing and editing.

Would it be possible to have an interview with you in Chicago during the week of March 1? To be even more specific, could it be arranged for 10 A.M. on Tuesday, March 3? I am going to be in Chicago that week, and this time and date would be best for me, but of course I would work out another time more convenient for you. In any event, I will call your office the week before to determine whether an interview can be worked out.

Sincerely yours,

Charles C. Thompson
1 Riverview Lane
Ann Arbor, Michigan 48106

factors relating to his qualifications that could be better described in a letter than in a resume; and

(3) A final paragraph suggested a course of action.

The fifth letter covered the same points in a different order. I remember it because it complemented a good but not outstanding resume. In that resume, [p. 252], a perceptive employer might see a person he would like, someone who is energetic and personable. Yet it didn't quite hang together because the work history and activities didn't seem to support what the writer wanted to do. But look at the letter that "made" the resume:

Mr. Paul Boynton, Manager of Employment
The United States Oil Company
1 Chicago Plaza
Chicago, Illinois 60607

March 10, 1986

Dear Mr. Boynton:

This June, following my graduation from the University of Puget Sound, I want to pursue a career in sales. Between April 10 and 23, I plan to call on leading companies whose products I would like to sell. The purpose of this letter is to determine whether you would like to have me include you in my itinerary.

Let me tell you why I believe I can sell. It seems to me that I am always selling. As a camp counselor, I persuaded the director to buy a fleet of small sailboats so I could start a sailing program. When our college housing co-op needed painting, I persuaded the members to give up a vacation to do the job. In thinking about how I enjoyed selling these and other projects, I decided to look into a sales career. I persuaded several sales representatives to let me spend a day or more traveling with them to see what it was like.

While with them I realized something more about myself that further convinced me I belong in sales. The best sales representatives were well organized, had high energy levels, and used their time efficiently, qualities I feel I have also. As evidence, I have enclosed a resume that outlines my accomplishments in college and during vacations.

I hope to hear from you, as United States Oil is in the top group of employers on my list.

Sincerely,

Lance Zarote

Encl: Resume

LANCE ZAROTE

Campus Address
101 Morril Hall
University of Puget Sound
Tacoma, Washington 95840
(206) 602-6206

Permanent Address
25 The Byway
Provincetown, Massachusetts
05840
(617) 206-6026

GOAL: A SALES CAREER

EDUCATION: UNIVERSITY OF PUGET SOUND Bachelor of Arts 1986

               Philosophy Major

               Business-related Courses
               Statistics   Introduction to Computers
               Economics   Calculus
               Accounting   English

EMPLOYMENT: UNIVERSITY OF PUGET SOUND (Work-Study Program)
               Dining Hall supervisor   1985–86
               Kitchen helper   1982–84

               OTHER WORK while in college
               Ma and Pa Motel, Tacoma—night clerk   1985
               Joe's Bar and Grill—weekend waiter & bartender
                                                            1984–86
               Baby-sitting, gardening, house cleaning   1981–86

               WATCHEE OUTEY SUMMER CAMP, Nome, Alaska
               Sailing coach and waterfront director   1985
               Counselor   1981–84

ACTIVITIES: CAMPUS
               Chair, Campus Chest Drive
               Intramural hockey, tennis, and volleyball

               LIVING UNIT
               House Manager, $25,000 budget
               Secretary
               Membership Committee

               CIVIC
               Reader-companion in nursing home
               Big Brother-Sister Program, Southside Youth Center

               CHURCH
               Choir
               Youth leader
               Sunday School Teacher

INTERESTS: Skiing   Music
               Chess   Dancing

An ordinary resume can become effective when attached to
a powerful letter.

Hard Work and Professional Typing Make a Good Letter

While only the five letters were effective, the rest of those who wrote could have done as well. The point is they didn't. Most people won't. Therein lies your opportunity, because, like Thompson and Zarote, you can write letters that set you apart. You don't have to create a literary masterpiece; just don't hastily knock off a letter with thoughts that wander all over the page. Write it and rewrite it, following Forbes's advice. Unless you are an exceptional typist, you are not good enough to type it yourself. Hire a professional. If you use a word processor, be sure the print is letter quality. Also, get an English teacher or someone in the word business to check your spelling, punctuation, and grammar. But be sure it is your letter. Somehow, a ghost-written letter always has a phony ring to it.

Don't Delegate the Job of Letter Writing

More important than style, however, is the thought process used in preparing letters and resumes. Don't shortchange yourself by delegating your thinking to someone else. When you write to employers, think about their needs; then think about yourself and what you offer, and relate this to what you would like to do. Putting your thoughts on paper—thoughtfully—will make you sort out your ideas and interrelate them. When you see them on paper they will talk back to you, at times to suggest better ideas, at other times to tell you that you are off the mark. To organize your ideas, create an outline. In other words, prepare a resume even if you decide not to use it. *The value of a resume is frequently more in its preparation than in its use.*

Resume Preparation

When you do give an employer your resume, make it a testimony to your ability to organize your thoughts. Remember, too, it must look sufficiently attractive to get an employer to read it. Unfortunately, most of the resumes I saw on employers' desks were just as unattractive as the letters; they had sloppy, crowded margins, were poorly organized, and were badly reproduced. At least 30 percent of the resumes had been put aside with hardly a glance because their physical appearance was awful. The rest got a twenty-second scan to see if they were worth studying.

Following are two resumes that pass the appearance test with flying colors. Let's see how they fare during a twenty-second scan and beyond.

Nancy Jones

Nancy Jones's resume has arrived at the desk of a laboratory director who needs an assistant to help run a quality-control laboratory in a pharmaceutical company.

With candidates far outnumbering openings in biology, the advertisement for the job has brought in hundreds of applications, and the director is wearily scanning them one by one to find the few that will be of interest to him. Conditions are not favorable for Nancy. She has to catch his eye with impressive qualifications or she is not going to get anywhere.

The director picks up Nancy's resume. Immediately, he is impressed, because it looks attractive. He thinks the resume reflects an orderly mind. Most resumes he has looked at just do not put it all together.

He begins to read. The job objective annoys him; it strikes him as being long-winded. Why couldn't she simply say she is interested in applied biology? What is this business about working with people? Is that there because she has doubts about biology?

If resumes are supposed to say only what needs to be said, what about this line?

Born January 6, 1964   5'7"   135 lbs.   Single   Excellent health

Does it say anything about her ability to do the job? The biologist doesn't think so. His eyes move down the page:

Education   Iowa State University, Ames, Iowa
             Bachelor of Science, June 1986
             Major: Biology   Concentration: Physiology
             GPA: 3.3 on a 4.0 scale

             Major Subjects   Minor Subjects
             Mammalian Physiology   Qualitative Analysis
             Vertebrate Anatomy   Quantitative Analysis
             Histology   Organic Chemistry
             Genetics   Biochemistry

She has used the outline form well, so he is able to take in a great deal of information in one look. She impresses him with her education.

Double spacing above and below her grade point average makes it stand out. However, if her average had not been quite as good, and if she had not wanted to feature it, she could have used single spacing to make it less conspicuous, like this:

Education   Iowa State University, Ames, Iowa
             Bachelor of Science, June 1986
             Major: Biology   Concentration: Physiology
             GPA: 2.7 on a 4.0 scale

Now that she has told him about her grades and her courses she wants to drive home the point that she was no ordinary student. She flags him down with the headline "Scholarships and Honors," and he sees her financial aid and

NANCY O. JONES

Present Address   After June 1, 1986
105 Belleville Place   1212 Centerline Road
Ames, Iowa 50011   Old Westbury, New York 11568
Phone: 515-924-6674   Phone: 516-544-7119

Born January 6, 1964   5'7"   135 lbs.   Single   Excellent health

Career   Research and development in most areas of applied
Objective   biology, with an opportunity to work with people as well

Education   Iowa State University, Ames, Iowa
                   Bachelor of Science, June 1986
                   Major: Biology   Concentration: Physiology

                   GPA: 3.3 on a 4.0 scale

Major Subjects	Minor Subjects
Mammalian Physiology	Qualitative Analysis
Vertebrate Anatomy	Quantitative Analysis
Histology	Organic Chemistry
Genetics	Biochemistry

Scholarships University Scholarship: $2850/year
and Honors   Iowa State Science and Research Award

                  Dean's List two semesters

Activities   Volunteer Probation Officer, 1983–84
                  Probation Department, Ames, Iowa

                  Tutor, Chemistry and Math, 1983–86
                  Central High School, Ames, Iowa

                  Member, Kappa Zeta social sorority

                  Women's Intercollegiate Hockey Team

Special   Familiarity with Spanish; PLC and FORTRAN computer
Skills   languages; typing

Work   Teaching Assistant and Laboratory Instructor
Experience   Freshman Biology   School year, 1985–86

                  Waitress, Four Seasons Restaurant
                  Catalina Island   Summers, 1984, 1985

The resume of Nancy O. Jones does not communicate her career-related
experience.

science awards, which make a favorable impression. Two times on the dean's list may not be important enough to set apart by double spacing, but it makes a modest impression.

Up until now, Nancy has made a favorable impression overall. The director is ready to take in the next batch of information:

Activities	Volunteer Probation Officer, 1983–84
	Probation Department, Ames, Iowa
	Tutor, Chemistry and Math, 1983–85
	Central High School, Ames, Iowa
	Member, Kappa Zeta social sorority
	Women's Intercollegiate Hockey Team

She almost loses him by featuring her work as a probation officer. That is not of primary interest to him, but through good spacing and placement, she draws his eye to the next item, which states that she has tutored chemistry and math. Unfortunately, Nancy now loses him permanently by ranking tutoring along with the sorority and the hockey team. He guesses she has made her major statement about biology, and so he turns to the next resume.

Good as it is, Nancy Jones's resume could be improved by reorganization. Her tutoring in chemistry and her two years as a teaching assistant and laboratory instructor in biology reveal more than an academic interest in biology. They should be featured. Everything related to biology and any other information of possible use to the employer should be put under a new marginal headline and statement, as follows:

Career-related Experience	Biology Lab Instructor and Teaching Assistant
	Freshman Biology (1985–86)
	Chemistry and Mathematics Tutor
	Central High School, Ames, Iowa (1983–86)

Skills and Interests	Microscopy	Computer Languages:
	Electron Microscopy	FORTRAN, PL/1,
	Histology	COBOL
	Spectrum Analysis	Statistics
	Small-Animal Surgery	

Now, the director is able to see things she can do. "Good," he says to himself, "She can use an electron microscope. We need someone with that skill."

By no means should Nancy eliminate mention of the hockey team, but since she is applying for a professional job, the first bait to throw out is credentials; they testify to her ability to do the work. After that, what may sink the hook is how the employer sees her as a person. He may have picked out bits here and there that testify to her diligence, but the picking out depends on chance reading; it would be best not to leave anything to chance. With a slightly different presentation, she might ensure that he receives an impression of her diligence.

There are other areas she could strengthen, things she has underplayed or totally neglected to mention. Sticking the waitress job in down at the bottom of the page is almost an apology for it. She may also have had other jobs, such as baby-sitting, household work, or door-to-door sales, that she belittles in her mind and has not even mentioned. Mention of such things might make a good impression on an employer looking for somebody who is not afraid to work and who is mature for her years.

If we quizzed Nancy, we might find that she could put something like this on her resume:

Scholarships and Financial Support	90% self-supporting through college as follows: University Scholarship: $2850/year Iowa State Science and Research Award
	Waitress, Four Seasons Restaurant Catalina Island (Summers, 1984, 1985)
	Teaching and instructing, baby-sitting, home maintenance, selling

And this, because her activities tell something about her as a person:

Activities	Volunteer Probation Officer (1983–84) Kappa Zeta social sorority Women's Intercollegiate Hockey Team Skiing, sailing, singing, tennis

Double spacing has been cut down so as not to overemphasize the less important items, yet a string of other things not terribly important in themselves has been inserted to support the impression of an active, interesting person. Sometimes you want to leave an impression, at other times you want to emphasize a qualification. For example, Nancy wanted to feature her studies, and the way she brought them out by listing them in a column was good. If she had listed them like this, they would not have stood out:

> Major Subjects: Mammalian Physiology, Vertebrate Anatomy, Histology, Genetics
> Minor Subjects: Quantitative Analysis, Qualitative Analysis, Organic Chemistry, Biochemistry

On the next page, you will see the Nancy Jones resume as she might have revised it to emphasize the strong points that would have been of interest to that director looking for a resourceful assistant. The added emphasis might have made the difference that would have landed the job for her.

Nancy's revised resume is pure outline, devoid of prose. It works well for her. When she states that she has studied quantitative and qualitative analysis, and knows PL/1 and FORTRAN, a scientist reading her resume knows what this means.

Janet Smith

Janet Smith, whose resume [is on page 260], has a different problem in presenting her qualifications. She needs to *describe* what she did in order to tell an employer about her qualifications, so her resume calls for a mixture of key words and prose to get her message across. Yet prose can destroy the effect of an outline. The solution lies in imitating newspaper editors, who use headlines and subheadlines to attract readers. Like a newspaper, a resume should lend itself to skimming, so the reader can quickly pick up a good overview of what is important. Then the reader can select specific things that interest him, and read further. There is an art to using headlines, but Janet Smith hasn't mastered it, at least not in the resume she used to apply for a job with Hermann Langfelder, a hard-bitten

---

NANCY O. JONES

Present Address	After June 1, 1986
105 Belleville Place	1212 Centerline Road
Ames, Iowa 50011	Old Westbury, New York 11568
Phone: 515-924-6674	Phone: 516-544-7119

Career Objective   Research and development

Education
Iowa State University, Ames, Iowa
Bachelor of Science, June 1986
Major: Biology   Concentration: Phsyiology

GPA: 3.3 on a 4.0 scale

Major Subjects	Minor Subjects
Mammalian Physiology	Qualitative Analysis
Vertebrate Anatomy	Quantitative Analysis
Histology	Organic Chemistry
Genetics	Biochemistry

Career-related Experience
Biology Lab Instructor and Teaching Assistant
Freshman Biology (1985–86)

Chemistry and Mathematics Tutor
Central High School, Ames, Iowa (1983–86)

Skills and Interests

Microscopy	Computer Languages:
Electron Microscopy	FORTRAN, PL/1
Histology	COBOL
Spectrum Analysis	Statistics
Small-Animal Surgery	

Scholarships and Financial Support
90% self-supporting through college as follows:
University Scholarship: $2850/year
Iowa State Science and Research Award

Waitress, Four Seasons Restaurant
Catalina Island (Summers, 1984, 1985)

Teaching and instructing, baby-sitting, home maintenance, selling

Activities
Volunteer Probation Officer (1983–84)
Kappa Zeta social sorority
Women's Intercollegiate Hockey Team
Skiing, sailing, singing, tennis

The revised resume of Nancy O. Jones effectively features her career-related experience in a separate section.

old hand with thirty years in personnel and labor relations in the machinery business. He picked up her resume and read:

CAREER OBJECTIVE	A challenging position in personnel administration requiring organizational ability and an understanding of how people function in business and industry.

That was pure baloney, and he choked on it. He thought of the hours he had spent in meetings, listening to a lot of hot air. "Challenging, my foot!" he muttered. Then he read the bit about her organizational ability and her understanding of how people function in business and industry. "I've been at this business for thirty years," he groused to himself, "and I still can't figure out how people function in industry. But *she* knows all about it."

Beware of Misleading Headlines

"Well, let's see what she's done," he said to himself, and then his eyes fell on "UNIVERSAL METHODIST CHURCH." That did it! He didn't want to bring any do-gooder into his factory to preach. He rejected her. And the fault was hers, in using the headline.

Janet's job at the church was administrative, not ministerial, and the church didn't care whether she was Jewish, Catholic, or agnostic. Only in its ministerial work does the Methodist Church need Methodists. But people—Langfelder and the rest of us—respond to symbols and make snap judgments on the basis of symbols. Janet had put the symbol of the church—its name—in a heading, when she could have done something better.

When you lay out your resume, think of symbols. Imagine you are a newspaper editor who wants to put a story across. As an editor planning headlines, you must imagine yourself in the position of the reader. Ask yourself, "What words will catch the reader's eye? What words will put him off?"

Use words that fit the job in question, and play down those that can lead an employer to think of you in terms that don't relate to the job. Ask yourself, "Does this say something to the employer?" Janet Smith missed the obvious. Her job titles would have made perfect headlines to attract Langfelder, and some of her duties would have yielded key words to send appropriate messages. The following arrangement would have been more effective for her.

WORK EXPERIENCE	ASSISTANT PERSONNEL OFFICER 1983–85 Universal Methodist Church 1 Central Square New York, New York 10027 Interviewing, placement, grievances, and training of applicants and employees in the clerical and support services of the church organization. Developed programs for the career advancement of employees.

JANET V. SMITH
111 Main Street
North Hero, Vermont 05073
(802) 772-4325

CAREER
OBJECTIVE

A challenging position in personnel administration requiring organizational ability and an understanding of how people function in business and industry.

EDUCATION

PURDUE UNIVERSITY
Hammond, Indiana
Master of Industrial Relations   June 1986

SMITH COLLEGE
Northampton, Massachusetts
Bachelor of Arts, Magna Cum Laude   June 1981

WORK
EXPERIENCE

UNIVERSAL METHODIST CHURCH
1 Central Square
New York, New York 10027
Assistant Personnel Officer.   1983–85
Responsible for interviewing applicants for clerical positions within the organization and for placing those who demonstrated appropriate skills, for accepting and dealing with employees' grievances, and for developing programs on career advancement.

CORTEN STEEL COMPANY
Akron, Ohio 44309
Assistant, Personnel Office.   1981–83
Responsible for all correspondence of Personnel Director and for interviewing some custodial applicants and referring them to appropriate supervisors for further interviewing.

BORG-WARNER, INC.
Ithaca, New York 14850
Assembly linewoman.   Summer 1980
Assembled parts of specialized drive chains in company with thirty other men and women.

COMMUNITY
SERVICE

PLANNED PARENTHOOD
North Hero, Vermont
Counselor.   Summers of 1978 and 1979
Explained various aspects of family planning and provided birth control information to clients of Planned Parenthood. Made referrals to other counselors and physicians where appropriate.

AUXILIARY
SKILLS

French: Fluent. Knowledge of office procedures.
Knowledge of IBM 360 Series.

The resume of Janet V. Smith misleads the reader with irrelevant headings.

ASSISTANT, PERSONNEL OFFICE
1981–83
Corten Steel Company
10 Lake Street
Akron, Ohio 44309
Interviewing, referring, and correspondence as an assistant
for Personnel Director. Responsible for all correspondence
and for interviewing some custodial applicants and referring
them to supervisors for further interviews.

Let's suppose that Janet Smith has a chance to submit a second resume to Langfelder. This time, she uses headlines that pinpoint the ideas she most wants to get across, so that he makes it past the Universal Methodist Church and gets down to the assembly line. "Hey, now, look at that!" he thinks. "She's worked out there on the floor. That means she's heard all the language and knows the gripes and the tedium. We have a lot of women in this factory, and it might be a good thing to have a down-to-earth, smart woman on my staff." (His sexism may have been showing, but this kind of employer is alive and kicking somewhere out there, and you may have to deal with him.)

What if Janet Smith wanted a job in the computer industry and had had ten years' experience with IBM? Employers are impressed by "graduates" of companies like IBM who are known as leaders in their fields. Ten years with them is significant. It might make sense to present her experience this way:

EXPERIENCE: 1976–86
IBM Corporation
Binghamton, New York
Assistant Personnel Officer

Were she an engineer after a technical job that could use her IBM experience, highlighting the name of the company would have been a good idea. Imagine employers giving the resume a twenty-second scan. What words should you use and how should they be placed to catch the eye and make employers want to read further?

Mark Meyers—The Functional Resume

Janet Smith and Nancy Jones were lucky. Their training and experience translated into satisfactory headlines to highlight their experience, but that doesn't always work. Sometimes the only way to get a message across is to create a resume based on functions. Mark Meyers, whose resume [is on p. 264], adopted that technique to help him get a job in community recreation.

When he began to write a resume, he tried time and time again to get his message across in a conventional resume in which he first listed his education,

JANET V. SMITH
111 Main Street
North Hero, Vermont 05073
(802) 772-4325

CAREER INTERESTS	Personnel Administration and Labor Relations
EDUCATION	PURDUE UNIVERSITY June 1986 Hammond, Indiana Master of Industrial Relations
	SMITH COLLEGE June 1981 Northampton, Massachusetts Bachelor of Arts, Magna Cum Laude
WORK EXPERIENCE	ASSISTANT PERSONNEL OFFICER. 1983–85 Universal Methodist Church 1 Central Square New York, New York 10027 Interviewing, placement, grievances, and training of applicants and employees in the clerical and support services of the church organization. Developed programs for the career advancement of employees.
	ASSISTANT, PERSONNEL OFFICE. 1981–83 Corten Steel Company Akron, Ohio 44309 Interviewing, referring, and correspondence as an assistant for Personnel Director. Responsible for all correspondence and for interviewing some custodial applicants and referring them to supervisors for further interviews.
	ASSEMBLY LINEWOMAN. Summer 1980 Borg-Warner Inc. Ithaca, New York 14850 Factory work experience on an assembly line. Worked with a team of thirty other men and women.
COMMUNITY SERVICE	COUNSELOR. Summers 1978 and 1979 Planned Parenthood North Hero, Vermont 05073 Explained various aspects of family planning and provided birth control information to clients of Planned Parenthood. Made referrals to other counselors and physicians where appropriate.
AUXILIARY SKILLS	French: Fluent. Knowledge of office procedures. Knowledge of IBM 360 Series.

The revised resume for Janet V. Smith stresses what she did rather than the less important point of where she did it.

then his experiences in chronological order, and finally his activities, hobbies, and interests. But writing it conventionally raised all sorts of problems. He wanted to highlight his public relations and promotion experience, some of which he had been paid for and some not. Some of it had also been secondary to a primary assignment. Dividing up this experience and placing bits and pieces of it in various parts of the resume to make it conform to a conventional style diluted its impact. Also, his athletic ability and experience would mean a great deal to an employer in his field, but how could he show it effectively? Some of it had been gained as a participant, some through training, and some as a coach. Could he expect an employer to sift through the various sections of the resume to find out all he had done in athletics? (Remember, you can only count on an employer giving a resume a quick scan before deciding whether or not to study it more fully.)

His solution, as you can see, was to feature the functions of the job he wanted and then describe things he had done that pertained to each area. Thus, under each function he developed the equivalent of a mini resume.

Preparing a Resume for a Specific Job

Mark stated his case well, but you can't get blood from a stone. He found he had to look outside his field, because jobs in it were virtually nonexistent due to cutbacks in government funding. In his search, he ran across the following job listing from the publisher of a magazine for parents:

EDITORIAL SECRETARY

B.A. in Liberal Arts

Interested in childhood training. Well organized, outstanding language skills. Typing and clerical skills, potential to use electronic text-editing equipment. Reporting to Coordinating Editor, Happy Days magazine. Assist in all editorial functions. Evidence of creativity essential. Entry-level position with career potential.

Can you put yourself in his shoes, analyze the job, and devise a resume that speaks to the stated needs of this employer? The clue to doing it is to go through the job description and step by step take your cue from the employer. Right off you will hit a bit of a snare because the employer has specified a B.A., while Mark has a B.S. His drama minor might give him appropriate credentials, however. If he shows his education something like the example below, it might reflect the liberal background the employer apparently prefers:

EDUCATION   HOBOKEN UNIVERSITY, B.S., 1982

Major: Recreation   Minor: Drama

MARK MEYERS

1414 South Harp Road
Dover, Delaware 19901
(501) 267-3087

CAREER INTEREST
Community recreation.

RECREATION PROGRAMMING EXPERIENCE
Planned and implemented programs in stagecraft and drama;
assisted with programming in ceramics, photography, and
physical fitness for Dover Youth Bureau summer program.
Summer, 1981.
Lectured and led tours at Atlantic County (Delaware) Park nature
trail and visitors' center. Prepared slides to illustrate lecture;
helped in construction of nature exhibits. Summer, 1980.
Coordinated men's intramural sports competitions for Hoboken
University. Had responsibility for equipment and scheduling.
1979–81.

PUBLIC RELATIONS AND PROMOTION EXPERIENCE
Directed publicity efforts of University Drama Club for several
productions. Developed innovative techniques—such as a costumed
cast parade to arouse interest in an avant-garde staging of "Alice
in Wonderland," which gained campuswide attention. 1979–80.
Advertised in various media and became familiar with advertising
methods, including writing news releases, taping radio
announcements, designing graphics for posters and fliers. Drama
Club, 1980–82; men's sports, 1979–82.

LEADERSHIP AND ATHLETIC ABILITIES
Trained in outdoor leadership and survival skills by Outward Bound.
Summer, 1978.
Coached hockey and basketball. Dover Youth Bureau, 1981.
Participate in hockey, swimming, backpacking.

RESEARCH AND EVALUATION ABILITIES
Prepared college research project on the recreational needs of
residents of a Hoboken neighborhood. Designed questionnaire to
solicit residents' own perceptions of their needs; interviewed
residents and local officials. Fall semester, 1981.
Reported on effectiveness of Dover Youth Bureau programming.
Summer, 1981.

OFFICE SKILLS
Dealt with unhappy and irate customers at McGary's Department
Store, Dover. Worked at service desk, tracking down problems and
rectifying errors. Summer, 1977.
Typing and use of office machinery.

EDUCATION
Bachelor of Science, June, 1982   Major: Recreation
Hoboken University, Hoboken, New Jersey   Minor: Drama

The resume of Mark Meyers illustrates the functional style.

<u>Humanities courses:</u>

Introduction to Dramatic Literature
British Drama to 1700
History of Theater
Playwriting
Introduction to Poetry
Shakespeare
English History

Next, the job calls for an interest in childhood training, then language skills, and so on. Each specification suggests a headline for a resume. Mark faces another stumbling block in being able to demonstrate an interest in childhood training, since his experience was only with older youths. Since a resume makes points by stating facts, he cannot demonstrate an interest in childhood training in his resume because he lacks the appropriate experience. However, he *can* describe his interest in the letter that usually goes hand in glove with a resume. He has a good basis for doing it, because the field of recreation certainly has much to do with the entire range of human development from childhood on. He should be able to point out corollaries in his education and experience with the work being done in childhood training, and he could check a library for information about childhood training to help develop the corollaries. Above all, he should read the magazine and try to tie in as many of his experiences as possible with the purpose of the magazine.

With his interest in childhood training brought out in a letter to complement his resume, he might then proceed to develop his outline as follows:

EXPERIENCE   HUMAN DEVELOPMENT

<u>Dover Youth Bureau</u>. Planned and implemented programs in drama, photography, athletics, health. Summer, 1981.
<u>Research Project</u>. Studied recreational needs of a Hoboken neighborhood. Interviewed residents, developed questionnaire. Project provided an insight into the family life and problems of parents in a neighborhood setting. Fall semester, 1981.
<u>Outdoor Leadership Training</u>. Practical experience in human development through a knowledge of nature and survival skills.

LANGUAGE SKILLS AND CREATIVITY

<u>Writing</u>. Wrote releases, developed advertising, and prepared radio announcements for Drama Club, men's sports programs, and other events. Wrote report on Hoboken research project. 1979–82.
<u>Lecturing</u>. Gave talks and led tours at Atlantic County (Delaware) Park nature trail and visitors' center. Summer, 1980.

Audiovisual. Prepared slides for audiovisual presentation for visitors' center. 1980.

Promotional. Created innovative techniques—such as costume parade of cast—to arouse interest in avant-garde staging of "Alice in Wonderland," which gained campuswide attention. 1980.

Design. Designed posters, fliers, and other graphics for sporting events, plays, and other campus events. 1979–82. Constructed nature exhibits at nature center. 1980.

CLERICAL AND ADMINISTRATIVE

Clerical. Typing and use of office machinery, McGary's Department Store. Summer, 1977.

Administration. Responsible for equipment, scheduling of programs, and coordinating of competitions. Hoboken University, 1979–81.

The functional resume allows you to develop a different message for each job, or type of job, you wish to apply for. Different functions can be highlighted, depending on what the job requires, and your specific experiences rearranged under different headings. It gives you the flexibility you need if your experience has been varied and diverse.

Bruce Gregory Robertson—A Resume Reflecting an Active Mind and Body

Finally, there are merit employers who are interested in candidates not so much for what they know as for what they can learn. They want to see a resume that reflects an active person with an active mind. Bruce Gregory Robertson is such a person, and he has designed his resume [page 268] as much to reflect his personality as his experience. . . .

The Job Objective

"Do I have to have a job objective?" According to my calculations, as of this writing I have been a career counselor for 2,028 weeks, and I have been asked that question at least six times a week, except for the 117 weeks when I was on vacation. When I answer, "No, I don't like the heading JOB OBJECTIVE," the sigh of relief is audible. The job seekers think I have let them off the hook for one of the most important parts of a resume. I haven't. With rare exceptions, a resume should open with an objective—it's the way it is phrased that can be changed.

I show them the preceding Robertson, Meyers, and Smith resumes and tell them that I prefer the headline CAREER INTEREST because it leads to a simple and direct way of stating the purpose of the resume. For example, I suggest they try rewriting the Robertson and revised Smith statements of interest as job objectives to see if they don't find it awkward. After a struggle they come up with the kind of baloney found in the unrevised Jones and Smith resumes.

They listen politely. I may have helped them with a minor problem of phrasing, but I know that I really haven't dealt with their question. Then they tell me what I already knew: They don't want to state a goal because they don't know what they want to do. I ask them to imagine themselves as the employers reading their resumes. If theirs is like the revised Nancy Jones resume that is so obviously slanted toward biology, then employers can figure out what the resume is for without a stated objective. However, I wouldn't fool with a resume that didn't tell me at the outset what it was all about. When I have to start studying a resume to guess what the writer wants, I throw it in the wastebasket.

Next I point to the Zarote and Robertson resumes, which wouldn't make any sense without a statement of purpose. And I can't get up much enthusiasm for a letter as a substitute for an objective. A letter stating a purpose accompanied by a resume without purpose is a wasted letter.

I remember a young woman who, on short notice, got a chance to be interviewed by a recruiter from a large department store. Knowing very little about merchandising, she headed for the nearest department store, where several managers were kind enough to give her information and the loan of their trade journals. In three hours of investigation, her eyes were opened to an industry in which people pursued careers in training, employee relations, promotion, credit, public relations, merchandising, and other occupations. Several of these looked interesting, so thanks to word processing, she easily changed a few things on her resume, then listed her objective as:

CAREER INTERESTS: Training, promotion, and public relations in a retail setting.

Like most of us, her range of aptitudes was wide, so like a chameleon she showed the recruiter only those that seemed to match retailing.

One Page or Two?

If a resume can be kept to one page, so much the better. The length depends on the message. In reading resumes where everything is jammed on one page with none of the white space or headings that can make them attractive and readable, I have wearied of trying to find information and have given up. On the other hand, it has never been the least bit tiring to lift a piece of paper and turn to a second page while scanning an interesting resume. A resume is an outline. It needs white space. It needs headings that stand out. Don't sacrifice them for some arbitrary notion about one-page maximums.

BRUCE GREGORY ROBERTSON

Home Address
105 Comstock Drive
Pierre, South Dakota 57501
(605) 257-7236

College Address
5 Erasmus Drive
St. Paul, Minnesota 55101
(612) 220-2020

CAREER INTERESTS
- The marketing of products or services in industries such as banking, publishing, and retailing.

EDUCATIONAL BACKGROUND
- Macalester College, St. Paul, Minnesota   A.B., May 1986
  Major: English   Minor: Economics
  Honors: Dean's List   1985–86

EMPLOYMENT
- Sales - Southwestern Publishing Company, Memphis, Tennessee.
  Educational dictionary sales to families with high school pupils: summer 1984 in Santa Fe, New Mexico; 1985 in Asheville, North Carolina; assisted in training new salesmen.

- Administrative and Clerical - Temporary Help, Inc. Typing and other business machine operations, bookkeeping, clerking, complaint adjustments; short-term assignments with auto dealers, banks, real estate operations, schools, and similar employers: summer 1983; part-time 1984.

- Miscellaneous - Camp counselor, stock clerk in grocery store, baby-sitter, newspaper boy. From high school on have earned money for clothes, travel, and purchase and maintenance of an automobile.

ACTIVITIES
- Vice President, Seven-Come-Eleven investment club
- Varsity basketball
- Coach and tutor, St. Paul Concordia Boys Club
- Debate Club
- Book and Bottle literary club

SKILLS
- Typing
- PLC and FORTRAN computer languages
- German: fluent

HONORS
- Dakota Interstate Scholarship
- Hubert H. Humphrey First Prize, Minnesota Intercollegiate Debate

INTERESTS
- Public speaking and debate
- Investments
- Writing
- Parachute jumping

A resume designed more to reflect an active, energetic personality than specific experience.

Additional Advice About Resumes

No matter how you develop your message, test it before you send it to employers. Get friends to give you a critique of your resume or vita, especially if they are in an occupation in which you hope to find a job. A word of caution, however. Unless you guide them, their critique may relate more to the ritual than to the message. One job hunter had modeled a resume after Janet Smith's. The critic took a red pencil and put all the dates of employment in the left-hand margin. That would have been a good idea if it had indicated long years of experience with a company such as 3M, signifying considerable experience with one of the best-managed companies in the country. But the dates in question referred to short-time summer jobs, which were of no consequence to the message and cluttered the margin with information that distracted from the headlines.

One way to get a resume criticized is to hold it up a few feet from the reader and ask for comments on its appearance. Does it look neat? Is the layout pleasing? Does it look easy to read? Is the print good-looking?

Next, give the critics the resume to read. Let them make all the comments they want. You may pick up valuable ideas for improving its style and layout, but be careful you don't get caught up in inconsequentials. What you really want is to have your critics look at the resume as if they didn't know you. You might even show them a resume with an alias, then ask:

What qualifications does this person have?

What do you see this person doing with these qualifications?

What kind of an employer would want to hire this person?

Does the resume project an image of a certain kind of person? What kind? Aggressive? Thoughtful? Energetic? What?

In other words, ask your critics the most important question about your resume: "What message do you get about me?"

---

[1] Daniel Melcher, *Book Publishing* (New York: Publishers Weekly). Pamphlet, out of print.

[2] Christopher Billy, ed., *Engineering, Science, and Computer Jobs* (Princeton, NJ: Peterson's Guides). Annual.

[3] Christopher Billy, ed., *Business and Management Jobs* (Princeton, NJ: Peterson's Guides). Annual.

[4] *CPC Annual* (Bethlehem, PA: College Placement Council, Inc.). Annual.

[5] Malcolm Forbes, *How to Write a Business Letter* (Elmsford, NY: International Paper Co., 1979). Handout and advertisement. [Editor's note: Forbes' complete remarks about how to write an effective business letter are reprinted on pages 115–18 in this anthology.]

Ten Tough Questions about Resumes

YANA PARKER

Yana Parker is a free-lance employment
consultant based in California.

1. "How do I account for that year when I wasn't employed?"

2. "What if I was 'just a housewife' for 20 years?"

3. "What do I do about dates on my job history . . . when I had two or
three little jobs with a month or so in between?"

4. "What if I was called a 'secretary' and never got the pay or job title
for all the things I really did?"

5. "Can't I skip the Job Objective? I don't want to limit myself."

6. "What if I don't have any work experience in the exact job that I
want now?"

7. "How long should a resume be? One page?"

8. "What if my experience was from a long time ago?"

9. "What if they insist on a chronological resume and a lot of dates?"
and finally . . .

10. "How should I use my resume?"

1. "How Do I Account for that Year When I Wasn't Employed?"

Tell the truth, creatively.
BE POSITIVE; refer to what you WERE doing rather than to what you WEREN'T
doing. Don't say "unemployed" because it MIGHT convey an UN-truth about
you, that you aren't interested in working, when in fact we both know you WANT
to work. Instead, look at what you WERE doing, allow yourself a reasonable
degree of "being human," and emphasize the positive aspects of what you did
that year.

EXAMPLE: Candidly from my own experience . . . in 1974 I was traveling
across the country "trying to figure out what to do with the rest of my life," coping

TEN TOUGH QUESTIONS ABOUT RESUMES   By Yana Parker. From *The Damn Good Resume Guide* by
Yana Parker. Copyright © 1983. Used with permission of Ten Speed Press, Box 7123, Berkeley, CA
94707.

with an unexpected traumatic illness, making some embarrassing and painful and wonderful experiments in group-living, and looking—sometimes desperately—for work that I could feel good about. I got by on unemployment for awhile, Medi-Cal for the illness, off-and-on Kelly Girl work, and loans from Mom. It was a very tough year.

What does it say on my resume?

"1974—Travel and independent study"

And that's true! I've just expressed it with more dignity than I was feeling at the time. I don't need to tell anybody, on my resume, what a bummer that year was. And believe me, I learned enough to justify calling it "independent study"!

2. "What If I Was 'Just a Housewife' for 20 Years?"

Change your attitude, for starters (more below);
Give yourself credit for all you've accomplished and learned;
Then, get help expressing it all creatively.

Every woman I've worked with, who started with "just a housewife" self-image, ended up with greatly improved self-esteem after doing a DAMN GOOD RESUME.[1] When you discard the myth that only PAID work is valuable, and start listing everything you ever did (home management activities, volunteer work, hobby and craft work, personal growth projects, reading of all kinds), an impressive body of skills, knowledge and experience emerges.

The task then is simply to identify what skills are demonstrated in all that, and learning to express them in world-of-work terms. Get help and support from places like "Displaced Homemaker" centers and community Women's Centers for the needed attitude change, and help in analyzing and writing about your skills. . . .

3. "What Do I Do about Dates on My Job History? . . . When I Had Two or Three Little Jobs, with a Month or so in Between?"

Delete very short-term jobs, OR
Combine several short jobs in one description. . . .
Stick to YEARS rather than precise dates by-the-month. Rounding off to years is a good general practice anyway:

- it looks better

- it keeps the reader from doing a lot of detailed arithmetic with your work record when you want them to focus on your SKILLS. . . .

[1A "damn good resume" is Yana Parker's term for a functional resume that starts with a clearly stated job objective and then presents an assessment of skills and experience in terms of that objective.]

4. "What If I Was Called a 'Secretary' and Never Got the Pay or the Job Title for All the Things I Really Did?"

You don't have to use THEIR job title! So MUCH fine and important work is done every day in millions of offices by intelligent women who aren't being adequately paid or recognized for the high levels of their skills and responsibilities.

"COME THE REVOLUTION . . . " Meanwhile, feel free to create a fairer job title that reflects the highest level of skills you used as a so-called "secretary."

EXAMPLE: One client's old resume listed "secretary" positions five times. Her NEW DAMN GOOD RESUME refers to those same jobs with the following reasonable, fair job titles:

> office supervisor
> director's assistant
> technical writer
> executive secretary
> administrative assistant

5. "Can't I Just Skip the Job Objective? I Don't Want to Limit Myself."

NO!

Clearly stating your Objective serves to FOCUS you, not to box you in. It's critically important to KNOW WHAT YOUR OBJECTIVE IS, as explicitly as possible, and to state it, and then to have everything else on your resume directly relate to it. THAT'S what makes it a DAMN GOOD RESUME.

And remember, you could have TWO or more resumes, each with different objectives. . . .

6. "What If I Don't Have Any Work Experience in the Exact Job that I Want to Do Now?"

A DAMN GOOD RESUME is the perfect format for you. If you really want a particular kind of job and are confident that you'd do well at it if only you got the chance, it's just about certain that you have enough transferable skills to show that you're a good candidate for the job.

Here's what your resume needs to show:

Transferable skills from paid or unpaid experience.

A credible progression from where you've been to where you want to go now. (If there's a leap the size of the Grand Canyon from where you are to the position you want, then be willing to state a current objective that bridges the gap.)

Evidence of motivation & potential—experience that used the same kind of personality traits and strengths that your Ideal Job calls for. . . .

7. "How Long Should a Resume Be?"

One page is best, occasionally two. And it WILL all fit—even if you have 25 years of fantastic experience. A good resume is like a handful of Aces . . . you DON'T deal out the whole deck! Prospective employers don't WANT your whole life history; they only need to see the essential points that make you qualified, plus the unique experience and attitudes that make you SPECIAL. Say the minimum, powerfully.

8. "What If My Experience Was from a Long Time Ago?"

The employer's attention is turned to your SKILLS, which appear first, rather than WHEN you acquired them, with THE DAMN GOOD RESUME format. Also, you can include your more recent activities of all kinds and show how the skills you acquired are transferable to the job you now seek.

9. "What If They Insist on a Chronological Resume, with All Those Dates in Order?"

You could point out that your resume DOES include a list of your jobs and the years you did them; it's at the end, and it's condensed. OR, you may decide to go for the chronological resume instead of the D.G.R. format. Some knowledgeable folks insist that a chronological resume is sometimes better—like when you're staying in the same field and trying to move up the career ladder. . . .

This question usually comes up in connection with a Job Application . . . which you are going to AVOID filling out until after you've had a personal interview with the Hiring Person. THEN attach your resume instead of filling out the "Job History" section, which is invariably designed to your disadvantage. You DO NOT have to give all that information before being interviewed.

EXCEPTION: for civil service jobs, we're advised, your application won't get processed unless you fill it out fully. In that case, don't fight it . . . do it THEIR way!

10. "How Should I Use My Resume?"

a) AS A "FIRST DRAFT" MODEL FOR A TAILORED RESUME. Always, when you apply for a specific advertised job opening, rewrite your resume using:

- THEIR job title as your Job Objective (word for word)
- THEIR stated skill requirements as your Skill Areas

b) AS A LAST RESORT FIRST CONTACT. When there's no way around it and you simply can't make the initial contact any other way. (But be creative . . . there usually is another way to reach the Hiring Person.) Send an excellent cover letter along with your resume.

c) BEFORE YOUR JOB INTERVIEW. To get you focused and clear. Tuck the resume in your pocket to look at just before you enter the new workplace; it will remind you of your objective and of your skills, in case you tend to space out about them.

d) AFTER YOUR JOB INTERVIEW. You can leave it with the employer as a concrete reminder and documentation of the information you provided during the interview. DO NOT hand it to the employer at the beginning of your meeting; she'll be looking at it instead of at you!

e) WHEN YOU MAKE PHONE CALLS TO STRANGERS for job information research. When lining up informational interviews, and such—especially if your morale is flagging—keep your DAMN GOOD RESUME in front of you as you work, to remind you of your skills and accomplishments, and to keep your mind from going blank about your objective.

The Style and Appearance of the Cover Letter

MARCIA R. FOX

When she wrote the book from which this selection is taken, Marcia R. Fox directed career counseling and job placement at New York University's Graduate School of Public Administration.

To an employer, your cover letter is the sole clue to your proficiency with the English language. Not only must your letters be grammatically and typographically *perfect* but you must also write them in an appropriate style.

1. Aim for simple but precise language. For example: "I am a forthcoming master's in electrical engineering interested in an engineering position with your company." Such virtues of simplicity were ignored in another version of this applicant's cover letter.

> Having graduated from the University of Colorado with a master's in electrical engineering, I have decided to pursue a career in a company such as yours.

2. If there is a reason for your particular interest in a certain employer, say so directly and succinctly. For example: "Professor John Sears, my research adviser, has repeatedly told me of your leadership in the field of prenatal nutrition."

3. Strive for precise, specific language. Avoid trite clichés and empty phrases:

> Employment at a highly diversified company such as yours represents a *challenging and stimulating beginning* to a career in business as well as the opportunity to significantly augment one's education.

> Although I am young, I have learned a great deal about human nature. I am in search of a *meaningful growth position* where I can use my talents and skills in a *responsible, challenging way*. I am a *creative thinker*.

Avoid vague terms such as "meaningful growth opportunity" and "creative thinker." Substitute "management trainee" or another specific term for "meaningful growth opportunity" or a "responsible" or "challenging" position. It's not the employer's job to figure out what you might find challenging; he has specific jobs to fill. Tell him what you want and assess whether or not the opportunity is meaningful at the interview!

4. Be concise. The best antidote for excessive wordiness is to read over a draft of your letter with a red pen in hand. Be prepared to justify each word. Notice, for example, how only the last sentence of the following paragraph is pertinent or substantive:

> I understand that your personal obligations in combination with the huge volume of applications through which you must wade, leave you with a limited amount of time to spend on each. With this in mind, thank you for your time and consideration.

In trying to identify with the employer's burden, the applicant unwittingly took up even more of the employer's time!

5. Use the active voice. The only way to sound energetic is to use the active voice. For example, state:

"I would welcome the opportunity for an interview," not "An interview at your convenience is requested." Write, "I acquired a skill in economic analysis from these courses," not "From these courses, a skill in economic analysis was acquired."

An applicant's discomfort at actually writing a cover letter or even applying for a job can often result in excessive abruptness.

To help you hear the tone of your letter, wait a day before mailing it out, or have someone else read your letters aloud or silently.

Many professionals equate a professional style with a cool tone. The ideal cover letter, however, conveys the person behind the applicant. To create the rapport that will win you interviews, you must reveal some human warmth. Read the following example aloud to hear the tone of commanding coldness to avoid:

> Contact me if you have a suitable opening.

Do not be afraid to sound enthusiastic for fear it will be misinterpreted as feigned interest by a cynical employer. Always convey your enthusiasm professionally, by anchoring it to a credential or relevant fact. For example: "As a result of my fascination with gerontology, I obtained an H.E.W. fellowship to write a dissertation on the problems of indigent elderly women."

Remember that the employer is the stranger who must be persuaded to interview you. Problems of inappropriate tone may occur if you confuse him with another group or person. For example, naïve job hunters often mistakenly perceive the employer as a career counselor or as a "buddy" with whom to share fantasies. Don't close a letter this way: "I would very much appreciate talking with you so as to obtain a clearer perspective on my career goals." It is not the employer's responsibility to counsel you. Get the advice elsewhere!

A second problem arises when applicants approach the employer in a narcissistic way. To win interviews you must convince the employer you can help him rather than vice versa, as in this unfortunate example:

> Employment at a highly diversified company such as yours offers many attractive health and vacation benefits. Moreover, it gives a challenging start to one who hopes to open his own business some day.

Some applicants mistakenly regard the employer as an audience in search of entertainment. This can lead to the kind of self-conscious "cuteness" exhibited in the following example:

> Is there something special about a person who graduated six months early from both high school and college and has never cut a class in her entire educational career?

If you are tempted to point to any perceived inadequacies, remind yourself that employers are not confessors. It is self-destructive to point out facts that can harm you and which might otherwise have gone unnoticed. For example:

> I am a forthcoming graduate of M.I.T.'s program in electrical engineering. While I did not win any significant research prizes, I . . .

Here is how a severe case of sour grapes was transmitted in a cover letter that manages to sound both confessional and hostile at the same time:

> Academically, I stand well within the top half of my class. A failure to be glib on exams prevented me from qualifying for Phi Beta Kappa. However, this failure has not prevented me from succeeding in any other endeavor.

Sometimes it will be necessary to carefully stress the positive aspects of a situation that could easily have negative connotations to an employer. One woman reentered the job market using this bad opening sentence in her cover letter:

> Seven years ago I resigned from a career in business to raise a family.

Her opening could easily have suggested an enterprising person had she thought to lead with her strengths:

> Your organization may be interested in a seasoned personnel administrator who has started her own successful business and consulted with an executive search firm concurrently with starting a family.

Do not indulge in subjective self-praise:

The enclosed resume sketches my background and shows my creativity, outstanding leadership skills, and writing ability.

Let the employer draw inferences from factual statements! Or if you wish to point to the clear inference, be modest and less blunt. For example:

While still a student, I have obtained useful managerial skills through various activities. For example, my work on the student newspaper helped to sharpen my business, editorial, and writing skills. During my second summer, an administrative-assistant position in a small office helped to train me in bookkeeping procedures, employee benefits, and general office systems. Recently, as a management intern assigned to the Deputy Mayor's Office, I obtained excellent exposure to public management problems.

Here is another good example:

During my graduate school career, I have tried to combine a seriousness of intellectual purpose with the development of interpersonal leadership skills. As chairman of the Student-Faculty Committee on Student Life, president of the student body, and senator-at-large in the university senate, I have gained useful training for a career in educational administration.

Sometimes a personality trait, such as leadership, is an important criterion of the job. If it seems important to stress such a quality do so substantively, as in the following example:

I have learned that an effective personality is an important asset in a successful public relations career. As a result, I have tried to polish and refine my interpersonal skills through a number of special workshops on leadership styles and interpersonal effectiveness. When I received the "Outstanding Student Leader" Award at Yale last year, I felt encouraged about my own future potential to work effectively with others.

Avoid the puffery of the alternative version:

I believe that I have the kind of sparkling personality that is essential to a successful career in public relations.

A good cover letter should not exceed one page. Save the elaborate detail for the interview, when the employer is certain to be more interested. Keep the paragraphs in your letter short for the greater visual ease of your reader.

Center the letter, and allow two to four inches as a border under your signature. The letter should not look crowded. Top and side margins should be generous.

Use bond paper in 8½" × 11" size. Ideally, the paper should match that of your resume, but if that proves too difficult, don't worry about it. Avoid corrasable paper unless you are such a poor typist that *not* using it will make it impossible for you to type letters. You might consider paying someone else to type the letter on bond for you. If at all possible, don't use an old college typewriter for your letters. As with your resume, an IBM Selectric or Executive typewriter will enhance your text.

Neatness is important. If your cover letters have obvious corrections, there may be adverse reactions. In any event you'll look unprofessional.

Proofread carefully for errors. A misspelled name, a run-on sentence, or a typographical error can easily cost you an interview! You cannot be too much of a perfectionist in this area.

If you plan to send out a hundred resumes to one specific kind of employer, convenience is important. Write one good cover letter and reproduce it as follows.

Have just the body of a form letter (e.g., no employer name or salutation) typed on an excellent typewriter. Then have it photo-offset in the desired quantities. Using the *original* typewriter, type in the necessary individual name and salutation. Then have each letter photocopied onto bond paper for about five cents each. No one will detect that the product is not an individual letter if your photocopy is on bond paper. A second, less complicated alternative is to follow precisely the same procedure but to stop at the photocopy step. Instead have your letters photo-offset onto bond paper. The disadvantage is that the employer will be able to see that you have used a form letter.

Do not type new details into the actual body of a reproduced letter; proper alignment is extremely difficult to achieve. Even the slightest variation will probably be detected.

A Checklist

Want to write a cover letter? Sit down and fill in the blanks:
1. I am *(June graduate; M.B.A., from N.Y.U.)* _____
2. I want a job as *(a junior accountant)* _____
3. I can offer you *(skills, experience)* _____
4. I am enclosing a resume _____
5. I want to see you *(request an interview)* _____
6. Thank you!

Now polish the language, flesh out the concepts, and you have an *effective* cover letter.

Preparing a Writing Sample

WARREN S. FELD

Warren S. Feld is President of Designed
Impacts

F or certain jobs, especially consulting, technical or research-oriented
jobs, you may be asked to submit a writing sample. (You may also feel it
is strategic to submit such a sample on your own.) A prospective
employer may also ask you to submit work samples of skill areas you cited in your
resume. Although you may want to submit a well written 20-page paper, a better
strategy is to submit four 5-7 page papers—each one demonstrating a different
kind of writing. In your cover letter accompanying the writing samples, identify
and explain the purposes of each one.

Type each writing sample separately. Use a 2″ left margin and 1″ margins on
the other 3 sides. Start the first page of each sample 14 lines from the top of the
paper. Start subsequent pages of each sample 7 lines from the top. Always use a
cover page with each sample.

If you have trouble figuring out how to write for a nontechnical audience,
picture yourself writing to a parent, sibling, or child. Your classwork, community
project, church work, or previous work on the job are all sources of possible
writing samples. You have done term papers, reports, evaluations, and the like
involving ideas, numbers, plans, proposals, presentations, financial analyses, etc.

You will probably send your writing sample after the first letter or personal
contact. Send either another copy of your resume or a 1-page capability statement with the writing sample(s).

Four Types of Samples to Demonstrate Four Types of Writing Styles/Skills

Writing Sample #1. Policy-Oriented Paper

This could be in the form of a policy memorandum or a condensed policy position
paper. This sample shows that you can (a) make comprehensive statements from
specific facts; (b) define and structure concepts, variables, and decision criteria in
a meaningful way; and (c) understand and have some control over emotionally

charged and often contradictory issues that must be resolved, albeit temporarily, in order to steer an organization or community through a crisis or problem resolution.

Writing the Policy-Oriented Paper

Policy memoranda are usually short documents that state a policy position, and then backtrack, analyze, and compare different key alternatives in a situation. They are used to gain agreement of a decision maker with your policy recommendation. As such, they must be designed with "influence exertion" in mind.

Common to all memoranda is the fact that the first page should "say it all." There should be no need to read beyond the first page. Also common to all memoranda is the fact that each page and each section is skimmable. The decision maker should be able to page through the document in a matter of seconds and understand your main points.

There are typically six sections in a policy memorandum:

Section 1. State the policy recommendation with which you want the decision maker to agree. A concise first sentence states what you want the decision maker to do. Subsequent sentences restate the recommendation with respect to the urgency of the problem. This should probably take ½ to 1 page.

Section 2. State decision criteria used to evaluate the feasibility of the desired recommendation and the infeasibility of alternative recommendations.

Be specific. *Do not write:* "Political Feasibility." *Do write:* "Mr. X will not support anything costing more than $$."

Aim for 5–10 criteria and arrange them by order of priority. When you use more than 4–5 criteria, cluster them into sets of 3–4 criteria because this aids interpretation. Give each set a cover label like Political Feasibility.

Section 3. Identify 3 or more relevant alternative courses of action. The way you order these alternatives is a strategic choice. You start usually with the most desirable alternative and end with the least because the decision maker will tend to read the first items in each section more thoroughly, and skim the rest. However, it makes sense sometimes to locate your most desired alternative second or third because the first alternative will get the most discussion and critique. Included as one of your alternatives is always the status quo or no change. Your range of alternatives should represent the range of ideas and positions that you know will bear on the debate—actually will come to bear, not potentially.

Section 4. For each course of action identify specific design components and resource needs; the pros and cons; and the relationship to the decision criteria as the basis for acceptance/rejection.

This section can be in narrative or list form. Do not forget to clearly restate and label each alternative from section to section. Do *not* assume the reader remembers what was said from page to page. The use of repetition, subheadings, underlining, white space on the page, and analogies in the narrative all help keep the reader's full attention.

Section 5. Summarize your evaluative strategy, conclusions, and recommendations.

Section 6. Add any words of advice, things to be concerned about, possible next steps in the policy/implementation process.

Writing Sample #2. Program-Oriented Paper

This is in the form of a program plan, a program design, an analysis or evaluation of a program, or discussion of a program. You might submit a condensed version of a paper already written. This sample shows that you can (a) write at a high degree of specificity, (b) define and structure program components and activities in a meaningful way; and (c) understand and have some control over how to build a program in anticipation of specific problems of implementation.

Writing the Program-Oriented Paper

The program plan should be written in plain, nontechnical English. Avoiding the literary, jargon, and broad-based generalities, it should cover the following kinds of information:

Section 1. Listing of information including
   a. Significant events preceding program planning efforts
   b. Significant events occurring during program
   c. Assessment or organizational climate, context, and resources for resisting or supporting ongoing program
   d. Scope and limit of writer's role vis-à-vis program design, implementation, and/or management

       e. Nature of interorganizational field, climate, and resources for resisting or supporting ongoing program

       f. Scope and limits of firm/agency vis-à-vis program's design, implementation, and/or management

       g. Other information necessary to better understand the program's history, present state, and prospects.

Section 2.   Identification of key program variables and their interrelationships.

       a. Internal variables and their interrelationships, namely:
1. Leadership
2. Doctrine/Mission
3. Program/Policy
4. Resources for Support/Resistance
5. Internal Organizational Structures (other factors that enhance or impede change and adaptation)

       b. External variables and their relationships to internal variables
1. Those that enable program to survive
2. Normative values and standards prevalent outside the organization
3. Functional ties with other programs or constituencies
4. Other ill-defined factors, such as public opinion, which seem important

       c. Final outputs
1. A definition of service or product
2. Creation of power, influence, persuasion, dependency, survival, adaptation
3. Reinvestment of outputs (such as new skills learned)
4. Feedback of information and evaluation.

Section 3.   Discussion of specific parameters of program in reference to goals it is designed to achieve. Give an understanding of what it takes to achieve program success in measurable terms.

Section 4.   Discussion of problems with the program and/or its implementation. Identify program's chances of continued success. Discuss viability of program alternatives should the program fail or not succeed as well as hoped.

Writing Sample #3. Paper Showing That You Can Write Using Numbers

This could be in the form of a data analysis or an explanation for using a particular quantitative methodology. This sample shows that you can (a) write narratives that include a lot of numbers; (b) draw a diagram or chart using numerical statistics or outcomes; (c) handle quantitative information; and (d) anticipate the difficulty a nontechnical audience will have in understanding any document with numbers or statistics in it.

Writing With Numbers

When writing quantitative information most people fall into one of the following traps:

1. Using too few numbers, and relying instead on broad but unsupported statements of fact (such as "most people agree that . . . " or "everyone knows that . . . ")

2. Using numbers in a boring, often confusing, manner that turns readers off

3. Hiding meanings in poorly designed or interpreted charts, assuming that the reader will recognize what is relevant on his own

4. Using too many numbers, failing to weed out those that are either redundant, unimportant, or superfluous to the writer's argument

5. Using numbers as space fillers to flesh out a page or a report that is thin rather than as a strategic technique to get a particular point across more effectively than a narrative or theoretical discussion would.

Think about the following uses/misuses of numbers:

Bad: The town of Hebringer was at risk for disease.
Better: One-third of the town—4,506 people, 68% of whom were male—were experiencing a 25% increased risk of getting cancer.

Bad: The report stated that 5,560,789 people, 36% of the total number of immigrants (2,001,884 people, 1,345,002 males and 656,882 females) had entered the country illegally in 1984.
Better: Illegal immigration last year rose 14%; that means that over 5 million more people (67% of them male) were being supported by the nation's economy than would normally be expected from examining Census figures.

Bad: Unbelievably, there were 12 more figures added to the book.
Better: Originally, space and money permitted only 6 figures to be included in the book, but the editor liked the figures so much she found money to include 12 more.

Diagrams, charts, tables, and graphs should be kept simple and tell a *persuasive* story. Each should illustrate only 2 to 3 points so that their meaning is immediately apparent to the reader. The diagram or chart should reflect a hierarchy that aids interpretation (most to least, best to worst, similar to dissimilar, first to last). Using a series of diagrams/charts with each illustrating 2 to 3 points is better than stating everything in a single, highly complex diagram or chart. Identify an audience and keep it in mind as you develop your diagram or chart. Since you will probably want the diagram or chart reproduced, you are limited to black and white.

Writing Sample #4. Paper Showing That You Can Use Theoretical or Complex Ideas

This could be in the form of a comparative analysis of organizational or administrative theories as these apply to an administrative, clinical or technical problem, or of an explanation for using a particular qualitative methodology. This sample shows that you can (a) write narratives that include a lot of theoretical or complex ideas and concepts; (b) draw a diagram or chart using categorical ideas/numbers or outcomes; and (c) anticipate the difficulty a nontechnical audience will have in understanding anything theoretical or complex.

Writing the Theory or Concept Paper

Many styles of writing use theories or complex ideas. A *scientific* style is analytical, explanatory, and often written as though an experiment had just been conducted (problem definition, literature review, strategies and justifications for data collection and analysis, description of results, conclusions, discussion of implications of findings, suggestions for next steps that might be taken). A *descriptive* or *non-scientific* style is best summarized by the journalists' 6-question approach: who, what, when, where, why, and how. A third style is a *change-oriented* or *policy* style (see writing sample #1) that presents facts and values in an organized, persuasive manner.

    Writing that uses theories or complex ideas can be written in any one of these styles. The choice of style depends on one condition: who your audience is and what that audience expects. The tasks involved are basic, no matter what the style of writing. These tasks are to:

    1. Collect and logically organize a set of facts, descriptions, values, impressions, and other data.

    2. Successfully explain the logic in your ordering, preferably in reference to either theories in the academic literature *or* well-known views of key players in your profession. (Taking a comparative approach strengthens the receptivity and credibility of any argument or statement you are trying to make.)

3. Discuss all barriers/contradictions/problems that force you to devise a less than perfect logical ordering or a less than perfect explanation of a logical ordering.

4. Identify which alternative explanation or ordering you might use, given the barriers, or what rationale you intend to use to support a theory or complex idea in the presence of these barriers.

No matter who your audience, try to minimize use of jargon and maximize demonstration of your abilities to think in complex terms without being overwhelmed.

Having Trouble Starting a Paper or a Section of a Paper?

If you have trouble starting a paper (or a section of a paper), you might address the first eight paragraphs to these eight topics in this order:

1. Problem statement and exemplars of the problem

2. Aim (social, general, or personal)

3. For this aim to be met, certain changes need to be made or certain things have to occur

4. List of barriers

5. What I used instead; objectives; procedures

6. Framework of presentation below

7. Scope and limitations of my efforts below

8. Statement of the larger problem of which I am only dealing with a small part for practical reasons.

Composition

Employing the clearest, most straightforward, and persuasive style of writing possible is important. Err on the side of boring rather than literary. Current conventions teach us to state an opinion persuasively, take a stand, give supporting detail and elaboration. This results in writing that is direct and powerful, easily grasped, and that triggers an active response. Aspects of this style include the use of active, transitive voice ("I did this"); the use of definite pronouns ("I, you, she, he, they, we"); the use of the first or second person ("I, we, you did it"); a focus on choice of thoughts rather than on choice of words ("she said hi" rather than "she effused greetings").

Rule of Cognitive Capacity: People can deal with only 3 to 5 categories, types, numbers or kinds of items at a time. If you find yourself exceeding 3 to 5, recategorize or regroup. For example, if you are presenting 6 previous job positions you have held, the reader more easily understands 2 groups (3 and 3 or 2 and 4) of job positions, for example, one set of positions directly relevant to the job you are pursuing and the second set only indirectly or functionally relevant.

Try not to overwhelm the reader with words. Avoid colloquialisms, fad words, and cliches. Avoid dead, colorless, or tired words such as *good, big, interesting, wonderful, terrific,* or *fabulous.* Make what you write believable and credible. Be enthusiastic when writing about yourself, but be truthful.

Gaining Tight Focus—The Technique of Matrix Ordering

Matrix Ordering is a tool of classification and categorization. It is useful in linking a set of ideas to an organized report narrative. The technique is simple. It involves redefining "reality" in terms of

- Items that can go into rows (of a matrix)
- Items that can go into columns
- Items that can go into cells

The task is one of managing meanings. The matrix serves to graphically represent a situation. You literally speak or write this matrix. You never include more information in your report or talk than you have put into the structure of your matrix, and never include less.

For example, suppose you set up the following matrix illustrating sales of two lines of men's clothes in the fall/winter and spring/summer seasons:

STORE LOCALE	FALL/WINTER SALES		SPRING/SUMMER SALES	
	K. Kline Line	D.I.B.S.	K. Kline Line	D.I.B.S.
Urban Stores	$5.6K	$3.4K	$3.2K	$6.2K
Suburban Stores	4.3K	4.8K	5.3K	4.5K
Rural Stores	5.1K	2.2K	3.9K	4.4K

The report looks like the following:

Introductory Paragraph/Section: Define whole matrix: identify the row, column, cell categories. You identify key issues such as differences among urban/suburban/rural stores, lines of clothes, and/or seasons of the year

Section 1/Paragraph 1: Discuss row 1

Section 2/Paragraph 2:   Discuss row 2

Section 3/Paragraph 3:   Discuss row 3

Concluding Section/Paragraph: Compare rows 1, 2, and 3

The pattern of matrix ordering is obvious. By forcing your report to tightly follow the confines of the matrix as you have decided to construct it, you end with a focused, organized, intelligent piece of writing.

ANNOTATED BIBLIOGRAPHY

This annotated bibliography provides more than 330 additional sources of information on business and technical writing.

For your convenience, the bibliography is divided into four sections:

1. Bibliographies

2. Books (including textbooks)

3. Anthologies

4. Journal articles.

BIBLIOGRAPHIES

Abshire, Gary M. "Writing on Writing." *IEEE Transactions on Professional Communication*, PC-25 (December, 1982), 211–219. A simple list divided into three sections—general, business, and technical writing—of 261 books, articles, and other materials published between 1953 and 1981.

Alred, Gerald, and others. *Business and Technical Writing: An Annotated Bibliography of Books, 1880–1980*. Metuchen, NJ: Scarecrow, 1981. An annotated list of 874 books.

Balachandran, Sarojini. *Employee Communication: A Bibliography*. Urbana, IL: ABCA, 1976. An annotated list of items published between 1965 and 1975 that discuss the communication gap between managers and employees.

———. *Technical Writing: A Bibliography*. Urbana, IL: ABCA; and Washington, DC: STC, 1977. An annotated list of publications on scientific and technical writing since 1965.

Bibliography of Publications Designed to Raise the Standard of Scientific Literature. Paris: UNESCO, 1963. An annotated list (in English) of 354 items (in English, French, Russian, Spanish, German, Bulgarian, Danish, Polish, and Czech) in six areas including general works on language and composition, technical writing, and readings in science for technical authors.

"Bibliography of Technical Writing." *Technical Writing Teacher*, 3 (Fall 1975–). A continuing list of bibliographies, books, book reviews, articles, and technical reports.

Blackman, Carolyn M. "A Bibliography for Beginning Teachers of Technical Writing." In *Technical and Professional Communication*. Thomas M. Sawyer, ed. Ann Arbor, MI: Professional Communication Press, 1977. A list of organizations, periodicals, conferences, meetings, institutes, bibliographies, articles, standard references, and general orientation materials on technical writing.

Bowman, Mary Ann. "Books on Business and Technical Writing in the University of Illinois Library." *Journal of Business Communication*, 12 (Winter 1975), 33–67. A list of books written in English between 1950 and 1973 whose titles appeared in the card catalogue of the University of Illinois Library under a variety of subject headings related to business and technical writing.

———, and Joan D. Stamas. *Written Communication in Business: A Selective Bibliography, 1967–1977*. Champaign, IL: ABCA, 1980. An annotated list of over 800 books and articles.

Brockmann, R. John. "Case Method Annotated Bibliography (1961–1982)." In *The Case Method in Technical Communication: Theory and Models*. R. John Brockmann, ed. Lubbock, TX: ATTW, 1984. More than 35 books and articles.

Burkett, Eva M. *Writing in Subject-Matter Fields: A Bibliographic Guide with Annotations and Writing Assignments*. Metuchen, NJ: Scarecrow, 1977. Brief individual sections with items on writing in law and science, technical and business writing, interdisciplinary writing, and other topics.

Burns, Shannon, and others. *An Annotated Bibliography of Texts on Writing Skills*. New York: Garland, 1976. Over 400 items on grammar and usage, composition, rhetoric, and technical writing.

Carson, Helen V., and others. *An Annotated Bibliography on Technical Writing, Editing, Graphics, and Publishing, 1966–1980*. Washington, DC: STC, 1983. More than 2600 books, articles, and papers.

Carter, Robert. *Communication in Organizations: An Annotated Bibliography and Sourcebook*. Detroit: Gale, 1972. More than 75 items on business writing.

Cunningham, Donald H. "Bibliographies of Technical Writing Materials." *Technical Writing Teacher*, 1 (Winter 1974), 9–10. A brief list of instructional materials.

———. "Books on Police Writing." *College Composition and Communication*, 23 (May, 1972), 199–201. A review of books published between 1957 and 1972 on the fundamentals of police writing.

————, and Vivienne Hertz. "An Annotated Bibliography on the Teaching of Technical Writing." *College Composition and Communication*, 21 (May, 1970), 177–186. Sixty-seven entries.

————. "Bibliography: Police Report Writing" *Police Chief*, 38 (August, 1971), 44, 49–50. One hundred and two items including books, sections of books, bound and unbound manuals and bulletins, articles, and materials indirectly related to police reporting.

Denton, L. W., and W. E. Rivers. "Consulting and In-House Writing Courses: A Selected Bibliography." In *Communication Training and Consulting in Business, Industry, and Government*. William J. Buchholz, ed. Urbana, IL: ABCA, 1983. An annotated list of sources for information on consulting, professional training, teaching methodology, and successful short courses in business communications.

Dorrell, Jean, and Betty Johnson. "A Comparative Analysis of Topics Covered in Twenty College-Level Communication Textbooks." *ABCA Bulletin*, 44 (September, 1982), 11–16. A breakdown by major and minor topics covered, an assessment of textbook readability using the Gunning Fog Index, and statistics on numbers of adoptions by colleges and universities.

Fearing, Bertie E., and Thomas M. Sawyer. "Speech for Technical Communicators: A Bibliography." *IEEE Transactions on Professional Communication*, PC-23 (March, 1980), 53–60. A list of 178 resources for technical communicators interested in improving their speaking skills.

Fielden, John S. "For Better Business Writing." *Harvard Business Review*, 43 (January-February, 1965), 164–166, 169–170, 172. A list of reference books designed to help people in business write more effectively.

Goldberg, Jay J. "A Survey of Scholarly Works in Technical Writing." *Technical Communication*, 22 (First Quarter 1975), 5–8. A discussion of 35 items dealing with readability, professional training, and information transfer.

Goldstein, Jone R., and Robert R. Donovan. *A Bibliography of Basic Texts in Technical and Scientific Writing*. Washington, DC: STC, 1982. An annotated bibliography of texts supplemented by a list of additional resource materials.

Griffing, John. "Teaching Graphics in Technical Writing Classes: A Selective Bibliography." In *Teaching Technical Writing: Graphics*. Dixie Elise Hickman, ed. Lubbock, TX: ATTW (Anthology #5), 1985. Nineteen items.

Keene, Michael L., and Merrill D. Whitburn. "Audience Analysis for Technical Writing: A Selective, Annotated Bibliography." In *Teaching Technical Writing: Teaching Audience Analysis and Adaptation*. Paul V. Anderson, ed. Morehead, KY: ATTW (Anthology #1), 1980. Detailed annotations of more than 25 articles and books discussing theoretical as well as practical considerations concerning audience.

Killingworth, M. J. "A Bibliography on Proposal Writing." *IEEE Transactions on Professional Communication*, PC-26 (June, 1983), 79–83. Annotations of 80 items.

Larson, Richard L. "Selected Bibliography of Research and Writing about the Teaching of Composition." *College Composition and Communication*, 26 (May, 1975), 187–195; 27 (May, 1976), 171–180; 28 (May, 1977), 181–193; 29 (May, 1978), 181–194; and 30 (May, 1979), 196–213. Some items on business and technical writing. (Bibliography resumed in 38 [October, 1987], 319–36.)

Leonard, Don. "An Annotated Bibliography of Recent Articles on Company Communications Training." *ABCA Bulletin*, 45 (June, 1982), 48–52. Thirty-four entries.

Lindemann, Erika, ed. *Longman Bibliography of Composition and Rhetoric. 1984–1985*. White Plains, NY: Longman, 1987. More than 3800 annotations including selected items on business and technical writing.

Lodge, Frank L. "Specifications and Catalogs Frequently Used in the Presentation of Technical Data." In *Handbook of Technical Writing Practices*. Stello Jordan and others, eds. Vol. 2. New York: Wiley, 1971. An annotated list of specifications and catalogues issued by agencies of the Defense Department.

McClure, Lucille. "Two Bibliographies: Technical Writing Books in Print. Photo-typesetting." *IEEE Transactions on Engineering Writing and Speech*, EWS-8 (December, 1965), 65–70. Fifty-nine books on technical writing.

Miller, Carolyn R., and Bertie E. Fearing. "Resources for Teachers of Business, Technical and Vocational Writing." In *Technical and Business Communication in Two-Year Programs*. W. Keats Sparrow and Nell Ann Pickett, eds. Urbana, IL: NCTE, 1983. An annotated list of organizations, institutes and workshops, journals, materials for teacher preparation, textbooks for freshmen and sophomore courses, standard reference works and resources, and bibliographies.

Moran, Michael G., and Debra Journet, eds. *Research in Technical Communication, A Bibliographic Sourcebook*. Westport, CT: Greenwood, 1985. Fifteen bibliographic essays and three appendices surveying the growing bibliography of business and technical communication.

Nancarrow, Paula Reed, and others, eds. *Word Processors and the Writing Process: An Annotated Bibliography*. Westport, CT: Greenwood, 1984. Approximately 600 entries on computer-aided writing instruction.

Oslund, R. R. "A Bibliography of Proposals." *STWP Review*, 11 (April, 1964), 13–14. Eighty-four items on proposal writing.

Philler, Theresa, and others. *An Annotated Bibliography on Technical Writing, Editing, Graphics, and Publishing, 1950–1965*. Washington, DC: STC; and Pittsburgh: Carnegie Library, 1966. Two thousand books, articles, and papers.

Rude, Carolyn D., and Rex W. Castle. "Technical Editing: A Selected, Annotated Bibliography." In *Teaching Technical Editing*. Carolyn D. Rude, ed. Lubbock, TX: ATTW (Anthology #6), 1985. More than 300 items.

Smith, Julian F., and others. "Style Manuals: Guides for Technical Writing." *Journal of Chemical Education*, 42 (July, 1965), 373–375. A review of 41 style manuals designed for technical writers.

Van Veen, Frederick. "An Index to 500 Papers through 1962 on Engineering Writing and Related Subjects." *IEEE Transactions on Engineering Writing and Speech*, EWS-6 (September, 1963), 50–58. Author-subject index; many of the papers listed have not been published.

Wagner, Carl G. "The Technical Writing Audience: A Recent Bibliography." *Technical Writing Teacher*, 14 (Spring 1987), 243–63. An annotated list of 109 items.

Walsh, Ruth M., and Stanley J. Birkin. *Business Communication: An Annotated Bibliography*. Westport, CT: Greenwood, 1980. Sixteen hundred books, articles, reviews, and dissertations written between 1960 and 1979.

Walsh, Ruth M., and others. "Business Communications: A Selected, Annotated Bibliography." *Journal of Business Communications*, 11 (Fall 1973), 65–112. A list of over 400 books and articles published between 1940 and 1972.

Walter, John A. "Basic Recommended Reference Shelf: A Selected Bibliography of Technical and Scientific Writing." In *Handbook of Technical Writing Practices*. Stello Jordan and others, eds. Vol. 2. New York: Wiley, 1971. An annotated list of reference books on grammar, style, usage, and business and technical communications.

———. "Style Manuals." In *Handbook of Technical Writing Practices*. Stello Jordan and others, eds. Vol. 2. New York: Wiley, 1971. An annotated list of more than 60 general, institutional, and industrial style manuals and authors' guides.

White, Jane F., and Patty G. Campbell. *Abstracts of Business Communication, 1900 through 1970*. Urbana, IL: ABCA, 1982. Abstracts of theses and dissertations in business communications.

BOOKS

Adelstein, Michael E., and W. Keats Sparrow. *Business Communications*. New York: Harcourt Brace Jovanovich, 1983. A comprehensive introductory textbook.

Alvarez, Joseph A. *Elements of Technical Writing.* New York: Harcourt Brace Jovanovich, 1980. A handbook taking a descriptive approach to principles of grammar, punctuation, and style.

Anderson, Paul V. *Technical Writing.* San Diego: Harcourt Brace Jovanovich, 1987. A comprehensive textbook offering a reader-centered approach to technical writing.

Andrews, Deborah C., and Margaret D. Blickle. *Technical Writing Principles and Forms.* 2nd ed. New York: Macmillan, 1982. A comprehensive introductory textbook that takes a rhetorical approach to technical writing.

Austen, David, and Tim Crosfield. *English for Nurses.* London: Longman, 1976. A basic textbook for students in nursing programs.

Backman, Lon F. *A Digest on the Elements of Proposal Writing.* Olympia, WA: State of Washington Planning and Community Affairs Agency, n.d. Detailed guidelines written in the form of an actual proposal.

Barnett, Marva T., and J. L. Smith. *Effective Communications for Public Safety Personnel.* New York: Delmar, 1978. An introductory textbook for students in police and fire training programs.

Barrass, Robert. *Scientists Must Write.* London: Chapman and Hall, 1978. A brief guide to better writing for working scientists and engineers.

Barzun, Jacques, and Henry F. Graff. *The Modern Researcher.* 4th ed. San Diego: Harcourt Brace Jovanovich, 1985. A scholarly discussion of the principles that should inform any kind of research.

Bates, Jefferson D. *Writing with Precision.* Washington, DC: Acropolis, 1978. A self-help textbook designed to enlist government writers in the ''war'' against gobbledygook in bureaucratic prose.

Beach, Mark. *Editing Your Newsletter.* Portland, OR: Coast to Coast Books, 1980. A brief guide to designing, writing, and producing newsletters.

Beatty, Richard. *The Resume Kit.* New York: Wiley, 1984. A comprehensive guide with a special section on ''problem resumes.''

Bennett, John B. *Editing for Engineers.* New York: Wiley, 1970. A brief handbook for engineers who write and managers who edit technical documents.

Berenson, Conrad, and Raymond R. Colton. *Research and Report Writing for Business and Economics.* New York: Random House, 1971. A comprehensive guide for beginning college students who need to write reports and research papers.

Bingham, Earl G. *Pocketbook for Technical and Professional Writers.* Belmont, CA: Wadsworth, 1982. A brief handbook.

Blicq, Ron S. *Technically Write!* 3rd ed. Englewood Cliffs, NJ: Prentice-Hall, 1986. A basic textbook using a modern engineering consulting firm as the setting for each assignment.

Blumenthal, Lassor A. *The Complete Book of Personal Letter Writing and Modern Correspondence.* Garden City, NY: Doubleday, 1969. A comprehensive guide to social, business, and professional letter writing.

Bolles, Richard Nelson. *What Color Is Your Parachute?* Berkeley, CA: Ten Speed Press, updated annually. A practical guide to the job hunt and career change.

Bostwick, Burdette. *Resume Writing.* 3rd ed. New York: Wiley, 1985. A comprehensive guide with discussions and examples of different resume formats.

Bowman, Joel P., and Bernadine P. Branchaw. *Business Report Writing.* 2nd ed. Chicago: Dryden, 1988. A comprehensive introduction to report writing for teachers, students, and professionals.

Brand, Norman, and John O. White. *Legal Writing: The Strategy of Persuasion.* 2nd ed. New York: St Martin's, 1988. A textbook applying the principles of advanced composition and persuasion to the specific writing needs of prelaw, paralegal, and law students.

Brinegar, Bonnie Carter, and Craig Barnwell Skates. *Technical Writing: A Guide with Models.* Glenview, IL: Scott, Foresman, 1983. An introductory textbook and reader emphasizing four basic technical writing models: information, investigation, evaluation, and persuasion.

Brown, Harry M. *Business Report Writing.* New York: Van Nostrand, 1980. A thorough discussion of all aspects of report writing for students and professionals.

————, and Karen K. Reid. *Business Writing and Communication*. New York: Van Nostrand, 1979. An introductory textbook.

Brunner, Ingrid, and others. *The Technician as Writer*. Indianapolis: Bobbs-Merrill, 1980. A technical report writing textbook for students in junior colleges.

Brusaw, Charles T., and others. *The Business Writer's Handbook*. 3rd ed. New York: St. Martin's, 1987. An easy-to-use, thorough handbook containing over 500 alphabetically arranged entries.

Carlsen, Robert D., and Donald L. Vest. *The Encyclopedia of Business Charts*. Englewood Cliffs, NJ: Prentice-Hall, 1977. A comprehensive reference guide to business charts and their style.

Carr-Ruffino, Norma. *Writing Short Business Reports*. New York: Gregg, 1980. A text-workbook for classes or industrial training programs emphasizing report writing.

Cheatham, T. Richard, and Keith V. Erickson. *The Police Officer's Guide to Better Communication*. Glenview, IL: Scott, Foresman, 1984. A basic guide for communicating effectively with witnesses, suspects, other officers, and the public.

The Chicago Manual of Style. 13th ed. Chicago: University of Chicago, 1982. A standard reference for authors, editors, copywriters, and proofreaders.

Cloke, Marjane, and Robert Wallace. *The Modern Business Letter Writer's Manual*. New York: Doubleday, 1974. A handy paperback guide for writers of business letters.

Cook, Claire K. *Line by Line*. Boston: Houghton Mifflin, 1985. The Modern Language Association's guide to editing.

Couture, Barbara, and Jone Rymer Goldstein. *Cases for Technical and Professional Writing*. Boston: Little, Brown, 1985. An introductory textbook that includes 30 cases for additional study.

Cremmins, Edward T. *The Art of Abstracting*. Philadelphia: ISI, 1982. A thorough discussion of the rules for reading and writing abstracts.

Cunningham, Donald H., and Gerald W. Cohen. *Creating Technical Manuals: A Step-by-Step Approach to Writing User-Friendly Instruction*. New York: McGraw-Hill, 1984. A guide for the writer with little or no technical background.

Damerst, William A. *Clear Technical Reports*. New York: Harcourt Brace Jovanovich, 1972. A comprehensive textbook emphasizing the need for clarity.

Davis, Ken. *Better Business Writing: A Process Approach*. Columbus: Merrill, 1983. An introductory textbook for junior college or short corporate business writing courses.

Dawe, J. *Writing Business and Economics Papers, Theses, and Dissertations*. Totowa, NJ: Littlefield, Adams, 1975. A comprehensive style manual.

Day, Robert A. *How to Write and Publish a Scientific Paper*. 2nd ed. Philadelphia: ISI, 1983. A "cookbook" for scientists to help the put their research into publishable form.

Dirckx, John H. *Dx + Rx: A Physician's Guide to Medical Writing*. Boston: G. K. Hall, 1977. A handbook emphasizing accuracy, clarity, and readability.

Dodds, Robert H. *Writing for Technical and Business Magazines*. 1969; rpt. Melbourne, FL: Krieger, 1982. Practical discussions of the publishing process from the points of view of writer and editor alike.

Dumont, Raymond A., and John M. Lannon. *Business Communications*. 2nd ed. Boston: Little, Brown, 1987. A comprehensive introductory textbook.

Ehrlich, Eugene, and Daniel Murphy. *The Art of Technical Writing*. New York: Crowell, 1969. A handbook.

Eisenberg, Anne. *Reading Technical Books*. Englewood Cliffs, NJ: Prentice-Hall, 1978. A basic junior-college textbook designed to show students how to find and organize technical information.

Elbow, Peter. *Writing without Teachers*. New York: Oxford, 1973. A brief introduction to the writing process.

Emerson, Lynn A. *How to Prepare Training Manuals*. Albany: University of the State of New York, Department of Education, 1952. Ten chapters following the order in which the steps for writing a manual should be carried out.

Enrick, Norbert L. *Handbook of Effective Graphic and Tabular Communication.* Huntington, NY: Krieger, 1980. A thorough discussion supplemented by numerous examples.

Fear, David E. *Technical Communication.* 2nd ed. Glenview, IL: Scott, Foresman, 1981. A rhetoric and handbook.

Flesch, Rudolf. *The ABC of Style.* New York: Harper and Row, 1980. A reference guide explaining how to avoid the pedantic, the trite, the pompous, and the verbose in writing.

————. *The Art of Readable Writing.* rev. ed. New York: Harper and Row, 1973. A general discussion based on the premise that one should as much as possible write the way one talks; includes an explanation of the Flesch Readability Formula.

————. *How to Write Plain English.* New York: Harper and Row, 1981. A guide for consumers and lawyers.

French, Christopher, and others, eds. *The Associated Press Style Book and Libel Manual.* rev. ed. Reading, MA: Addison-Wesley, 1987. The working journalist's bible covering the rules of grammar, punctuation, and usage.

Gallagher, William J. *Writing the Business and Technical Report.* Boston: CBI, 1981. A detailed, process approach to report writing.

Garrison, Roger. *How a Writer Works.* rev. ed. New York: Harper and Row, 1985. A concise guide for professionals that emphasizes revision as the key to effective writing.

Gelderman, Carol. *Better Writing for Professionals.* Glenview, IL: Scott, Foresman, 1983. A concise guide offering advice on writing and publishing articles for career advancement.

Goswami, D., and others. *Writing in the Professions.* Washington, DC: American Institutes for Research, 1981. A systematic, process-oriented resource book.

Griffin, C. W. *Writing, A Guide for Business Professionals.* San Diego: Harcourt Brace Jovanovich, 1987. A comprehensive, process-oriented textbook.

Gunning. Robert. *New Guide to More Effective Writing in Business and Industry.* Boston: Industrial Education Institute, 1963. A quick reference designed for the technician on the job.

————. *The Technique of Clear Writing.* rev. ed. New York: McGraw-Hill, 1968. A detailed discussion of the Fog Index and selected principles of clear writing.

Hafer, W. Keith, and Gordon E. White. *Advertising Writing.* 2nd ed. St. Paul: West, 1982. A comprehensive textbook on public relations and advertising writing.

Harris, John S., and Reed H. Blake. *Technical Writing for Social Scientists.* Chicago: Nelson Hall, 1976. A rhetoric for social scientists and students in social science programs.

Hart, Andrew W., and James A. Reinking. *Writing for Career-Education Students.* 3rd ed. New York: St. Martin's Press, 1986. A comprehensive introductory textbook for students in vocational and technical programs.

Harty, Kevin J., and John Keenan. *Writing for Business and Industry, Process and Product.* New York: Macmillan, 1987. A comprehensive, process-oriented textbook.

Haughney, John. *Effective Catalogs.* New York: Wiley, 1968. A set of procedures for producing a basic marketing tool, the company catalog.

Henze, Geraldine. *From Murk to MASTERPIECE.* Homewood, IL: Irwin, 1984. A brief style guide.

Herbert. A. J. *The Structure of Technical English.* London: Longman, 1965. A grammar book designed to give foreign technicians and engineers practice in mastering the skills they need to communicate effectively in English.

Hill, L. Brooks. *The Military Officer's Guide to Better Communication.* Glenview, IL: Scott, Foresman, 1984. A brief guide designed to show military personnel how to improve their effectiveness as leaders and managers through better oral and written communication skills.

Himstreet, William C., and Wayne M. Baty. *Business Communications.* 8th ed. Boston: Kent, 1987. A comprehensive introductory textbook.

Hirschhorn, Howard H. *Writing for Science, Industry, and Technology.* New York: Van Nostrand, 1980. An introductory textbook for students majoring in the physical or social sciences, business, and technological areas.

Holcombe, Marya W., and Judith K. Stein. *Writing for Decision Makers: Memos and Reports with a Competitive Edge*. Belmont, CA: Lifetime Learning Publications, 1981. An advanced textbook stressing the writing process.

Holtz, Herman. *The Consultant's Guide to Proposal Writing*. New York: Wiley, 1986. A comprehensive guide to proposal writing.

———, and Terry Schmidt. *The Winning Proposal: How to Write It*. New York: McGraw-Hill, 1981. A thorough overview of the proposal process offering valuable insights into the way government works.

Hoover, Hardy. *Essentials for the Technical Writer*. rev. ed. New York: Dover, 1981. A brief guide to writing reports and specifications.

Houp, Kenneth, and Thomas Pearsall. *Reporting Technical Information*. 5th ed. New York: Macmillan, 1984. Well-illustrated textbook for advanced writing courses.

Howard, C. Jeriel, and David A. Gill. *Desk Copy: Modern Business Communications*. San Francisco: Canfield, 1971. A basic textbook for students in business and secretarial programs.

Huckin, Thomas N., and Leslie A. Olsen. *English for Science and Technology, A Handbook for Nonnative Speakers*. New York: McGraw Hill, 1983. An adaptation of the authors' *Principles of Communication for Science and Technology* designed to meet the writing and reference needs of nonnative students who have a fairly good command of English.

Huseman, Richard C., and others. *Business Communication, Strategies and Skills*. 3rd ed. Hinsdale, IL: Dryden, 1988. A basic textbook in communication theory and its practical application to the world of business.

Jackson, Tom. *The Perfect Resume*. Garden City, NY: Anchor, 1980. A guide to cover letters, resumes, and job-finding and salary-negotiating strategies supplemented by 55 sample resumes.

Jacobi, Ernest. *Work at Writing*. Rochelle Park, NJ: Hayden, 1980. A workbook to accompany *Writing at Work*; see below.

———. *Writing at Work*. Rochelle Park, NJ: Hayden, 1976. A textbook with emphasis on general principles rather than mechanics; intended for writers on the job.

Janis, J. Harold. *The Business Research Paper*. New York: Hobbs, Dorman, 1967. A compact guide to report formats and mechanics.

———. *Writing and Communicating in Business*. 3rd ed. New York: Macmillan, 1978. A comprehensive textbook for beginning or advanced courses.

———, and Howard R. Dressner. *Business Writing*. 2nd ed. New York: Barnes and Noble, 1972. A self-help guide to letter and report writing.

Keene, Michael L. *Effective Professional Writing*. Lexington, MA: Heath, 1987. A comprehensive textbook taking a reader-centered approach to technical writing.

Keithley, Erwin M., and Philip J. Schreiner. *A Manual of Style for the Preparation of Papers and Reports*. 3rd ed. Cincinnati: South-Western, 1980. A style guide.

Keithley, Erwin M., and Margaret H. Thompson. *English for Modern Business*. 5th ed. Homewood, IL: Irwin, 1986. A basic textbook for a refresher course in the fundamentals of grammar and writing.

Kett, Merriellyn, and Virginia Underwood. *How to Avoid Sexism*. Chicago: Lawrence Ragan Communications, 1978. A guide for writers, editors, and publishers that offers detailed discussions of sexism and the law, the generic "he," problems with forms of address, sex-role stereotyping, and acceptable practices for writing about both men and women.

King, Patricia. *Mind to Disk to Paper*. New York: Franklin Watt, 1984. A guide to business writing on a word processor.

Kleppner, Otto, and Thomas Russell. *Advertising Procedure*. 8th ed. Englewood Cliffs, NJ: Prentice-Hall, 1983. The standard textbook on all aspects of advertising.

Kolin, Philip C. *Successful Writing at Work*. 2nd ed. Lexington, MA: Heath, 1986. An introductory textbook emphasizing product rather than process.

———, and Janeen L. Kolin. *Models for Technical Writing*. New York: St. Martin's, 1985. An introductory textbook constructed around 65 models of actual on-the-job technical writing.

————. *Professional Writing for Nurses in Education, Practice, and Research.* St. Louis: Mosby, 1980. A technical writing textbook for nurses at all professional levels.

Krey, Isabella, and others. *Principles and Techniques of Effective Business Communication.* 2nd ed. San Diego: Harcourt Brace Jovanovich, 1985. An introductory text-workbook.

Krupa, Gene. *Situational Writing.* Belmont, CA: Wadsworth, 1982. A basic textbook built around a sequence of writing situations.

Lanham, Richard A. *Revising Business Prose.* 2nd ed. New York: Macmillan, 1987. A brief handbook and style guide.

Lannon, John M. *Technical Writing.* 3rd ed. Boston: Little, Brown, 1985. A comprehensive introductory textbook.

Laster, Ann A., and Nell Ann Pickett. *Occupational English.* 4th ed. New York: Harper and Row, 1986. A process-oriented textbook for junior college students.

Lauer, Janice, and others. *Four Worlds of Writing.* New York: Harper and Row, 1981. An introductory textbook that applies a process-oriented approach to private, public, academic, and business writing.

Lay, Mary K. *Strategies for Technical Writing.* New York: Holt, 1982. An introductory rhetoric with readings.

Lefferts, Robert. *Getting a Grant in the 80's.* 2nd ed. Englewood Cliffs, NJ: Prentice-Hall, 1982. A primer for preparing research proposals directed at corporations and foundations.

Leonard, Donald J. *Shurter's Communication in Business.* New York: McGraw-Hill, 1979. An introductory textbook for undergraduates or those already in business; a revision of the third edition of Robert Shurter's *Written Communication in Business* (1971).

Lesikar, Raymond V. *Basic Business Communication.* 3rd ed. Homewood, IL: Irwin, 1985. A comprehensive introductory textbook emphasizing practical applications rather than theory.

————. *Business Communication, Theory and Application.* 4th ed. Homewood, IL: Irwin, 1980. A comprehensive advanced textbook.

————, and Mary P. Lyons. *Report Writing for Business.* 7th ed. Homewood, IL: Irwin, 1986. A comprehensive discussion of the process of organizing and writing business reports.

Levine, Norman. *Technical Writing.* New York: Harper and Row, 1979. A brief introductory textbook.

Lico, Laurie. *Resumes for Successful Women.* New York: Pocket, 1985. A brief guide with advice especially valuable to women who are returning to the world of work.

Locke, Lawrence F., and W. W. Spirduso. *Proposals That Work.* New York: Teachers College Press, 1976. Guidelines for graduate students in the sciences.

Lodwig, Richard. *Career English.* Rochelle Park, NJ: Hayden, 1981. A basic textbook offering vocational guidance as well as instruction in writing; includes a series of short interviews in which people talk about why they enjoy their jobs.

Londo, Richard J. *Common Sense in Business Writing.* New York: Macmillan, 1982. A textbook stressing the writing process and emphasizing the basic essentials of composition and clarity in writing.

Maizell, Robert E., and others. *Abstracting Scientific and Technical Literature.* New York: Wiley, 1971. Tips for beginning abstractors, information scientists, and managers.

Maki, Peggy, and Carol Schilling. *Writing in Organizations.* New York: McGraw-Hill, 1987. A comprehensive introductory textbook using a problem-solving approach to business writing.

Mandel, Siegfried, and David L. Caldwell. *Proposal and Inquiry Writing.* New York: Macmillan, 1962. An example-filled textbook that takes the reader through the logical steps of initial inquiry, proposal preparation, and contract.

McCloskey, Donald. *The Writing of Economics.* New York: Macmillan, 1987. A brief handbook and style guide designed for anyone who writes for the world of work.

Mehaffey, Robert E. *Writing for the Real World.* Glenview, IL: Scott, Foresman, 1980. A textbook designed to prepare beginning students for the writing demands of the working world.

Messer, Ronald K. *Style in Technical Writing.* Glenview, IL: Scott, Foresman, 1982. A text-workbook for vocational students.

Meyer, Harold E. *Lifetime Encyclopedia of Letters*. Englewood Cliffs, NJ: Prentice-Hall, 1983. Guidelines for writing over 500 different kinds of business and personal letters.

Michaelson, Herbert. *How to Write and Publish Engineering Papers and Reports*. 2nd ed. Philadelphia: ISI, 1986. A practical guide to the production of manuscripts, theses, and dissertations.

Miller, Casey, and Kate Swift. *The Handbook of Nonsexist Writing*. New York: Barnes and Noble, 1980. Guidelines for eliminating sexism from oral and written communication.

Mills, Gordon H., and John A. Walter. *Technical Writing*. 5th ed. New York: Holt, 1986. A comprehensive advanced textbook—one of the standards in the field

Mitchell, John N. *Writing for Professional and Technical Journals*. New York: Wiley, 1968. A discussion of the characteristics of and style guides for professional and technical articles.

Monroe, Judson, *Effective Research and Report Writing in Government*. New York: McGraw-Hill, 1980. A self-help textbook for staff specialists and researchers in public agencies.

———, and others. *The Science of Scientific Writing*. Dubuque: Kendall/Hunt, 1977. A brief guide designed to help students and laboratory researchers write term papers, dissertations, and journal articles.

Moyer, Ruth, and others. *The Research and Report Handbook for Business, Industry, and Government*. New York: Wiley, 1981. An advanced textbook discussing reports, proposals, policies, legal briefs, memos, letters, and minutes.

Mullins, Carolyn J. *The Complete Writing Guide to Preparing Reports, Proposals, Memos, etc.* Englewood Cliffs, NJ: Prentice-Hall, 1980. A guide for writing on-the-job reports.

Munter, Mary. *Guide to Managerial Communication*. 2nd ed. Englewood Cliffs, NJ: Prentice-Hall, 1987. A brief handbook on written and oral communications.

Murphy, Herta A., and Charles Peck. *Effective Business Communication*. 3rd ed. New York: McGraw-Hill, 1980. A comprehensive textbook for advanced or beginning courses.

Nauheim, Ferd. *Letter Perfect*. New York: Van Nostrand Reinhold, 1982. A guide to writing business letters that work.

O'Hayre, John. *Gobbledygook Has Gotta Go*. Washington, DC: GPO, 1966. Suggestions about how to write direct and uncluttered reports, memos, and letters.

Oliu, Walter E., and others. *Writing That Works*. 3rd ed. New York: St. Martin's, 1988. An introductory textbook with a brief handbook.

Olsen, Leslie A., and Thomas N. Huckin. *Principles of Communication for Science and Technology*. New York: McGraw-Hill, 1983. A comprehensive textbook for intermediate and advanced students.

Olson, Gary A., and others. *Style and Readability in Business Writing: A Sentence-Combining Approach*. New York: Random House, 1985. A guide to the grammar business writers need to know.

———. *Style and Readability in Technical Writing: A Sentence-Combining Approach*. New York: Random House, 1984. A guide to the grammar technical writers need to know that uses the sentence-combining approach.

Pauley, Steven E., and Daniel G. Riordan. *Technical Report Writing Today*. 3rd ed. Boston: Houghton Mifflin, 1985. A brief introductory textbook asking students to write on topics in their specialized technical fields for an uninformed audience—the instructor.

Paxson, William C. *Write It Now!* Reading, MA: Addison-Wesley, 1985. A brief guide for writers of reports, memos, and letters.

Pearsall, Thomas. *Audience Analysis for Technical Writing*. Beverly Hills, CA: Glencoe, 1969. A pioneering study delineating audiences in terms of their technical expertise.

———. *Teaching Technical Writing: Methods for College English Teachers*. Washington, DC: STC, 1975. A short booklet for composition teachers interested in teaching more advanced or specialized courses in technical writing.

———, and Donald H. Cunningham. *How to Write for the World of Work*. 3rd ed. New York: Holt, 1986. An introductory textbook especially helpful in courses where the teacher is new to the fields of technical or business writing.

Pickett, Nell Ann, and Ann A. Laster. *Technical English: Writing, Reading, and Speaking*. 5th ed.

New York: Harper and Row, 1988. A comprehensive introductory text-workbook for students at two-year colleges.

Rathbone, Robert R. *Communicating Technical Information*. Reading, MA: Addison-Wesley, 1966. A self-help textbook for engineers and scientists who want to write more effective reports, abstracts, and journal articles.

Reid, James M., Jr., and Robert M. Wendlinger. *Effective Letters*. 3rd ed. New York: McGraw-Hill, 1978. A self-help textbook prepared in collaboration with the New York Life Insurance Company.

Roberts, Louise A. *How to Write for Business*. New York: Harper and Row, 1978. A brief introductory textbook.

Roman, Kenneth, and Joel Raphaelson. *Writing That Works*. New York: Harper and Row, 1981. Advice from two advertising executives on how to write letters, memos, reports, and fundraising literature.

Roundy, Nancy (with David Mair). *Strategies for Technical Communication*. Boston: Little, Brown, 1985. A textbook offering a process-oriented approach to technical writing.

Sandman, Peter M., and others. *Scientific and Technical Writing*. New York: Holt, 1985. An introductory textbook supplemented with numerous examples of scientific writing.

Schwartz, Helen J. *Interactive Writing*. New York: Holt, 1985. A guide to composing with a word processor.

Sharf, Barbara F. *The Physician's Guide to Better Communication*. Glenview, IL: Scott, Foresman, 1984. A brief guide examining and offering solutions to the problems physicians face in communicating with patients and colleagues.

Sherman, Theodore A., and Simon S. Johnson. *Modern Technical Writing*. 4th ed. Englewood Cliffs, NJ: Prentice-Hall, 1983. A comprehensive introductory textbook emphasizing letter and report writing.

Shurter, Robert, and Donald J. Leonard. *Effective Letters in Business*. 3rd ed. New York: McGraw-Hill, 1984. Popular paperback that examines the psychological principles that lie behind effective letters.

Sigband, Norman, and Arthur H. Bell. *Communication for Management and Business*. 4th ed. Glenview, IL: Scott, Foresman, 1986. A comprehensive introductory textbook supplemented by 15 reading selections.

Sorrels, Bobbye D. *The Nonsexist Communicator*. Englewood Cliffs, NJ: Prentice-Hall, 1983. Solutions to problems with gender and awkwardness in business, technical, and other kinds of writing.

Souther, James W., and Myron L. White. *Technical Report Writing*. 2nd ed. New York: Wiley, 1977. A discussion of the writing process and its application to scientific and technical report writing.

Steward, Joyce S., and Marjorie Smelstor. *Writing in the Social Sciences*. Glenview, IL: Scott, Foresman, 1983. A reader and textbook designed for students in the fields of psychology, sociology, anthropology, history, and economics.

Stuart, Ann. *Writing and Analyzing Effective Computer Systems Documentation*. New York: Holt, 1985. An interdisciplinary textbook designed to show students how to analyze, write, and evaluate standard computer system documents.

Taylor, K. Phillip, and others. *Communication Strategies for Trial Attorneys*. Glenview, IL: Scott, Foresman, 1984. A brief guide offering techniques for persuading judges and juries.

Tibbets, Arn. *Practical Business Writing*. Boston: Little, Brown, 1987. A comprehensive introductory textbook.

Tichy, H. J. *Effective Writing for Engineers, Managers, and Scientists*. New York: Wiley, 1967. A comprehensive textbook that includes a brief discussion of the writing process.

Trelease, Sam F. *How to Write Scientific and Technical Papers*. Cambridge, MA: MIT Press, 1969. A handy desk manual for technical writers.

Trimble, John R. *Writing with Style, Conversations on the Art of Writing*. Englewood Cliffs, NJ: Prentice-Hall, 1975. A writer's "survival kit" blending theory with practical advice.

Turner, Rufus P. *Grammar Review for Technical Writers*. 1971; rpt. Melbourne, FL: Krieger, 1981. A brief review of practical English grammar for technicians.

Ulman, Joseph N., and Jay R. Gould: *Technical Report Writing*. 3rd ed. New York: Holt, 1972. A comprehensive textbook and reference for technical report writers.

U.S. Government Correspondence Manual. Washington, DC: GSA, 1977. Standards for the appearance and style of government correspondence.

U.S. Government Printing Office Style Manual. Rev. ed. Washington, DC: GPO, 1973. The official government style guide.

Van Duyn, J. A., ed. *Director's and Officer's Complete Letter Book*. 2nd ed. Englewood Cliffs, NJ: Prentice-Hall, 1983. A how-to book containing 102 model letters and 950 alternate phrases, sentences, and paragraphs.

Visco, Louis J. *The Manager as an Editor*. Boston: CBI, 1981. Guidelines for managers on how to issue clear instructions, edit effectively, and educate subordinates to improve their writing without undermining their morale.

Weeks, Francis W., and Kitty O. Lockner. *Business Writing Cases and Problems*. Champaign, IL: Stipes. 1980. Ninety-six cases.

Weisman, Herman W. *Technical Correspondence*. New York: Wiley, 1968. A handbook.

———. *Technical Report Writing*. 2nd ed. Columbus: Merrill, 1975. A brief report writing handbook.

Weiss, Edmond H. *How to Write a Usable User Manual*. Philadelphia, ISI, 1985. A guide offering a structured approach to generating reports, proposals, and other business forms.

———. *The Writing System for Engineers and Scientists*. Englewood Cliffs, NJ: Prentice-Hall, 1982. A comprehensive introduction to the writing process.

Whalen, Doris H. *Handbook for Business Writers*. New York: Harcourt Brace Jovanovich, 1978. A ready reference manual discussing the forms of business writing.

———. *Handbook of Business English*. Orlando: Academic Press, 1986. A guide to style, grammar, spelling, word usage, and sentence mechanics.

Wilkinson, C. W., and others. *Communicating through Writing and Speaking in English*. 9th ed. Homewood, IL: Irwin, 1986. A comprehensive introductory textbook.

Williams, Joseph W. *Style: Ten Lessons in Clarity and Grace*. 2nd ed. Glenview, IL: Scott, Foresman, 1984. A guide offering advice on quick and effective written communication.

Woodford, F. Peter, ed. *Scientific Writing for Graduate Students*. New York: Rockefeller University Press, 1968. A comprehensive guide to scientific writing prepared by the Council of Biology Editors.

Wydick, Richard. *Plain English for Lawyers*. 2nd ed. Durham, NC: Academic Press, 1985. A guide for improving the writing or editing of legal and bureaucratic documents.

Wyld, Lionel D. *Preparing Effective Reports*. New York: Odyssey, 1967. A brief handbook.

Zimmerman, Donald E., and David G. Clark. *The Random House Guide to Technical and Scientific Communication*. New York: Random House, 1987. A comprehensive process approach to technical writing.

Zinsser, William. *Writing with a Word Processor*. New York: Harper and Row, 1983. A step-by-step "confession" of Zinsser's encounters with his IBM Displaywriter as he wrote this book.

ANTHOLOGIES

Anderson, Paul V., ed. *Teaching Technical Writing: Teaching Audience Analysis and Adaptation*. Morehead, KY: ATTW (Anthology #1), 1980. Four original essays and a selective annotated bibliography that provide materials for teaching audience analysis and adaptation.

———, and others, eds. *New Essays in Technical and Scientific Communication: Research, Theory, Practice*. Farmingdale, NY: Baywood, 1983. Twelve essays discussing readability and important pedagogical concerns for teachers and practitioners of technical and scientific writing.

Anderson, W. Steve, and Don Richard Cox, eds. *The Technical Reader*. 2nd ed. New York: Holt, 1984. Eighty introductory readings in technical, business, and scientific communication.

Armour, Richard, ed. *How to Write Better*. Boston: Christian Science Publishing Society, 1977. Reprints of articles on writing that appeared in the *Monitor* together with illustrative articles on a wide variety of subjects.

Boston, Bruce O., ed. *STET! Tricks of the Trade for Writers and Editors*. Alexandria, VA: Editorial Experts, Inc., 1986. A collection of 124 items previously published in *The Editorial Eye*, a newsletter providing tips, brief notes and articles, and occasional book reviews for professional writers and editors.

Bovee, Courtland, ed. *Business Writing Workshop*. Sherman Oaks, CA: Roxbury, 1980. Reprints of 41 articles discussing the forms of business writing.

Brockmann, R. John, ed. *The Case Method in Technical Communication: Theory and Models*. Lubbock, TX: ATTW, 1984. Seventeen essays and an annotated bibliography.

Buchholz, William J., ed. *Communication Training and Consulting in Business, Industry, and Government*. Urbana, IL: ABCA, 1983. Twenty-nine essays, some previously published, and an annotated bibliography.

Cunningham, Donald H., and Herman A. Estrin, eds. *The Teaching of Technical Writing*. Urbana, IL: NCTE, 1975. Twenty-four previously published essays addressing the central pedagogical concerns of technical and scientific writing.

DiGaetani, John Louis, ed. *The Handbook of Executive Communication*. Homewood, IL: Dow Jones-Irwin, 1986. A comprehensive reference book that contains 64 essays discussing business writing, reading, listening, speaking, and interviewing skills.

Douglas, George H., ed. *The Teaching of Business Communication*. Champaign, IL: ABCA, 1978. Reprints of 40 essays that appeared from 1972 to 1977 in the *ABCA Bulletin*.

Effective Communication for Engineers. New York: McGraw-Hill, 1974. Reprints of more than 50 articles from *Chemical Engineering* that discuss a wide range of topics in oral and written technical communication.

Estrin, Herman A., ed. *Technical and Professional Writing, A Practical Anthology*. 1963; rpt. New York: Preston, 1976. More than 40 articles on important aspects of business and technical writing.

Gieselman, Robert D., ed. *Readings in Business Communication*. Champaign, IL: Stipes, 1974. Twenty-two essays on a broad range of topics related to business communication.

Golen, Steven P., and others, eds. *Readings and Cases in Business Communication*. New York: Wiley, 1984. More than 50 essays and cases cross-referenced to chapters in 25 major business communication textbooks.

Gootnick, David, and Margaret Mary Gootnick, eds. *The Standard Handbook of Business Communication*. New York: Free Press, 1984. Twenty-one essays covering career planning and development and business communication.

Gould, Jay R., ed. *Directions in Technical Writing and Communication*. Farmingdale, NY: Baywood, 1978. Fourteen essays, all previously published in the *Journal of Technical Writing and Communication*, that discuss the major forms of technical writing.

Halpern, Jeanne W., ed. *Teaching Business Writing*. Urbana, IL: ABCA, 1983. Thirteen essays discussing approaches, plans, pedagogy, and research.

Harris, John, ed. *Teaching Technical Writing: The Training of Teachers of Technical Writing*. Lubbock, TX: ATTW (Anthology #4), 1984. Seven pedagogical essays.

Hickman, Dixie Elise, ed. *Teaching Technical Writing: Graphics*. Lubbock, TX: ATTW (Anthology #5), 1985. Six essays and a brief annotated bibliography.

Hildebrandt, Herbert W., ed. *International Business Communication: Theory, Practice, Teaching throughout the World*. Ann Arbor, MI: Division of Research, Graduate School of Business Administration, University of Michigan, 1981. Fourteen essays examining business communication and marketing concepts in Europe, the Far East, North and South America, and Africa.

Huseman, Richard C., and others, eds. *Readings in Business Communication*. Hinsdale, IL: Dryden, 1981. Reprints of 36 articles discussing theoretical considerations and strategies for written and oral business communications.

Jordan, Stello, and others, eds. *Handbook of Technical Writing Practices*. 2 vols. New York:

Wiley, 1971. Thirty-two essays offering a complete guide to technical writing and its various support services.

Journet, Debra, and Julie Lepick Kling, eds. *Readings for Technical Writers*. Glenview, IL: Scott, Foresman, 1984. Thirty-six selections written by professional technical writers and drawn from on-the-job situations in government, business, and industry.

Leonard, David C., and Peter J. McGuire, eds. *Readings in Technical Writing*. New York: Macmillan, 1983. Reprints of 21 articles and 5 samples that address the issues of style, audience, arrangement, and readability.

[Mann, Gerald A., and Harold E. Osborne, eds.] *Proposals and Their Preparation*. STC Anthology Series No. 1. Washington, DC: STC, 1973. Sixteen essays, all previously published by the Society for Technical Communication, discussing procedures and guidelines for writing proposals.

Nilsen, Alleen Pace, and others, eds. *Sexism and Language*. Urbana, IL: NCTE, 1977. Eighteen essays on sexism as a social, educational, and linguistic issue; an appendix reprints the NCTE Guidelines for Nonsexist Use of Language.

Odell, Lee, and Dixie Goswami, eds. *Writing in Nonacademic Settings*. New York: Guilford, 1985. Fourteen essays surveying the diversity and importance of writing done in non-academic settings.

Pickens, Judy E., and others, eds. *Without Bias: A Guidebook for Nondiscriminatory Communication*. San Francisco: International Association of Business Communicators, 1977. Six essays and a case study that set guidelines for avoiding discrimination on the basis of race, ethnic bias, sex, or physical handicap in written communication, visual media, and meetings, conferences, and workshops.

Richards, Jack C., ed. *Teaching English for Science and Technology*. SEAMO Regional English Language Centre Anthology Series No. 2. Singapore: Singapore University Press, 1976. Thirteen essays on the differences among scientific, technological, and technical English and the special problems they create for non-native speakers of English.

Rivers, William E., ed. *Business Reports: Samples from the "Real World."* Englewood Cliffs, NJ: Prentice-Hall, 1981. Thirty-eight sample reports written for various companies.

Rude, Carolyn D., ed. *Teaching Technical Editing*. Lubbock, TX: ATTW (Anthology #6), 1985. Eighteen essays and an extensive annotated bibliography.

Sawyer, Thomas M., ed. *Technical and Professional Communication*. Ann Arbor, MI: Professional Communication Press, 1977. Twenty pedagogical essays.

Shaw, James, ed. *Teaching Technical Writing and Editing—In-House Programs That Work*. STC Anthology Series No. 5. Washington, DC: STC. 1976. Twelve essays, all previously published by the Society for Technical Communication, discussing problems of designing and teaching in-house technical writing courses.

Siegel, Muffy E. A., and Toby Olson, eds. *Writing Talks*. Upper Montclair, NJ: Boynton Cook, 1983. Twelve original essays by authors with divergent backgrounds (a poet, a philosopher, a social worker, a psychologist, the director of a writing program, an EPA official, an international banker, and several college professors) who discuss problems in the teaching of writing.

Sparrow, W. Keats, and Donald H. Cunningham, eds. *The Practical Craft: Readings for Business and Technical Writers*. Boston: Houghton Mifflin, 1978. Twenty-eight essays.

Sparrow, W. Keats, and Nell Ann Pickett, eds. *Technical and Business Communication in Two-Year Programs*. Urbana, IL: NCTE, 1983. Twenty-five essays addressed directly to teachers of business and technical communication courses at junior and community colleges.

Stevenson, Dwight W., ed. *Courses, Components, and Exercises in Technical Communication*. Urbana, IL: NCTE, 1981. Twenty-one essays addressing a variety of pedagogical concerns.

Stratton, Charles R., ed. *Teaching Technical Writing: Cassette Grading*. Morehead, KY: ATTW (Anthology #2), 1979. Six previously published essays with updated postscripts by their authors and a brief bibliography.

Teaching Scientific Writing. English Journal, 67 (April, 1978). Seventeen articles.

Vervalin, Charles H., ed. *Communication and the Technical Professional*. Houston: Gulf, 1981. Twenty-six essays discussing communication dynamics and skills for engineers and scientists.

Weeks, Francis W., ed. *Readings in Communication from Fortune.* New York: Holt, 1961. Reprints of 28 articles from *Fortune.*

Whitburn, Merrill, ed. *Teaching Technical Writing: The First Day in the Technical Writing Course.* Morehead, KY: ATTW (Anthology #3), 1980. Five essays discussing writing assignments.

Wilkinson, C. W., and others, eds. *Writing for Business, Selected Articles on Business Communication.* 3rd ed. Homewood, IL: Irwin, 1960. More than seventy articles on the theory and practice of business communication.

Zook, Lola M., ed. *Technical Editing: Principles and Practices.* STC Anthology Series No. 4. Washington, DC: STC, 1975. Reprints of 18 papers and journal articles.

JOURNAL ARTICLES

Adams, Tom. "Developing a Meeting Memo." *Supervisory Management,* 25 (July, 1980), 39–42. The 13 essentials of an effective meeting memo.

Ammannito, Theresa A. "The Introduction." *STWP Review,* 9 (July, 1962), 11–14. An examination of the correlation between reader expertise and the length and complexity of introductions to technical reports and articles.

Arnold, Christian K. "The Construction of Statistical Tables." *IRE Transactions on Engineering Writing and Speech, EWS-5* (August, 1962), 9–14. Guidelines for constructing statistical tables, criteria for choosing vertical or horizontal presentations, and rules for the use of captions.

Aziz, A. "Article Titles as Tools of Communication." *Journal of Technical Writing and Communication,* 4 (Winter 1974), 19–21. Suggestions for forming titles that contain as much information in as few words as possible.

Bergwerk, R. J. "Effective Communication of Financial Data." *Journal of Accountancy,* 129 (February, 1970), 47–54. Suggestions on using tables to compare several pieces of data and graphs to show trends.

Bernheim, Mark. "The Written Job Search—Doubts and 'Leads.'" *The Technical Writing Teacher,* 10 (Fall 1982), 3–7. Practical strategies for job seekers.

Biskind, Elliot. "Writing Right." *New York State Bar Journal,* 42 (October, 1970), 548–554. Suggestions for improving the quality of legal writing.

Booth, Vernon. "Writing a Scientific Paper." *Biochemical Society Transactions,* 3 (1975), 2–26. A discussion of prewriting techniques, style, visual aids, and manuscript submission guidelines.

Bram, V. A. "Factors Affecting the Readability of Scientific and Engineering Texts." *The Communicator of Scientific and Technical Information,* 33 (October, 1977), 3–5. Suggestions for using effective sentences as a basis for successful communication with readers regardless of their expertise.

Bromage, Mary C. "Gamesmanship in Written Communication." *Management Review,* 61 (April, 1972), 11–15. Techniques for improving business writing diction.

Christenson, Larry. "How to Write an Office Manual." *American Business,* 25 (July, 1955), 26–27, 32–34. Nine principles for writing effective manuals.

Clark, Andrew K. "The Abstract Way to Concrete Writing." *Journal of Technical Writing and Communication,* 11 (1981), 131–138. Guidelines for teaching the writing of abstracts.

Cortelyou, Ethaline, "Abstract of the Technical Report." *Journal of Chemical Education,* 30 (October, 1955), 52–533. A discussion of the differences between abstracts and summaries.

Darian, Steven. "Using Spoken Language Features to Improve Business and Technical Writing." *ABCA Bulletin,* 44 (September, 1982), 25–30. Suggestions on the ways the differences between spoken and written communication can be used to improve business and technical writing.

Davidson, Jeffrey. "How to Spot a Phony Resume." *Supervisory Management,* 28 (May, 1983), 40–43. Guidelines for personnel managers that can serve as a warning to job applicants when preparing resumes and cover letters.

Davis, Jeffrey. "Protecting Consumers from Overdisclosure and Gobbledygook." *Virginia Law Review*, 63 (October, 1977), 841–920. A thorough discussion by a lawyer of the problems excessive disclosure, extraneous clauses, and intractable language cause consumers when they must agree to credit contracts.

DeBakey, Lois. "The Persuasive Proposal." *Journal of Technical Writing and Communication*, 6 (Winter 1976), 5–25. A discussion of the skills needed by investigators who write research proposals.

DeBeaugrande, Robert. "Information and Grammar in Technical Writing." *College Composition and Communication*, 28 (December, 1977), 325–332. A discussion of how grammar helps writers organize information.

DeRoche, W. Timothy. "Addressing Mail in the Eighties." *Balance* Sheet, 62 (February, 1981), 219–222. General recommendations that conform to the USPS's preferences for addressing mail.

Deutsch, Arnold R. "Does Your Company Practice Affirmative Action in Its Communication?" *Harvard Business Review*, 54 (November-December, 1976), 16 and 186–187. Suggestions for eliminating sexism.

Dittman, Nancy A. "Job Winning Resumes." *ABCA Bulletin*, 46 (June, 1983), 16–22. A discussion loaded with practical advice and supported by examples of traditional, functional, and mixed resumes.

Dodge, W. J. "Writing the Appropriation Request." *Chemical Engineering*, 73 (March 14, 1966), 152–154. Guidelines for requesting funding.

Dolphin, Robert, Jr., and Robert A. Wagley. "Reading the Annual Report." *Financial Executive*, 45 (June, 1977), 20–22. Suggestions for improving the readability of annual reports.

Dover, J. C. "How to Tell Your Profits Story." *Nation's Business*, 48 (May, 1960), 38–39, 117–120. Tips for avoiding harmful confusion about the size and use of profits.

Dulek, Ron. "To Question or Not to Question: A Study of Wordiness and Impact." *ABCA Bulletin*, 45 (March, 1982), 11–14. A suggestion on using questions initially in correspondence to ensure economy in writing.

Elliott, Colin R. "Must Scientific English Be Dull?" *English Language Teaching Journal*, 31 (October, 1976), 29–34. Suggestions for producing lively scientific and technical writing.

Encke, C. G. "Scientific Writing: One Scientist's Perspective." *English Journal*, 67 (April, 1978), 40–43. Comments on the rhetorical problems that accompany the use of illustrations and figures in scientific writing.

Evered, James. "How to Write a Good Job Description." *Supervisory Management*, 26 (April, 1981), 14–19. A process approach to writing effective job descriptions and meaningful performance standards.

Farkas, David K. "The Concept of Consistency in Writing and Editing." *Journal of Technical Writing and Communication*, 15 (1985), 353–364. Guidelines for establishing consistent patterns in technical writing.

Fielden, John S. "What Do You Mean I Can't Write?" *Harvard Business Review*, 42 (May-June, 1964), 144–156. A discussion of readability, appropriateness, grammatical correctness, and thought content.

Flesch, Rudolf. "How to Say It with Statistics." *Printers' Ink*, 233 (December 8, 1950), 23–24. Twelve suggestions for making statistics readable.

Francis, Henry E. "The Literary Aspects of Business Writing." *Journal of Business Communication*, 4 (October, 1966), 13–18. A discussion of form, style, and tone.

Guccione, Eugene, "Preparing Better Flowsheets." *Chemical Engineering*, 73 (March 14, 1966), 155–157. Suggestions about how to design complete, accurate, and easy-to-follow flowsheets.

Halatin, T. J. "Writing Letters of Reference That Get Results." *Supervisory Management*, 25 (December, 1980), 32–34. Seven tips for writing useful references.

Hanna, J. S. "Six Steps Toward Better Charts." *Technical Communication*, 29 (Third Quarter 1982), 4–8. Practical advice on the design, construction, and revision of tables and charts.

Happ, W. W. "Guidelines and Checklists for Preparing the Planning Report." *IEEE Transactions on Professional Communication*, PC-16 (December, 1973), 209–214. A checklist of more than 100 items.

Harty, Kevin J. "Some Guidelines for Saying 'No.'" *ABCA Bulletin*, 44 (December, 1980), 23–25. Five suggestions on how to soften the impact bad-news messages have on readers.

Hays, Robert. "Model Outlines Can Make Routine Writing Easier." *Technical Communication*, 29 (First Quarter 1982), 4–7. Models for progress or status reports, trip or site visit reports, experiment test or lab reports, investigation reports, analyses of competing ideas or plans, minutes of or confirmation reports on meetings, and long research or feasibility studies.

Jordan, Michael P. "As a Matter of Fact." *Journal of Business Communication*, 15 (Winter 1978), 3–11. A discussion of the distinctions among facts, opinions, and assumptions.

Kiritz, Norman. "Program Planning and Proposal Writing." *Grantsmanship Center News*, 7 (May-June, 1979), 33–79. Detailed, step-by-step instructions designed to assist both grant-making agencies and applicants for funding; the format suggested has been adopted by both government agencies and private foundations.

Krantz, Shelley. "Five Steps to Making Performance Appraisal Writing Easier." *Supervisory Management*, 28 (December, 1983), 7–10. Guidelines for writing job appraisals that will have a positive effect on employee performance.

Lay, Mary M. "Procedures, Instructions, and Specifications: A Challenge in Audience Analysis." *Journal of Technical Writing and Communication*, 12 (1982), 235–242. A discussion of the differences in audience and purpose for procedures, instructions, and specifications.

Limaye, Mohan R. "Approaching Punctuation as a System." *ABCA Bulletin*, 46 (March, 1983), 28–33. An argument that punctuation is a rational system of easy-to-learn rules rather than a conglomeration of seemingly unrelated rules and exemptions to rules.

McGirr, Clinton J. "Guidelines for Abstracting." *Technical Communication*, 25 (Second Quarter 1978), 2–5. A discussion of the differences between abstracts and introductions and of the appropriate length and contents of a good abstract.

Messer, Donald K. "Six Common Causes of Ambiguity." *The Technical Writing Teacher*, 7 (Winter 1980), 50–52. Implication, word order, ambiguous words, dangling participles, missing or improper punctuation, and faulty reference.

Motley, Robert J. "'Sexism' and Modern Business Communications." *Business Education Forum*, 33 (November, 1978), 28–31. Eight suggestions for eliminating sexism in business communication.

Palmer, Stacy E. "What to Say in a Letter of Recommendation." *Chronicle of Higher Education*, 27 (September 7, 1983), 21–22. Guidelines to ensure that recipients of written recommendations receive the information they really need about applicants.

Peterson, Becky K. "Tables and Graphs Improve Reader Performance and Reader Reaction." *Journal of Business Communication*, 20 (Spring 1983), 47–55. Results of a study suggesting how effective tables and graphs improve reader comprehension of written materials.

Plung, Daniel L. "Writing the Persuasive Business Letter." *Journal of Business Communication*, 17 (Spring 1980), 46–49. Guidelines for arranging ideas in a pattern corresponding to a reader's decision making processes.

Richards, Paul. "Sentence Control: Solving an Old Problem," *Supervisory Management*, 25 (May, 1980), 37–43. Suggestions for improving readability by varying sentence length and punctuation.

Samora, Julian, and others. "Medical Vocabulary Knowledge among Hospital Patients." *Journal of Health and Social Behavior*, 2 (1961), 83–92. Results of a study with important implications about the problems lay audiences can have with even basic specialized terminology.

Schindler, George E., Jr. "Why Engineers and Scientists Write as They Do—Twelve Characteristics of Their Prose." *IEEE Transactions on Professional Communication*, PC-18 (March, 1975), 5–10. A discussion of structural and grammatical problems commonly found in the sentences engineers and scientists write.

Selzer, Jack. "Readability Is a Four-Letter Word." *Journal of Business Communication*, 18 (Fall 1981), 22–34. An argument against the validity of readability formulas.

Shelby, Anne. "How to Type Your Paper." *The Technical Writing Teacher*, 1 (Winter 1974), 11–22. Easy-to-follow directions for typing formal reports.

Spangler, E. R. "Modern Grammar and Its Application to Technical Writing." *Journal of Chemical Education*, 33 (February, 1956), 61–64. An application of some basic principles of descriptive grammar to technical writing.

Sparrow, W. Keats. "Six Myths about 'Writing for Business and Industry.' " *The Technical Writing Teacher*, 3 (Winter 1976), 49–59. Practical advice for beginning teachers of business and technical writing.

Stiegler, Christine B. "Are You a Closet Sexist?" *Supervisory Management*, 24 (May, 1979), 38–41. A brief discussion of sexism in verbal and nonverbal communication.

Stine, Donna. "The Writing of Performance Appraisals: A Survey of Personnel Directors." *ABCA Bulletin*, 45 (March, 1982), 29–33. A discussion of common weaknesses in, goals for, and potential legal problems with written performance appraisals of employees.

Storm, A. Allman. "In Search of Money." *Management Accounting*, 53 (August, 1971), 29–32. Guidelines for those seeking capital.

Swift, Marvin. "Writing a Problem-Centered Report." *ABCA Bulletin*, 46 (September, 1983), 19–23. Guidelines for investigating and reporting on problems.

Tibbets, Arn. "Ten Rules for Writing *Readably*." *Journal of Business Communication*, 18 (Fall 1981), 53–62. Suggestions on how to write like "a human being."

Van DeWeghe, Richard. "Writing Models, Versatile Writers." *Journal of Business Communication*, 20 (Winter 1983), 13–23. Five models of the composing process.

Waters, Max L. "Abstracting—An Overlooked Management Writing Skill." *ABCA Bulletin*, 45 (June, 1982), 19–21. A general discussion distinguishing among descriptive, informative, analytical, and critical abstracts.

Weightman, Frank C. "The Executive Summary: An Indispensable Management Tool." *ABCA Bulletin*, 45 (December, 1982), 3–4. Suggestions for using effectively written executive summaries to involve the reader immediately in business reports.